"If the Workers Took a Notion"

If the workers took a notion they could stop all speeding trains;

Every ship upon the ocean they can tie with mighty chains.

Every wheel in creation, every mine and every mill;

Fleets and armies of the nations, will at their command stand still.

—JOE HILL,

from "Workers of the World Awaken,"

written in jail in 1915

"If the Workers Took a Notion"

The Right to Strike and American Political Development

JOSIAH BARTLETT LAMBERT

ILR PRESS
an imprint of CORNELL UNIVERSITY PRESS
Ithaca and London

First published 2005 by Cornell University Press
First printing, Cornell Paperbacks, 2005

Printed in the United States of America

Library of Congress Cataloging-in-Publication Data

Lambert, Josiah Bartlett, 1954–
  "If the workers took a notion" : the right to strike and American political development / Josiah Bartlett Lambert.
    p. cm.
  Includes bibliographical references and index.
  ISBN-13: 978-0-8014-4327-5 (cloth : alk. paper)
  ISBN-10: 0-8014-4327-X (cloth : alk. paper)
  ISBN-13: 978-0-8014-8945-7 (pbk. : alk. paper)
  ISBN-10: 0-8014-8945-8 (pbk. : alk. paper)
  1. Industrial relations—United States—History—20th century. 2. Strikes and lockouts—United States—History—20th century. 3. Political culture—United States—History—20th century. 4. Labor unions—United States—History—20th century. 5. Labor laws and legislation—United States—History—20th century. 6. Employee rights—United States—History—20th century. I. Title: Right to strike and American political development. II. Title.
  HD8072.5.L357 2005
  331.8'0973—dc22
                              2005008839

Cornell University Press strives to use environmentally responsible suppliers and materials to the fullest extent possible in the publishing of its books. Such materials include vegetable-based, low-VOC inks and acid-free papers that are recycled, totally chlorine-free, or partly composed of nonwood fibers. For further information, visit our website at www.cornellpress.cornell.edu.

Cloth printing   10 9 8 7 6 5 4 3 2 1
Paperback printing   10 9 8 7 6 5 4 3 2 1

To William Clark Breckenridge Lambert,

1918–2001,

and Linda Meyer Lambert

Contents

Acknowledgments

It is an honor and a pleasure to thank everyone who has supported me intellectually and personally throughout the writing of this book. Although many encouraged me along the way, special thanks go to my wife, Linda, and to Booth Fowler. Linda helped by preparing figures, reading numerous drafts of the manuscript, and helping to clarify the wording in the text. More important, she gave personal support during the years I conceived, researched, wrote, and revised this book. Booth was also crucial for the development and completion of this project. All who know Booth can attest to his intellectual rigor and high standards, as well as his good will and wonderful sense of humor. Booth always encouraged me to question my assumptions, but also to press ahead. Without his and Linda's support, I might not have brought this book to publication.

In addition, I give special thanks to members of the Political Science Department at the University of Wisconsin-Madison, and especially Graham Wilson, Dennis Dresang, and John Coleman. Charlie Anderson was also especially helpful for developing my interest in values and public policy.

Others beyond the University of Wisconsin-Madison have encouraged me as well. Carole Nackenoff of Swarthmore College provided early encouragement as I was conceiving my thesis and later insight as one of the readers for ILR Press. She helped me see beyond my own topic toward broader questions and implications in the field of American political development. An anonymous reader for ILR Press offered critical insights into how better to present my arguments. Others who read conference paper versions of the chapters and provided meaningful feedback include Paul Frymer, Ruth O'Brien, Sanford Schram, Kristen Kelly, Stephen Amberg, and Kevin McMahon.

I also want to thank my colleagues at St. Bonaventure University for their support. Jim Moor was very indulgent during the months I devoted to revisions. Jim Fodor, Chuck Gannon, and Richard Simpson read earlier versions of chapters and provided helpful suggestions. St. Bonaventure University also provided financial support in the form of two summer research fellowships and travel money.

Finally, I wish to thank everyone at Cornell University Press for assisting in the preparation of this manuscript, and especially Fran Benson, whose enthusiasm and practical advice helped bring this book to fruition.

"If the Workers Took a Notion"

I

"An inevitable and irresistible conflict" The Strange Case of the Disappearing American Strike

The United Paperworkers' strike against International Paper in Jay, Maine, during the late 1980s provides a bitter object lesson in the fate that awaits strikers today.[1] IP, following a year of record profits, took a hard bargaining position during labor contract negotiations with the union, demanding the elimination of the Christmas Day holiday, the end of premium pay on Sunday, and greater management flexibility, which meant the elimination of jobs. When time ran out on the negotiations, the union offered to continue working under the previous contract, but IP refused to budge and unilaterally imposed the new contract on the paper workers, causing hundreds to lose their jobs. Cornered, the paper workers walked out. Although the National Labor Relations Act (NRLA), or Wagner Act, prohibits employers from firing strikers, under a peculiar provision of the law known as the *Mackay* doctrine, an employer may permanently replace them. IP subsequently hired a permanent striker replacement firm, installed thirty trailers to house them, and, by the end of summer, had replaced all of the 2,300 strikers.

The strike continued for seventeen months, during which the local struggled to gain the support of the international leadership and other United Paperworkers locals. United Paperworkers hired Ray Rogers, director of Corporate Campaign, Inc., to lead a corporate campaign, sponsored a Jesse Jackson rally, and worked with Ralph Nader to publicize IP's environmental and worker safety violations. The local union, however, was no equal to the world's largest paper company, and, in October 1988, it conceded defeat. By law, defeated strikers may return to their jobs only after positions become available, and employers may not fire strikebreakers to make room for replaced workers, so most of the strikers never returned. Eventually, some of the strikebreakers petitioned the National Labor Relations Board (NLRB) to decertify the union, and three years later they voted to dissolve the local. The broken strike not only destroyed the local union and cost thousands of loyal employees their livelihoods but it also led to bankruptcies, divorces, and a shattered community. According to a former striker, "It has put brother against brother, friend against friend, and neighbor against neighbor."[2]

The breaking of the Jay, Maine, paper workers' strike was not an isolated incident. Employers hired permanent replacement workers in a variety of strikes throughout the 1980s and 1990s: Caterpillar, Midland Steel, Oregon Steel, Phelps-Dodge Copper, Ravenswood Aluminum, Pittston Coal, Bridgestone/Firestone Tire, Greyhound Bus; Eastern, Continental, United, and Trans-World Airlines; *New York Daily News, Chicago Tribune, Detroit News,* and the *San Francisco Chronicle* were among the companies that employed strikebreakers during this period. Even the National Football League used replacements during the 1987 football strike. In countless other labor disputes workers decided not to challenge their employers' resolve. In others, employers prevailed with different tactics that violated the spirit of the law that affirms the right to strike.

Strike data gathered by the Bureau of Labor Statistics (BLS) document the unprecedented drop in the U.S. strike rate over the past thirty years and provide further evidence of the erosion of the right to strike.[3] During the 1970s, about 289 major work stoppages occurred annually in the United States, but during the 1990s that number plummeted to about 35 per year, falling to just 14 in 2003, despite the fact that the private nonfarm workforce had grown from about 64 million in the 1970s to nearly 108 million in 2003. Other BLS strike statistics demonstrate that whereas 4 percent of the private nonfarm workforce participated in major work stoppages in 1970, fewer than .5 percent did so 1997. Depending on the statistical measure—number of work stoppages, number of workers involved, or percent of estimated working time idle—the overall strike rate in the United States has dropped by 60 percent to 90 percent over the past thirty years.

From the standpoint of American labor history, this decline in strike activity is unprecedented. Despite the lack of working-class consciousness in the labor movement, one of the American labor movement's most notable features has been the frequency and intensity of industrial conflict. As Philip Taft and Philip Ross noted, "the United States has had the bloodiest and most violent labor history of any industrial nation in the world."[4] This high level of industrial conflict was not just characteristic of the distant past;

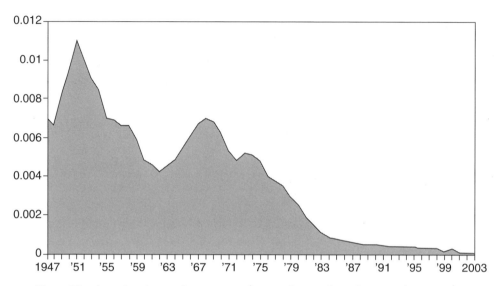

Fig. 1. Number of major work stoppages per one thousand nonfarm employees, 1947–2003. *Sources*: United States Bureau of Labor Statistics, *Compensation and Working Conditions* and *Monthly Labor Review*.

Walter Korpi and Michael Shalev provide statistical evidence of the comparatively high level of industrial conflict in the United States during the postwar years.[5] Between 1946 and 1976 the United States had the third highest relative volume of industrial conflicts of eighteen Western countries, averaging 585 days of idleness per 1,000 workers per year, exceeded only by Italy (with 631 days) and Finland (with 630). By comparison, Sweden averaged 43 days, Austria, 44 days, and Germany, 31 days.[6]

Granted, a decline in the number of strikes does not *prove* that the right to strike has eroded. Thus, in 1960 Arthur Ross and Paul Hartman hypothesized the "withering away of the strike," as mature industrial relations practices channeled industrial conflict into less confrontational and more accommodative collective bargaining procedures.[7] Strikes, according to this perspective, are obsolete. However, Michael Goldfield; Richard Freeman and James Medoff; Thomas Kochan, Harry Katz, and Robert McKersie; among others, have documented the breakdown in collective bargaining and the growing bitterness of industrial relations since the 1960s.[8] It is well known that whereas 35 percent of the private sector workforce belonged to unions in the early 1950s, less than 10 percent belong today. Moreover, the number of unfair labor practice complaints against employers brought to the NLRB increased over this period, from fewer than fifteen thousand per year before 1970 to well over twenty thousand per year since 1975. At the same time, the mean duration of strikes increased from sixteen days during the period from 1945 to 1977 to twenty-three days during the period from 1978 to 2000.[9] These alternative measures of industrial conflict indicate that the dramatic decline in the strike rate is not due to the withering away of the strike.

Nor is this drop in the strike rate due to the decline in union membership. While it seems intuitive that fewer unionized workers would mean fewer strikers, this hypothesis has no historical or factual support. Nonunionized workers have a long history of engaging in strikes. The massive 1877 railroad strikes and the industrial workers' movement of the 1930s, for example, illustrate that strikes frequently *precede* formal organization. Moreover, the strike rate has also decreased among unionized workers, from 11 percent in 1969–1970 to 1 percent in 1987, the last year the BLS measured it.[10]

Others have suggested that the disappearance of strikes is due to the 1980 election of Ronald Reagan and a rightward shift in U.S. politics.[11] President Reagan's breaking of the air traffic controllers' strike in 1981 and his appointment of promanagement lawyers to the NLRB was part of a concerted attempt to reduce the power of the labor movement. Employers in the private sector, according to this view, followed Reagan's lead and used similar strategies to create union-free workplaces. The decline in U.S. strike rates, however, had already begun by the mid-1970s, years before Reagan took office. Moreover, the theoretical literature predicts that the opposite would have occurred—that the election of a conservative government would provoke an increase in strikes, as workers turn to other power resources to defend previous gains in public policy.[12]

How, then, did the American labor movement come to a point where only 10 percent of the private sector workforce is unionized, and where even unionized workers are reluctant to strike because they fear permanent replacement and union decertification? How did one of the most militant labor movements become cowed, with a strike rate today a mere one-tenth of what it was a generation ago? Many labor scholars today point to American labor law, arguing that it is rigged against the labor movement. According to this view, the *Mackay* doctrine, employer free speech, the weakness of the duty to bargain in good faith, appropriate bargaining unit challenges, as well as a wide range of antiunion provisions in the 1947 Taft-Hartley Act (Labor Management Relations Act) and in the case law have tipped the playing field in favor of antiunion employers and have contributed to the erosion of the right to strike. Supporters of the labor movement consequently have advocated a variety of labor law reforms, from banning permanent striker replacements to repealing the Taft-Hartley Act. However, the labor movement has sought labor law reform for over fifty

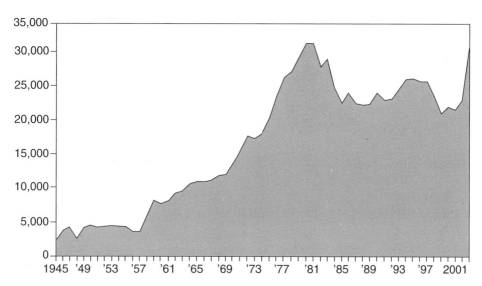

Fig. 2. Unfair labor practice charges filed against employers, 1945–2003.
Sources: Annual reports of the National Labor Relations Board.

years, and for over fifty years the labor movement has encountered congressional inertia, filibusters, vetoes, and failure. The "law turn" in labor studies appears to have reached a dead end of disillusion and hopelessness.

These inconsistencies and loopholes in American labor law are symptomatic of more fundamental problems with the right to strike, problems deeply rooted in American political development and the rise of the modern American liberal state. In *"If the Workers Took a Notion"* I argue that the rise of the modern American liberal state transformed the right to strike from what had been a stalwart citizenship right, founded on civic republican principles, into a tentative and conditional commercial right based on modern liberal precepts. Before this transformation, labor leaders and social reformers supported a robust right to strike as essential for the citizenship of working Americans and for the defense of republican institutions. The evolution of the early American republic into the new American state challenged this conception of the right to strike and eventually recast it to conform to the principle of voluntarism and a narrow conception of free collective bargaining. Modern American liberalism remains ambivalent and equivocal and lacks a steadfast commitment to the right to strike.

By modern American liberalism, I mean the framework of political principles, arguments, public policies, and institutions that originated during the Progressive Era and has dominated thinking about domestic policy since World War II. Most branches of modern American liberalism support a mildly interventionist state to promote the liberty and equality of citizens. What "liberty," "equality," and "citizenship" consist of remains disputed; modern American liberalism is not a single, monolithic ideology but an ongoing conversation, in which the participants express some shared concerns, some differing perspectives, and some fundamental disagreements. Four branches that shaped the modern liberal right to strike include industrial pluralism, Keynesian liberalism, economic liberalism, and rights-based liberalism. None, however, defends the right to strike as a fundamental citizenship right.

Granted, modern American liberalism transformed industrial conflict by replacing the law of the jungle with the rule of law, and by providing federal protections for the rights of workers to organize, to bargain collectively, and to strike. The Wagner Act, one of the most important social policies of the New Deal era, specifically affirms the right to strike. But modern American liberalism provides only a grudging acceptance of the right to strike, a "yes, but . . ." that concedes this right, then, with a series of reservations and conditions, retracts most of what it has granted. Wage earners have the right to strike, but not during the term of their contract. Employees are free to participate in a work stoppage, but only over issues of wages and working conditions. Job holders may engage in concerted activities, but not against someone else's employer. Working men and women may stop production, but they may not strike for political purposes. They may refuse to work, but not if it disrupts essential services. Workers may strike, but they may not interfere with strike breakers. Modern American liberalism accedes to the right to strike, but it quickly draws the line; what it gives with the one hand, it takes away with the other.

By contrast, a broad array of other traditions consider the right to strike to be indispensable for a just and democratic society, and regard its absence as a sign of oppression.[13] Modern Catholic social thought has acknowledged the rights of wage earners to withhold their labor for over a century. Despite their rejection of socialism, Pope Leo XIII's *Rerum Novarum* (1891) and Pope Pius XI's *Quadragesimo Anno* (1931) implicitly supported the right to strike.[14] The Second Vatican Council (1962–1965) explicitly defended this right, stating that the strike is "a necessary, though not ultimate, means for the defense of the workers' own rights and the fulfillment of their desires."[15] Likewise, Protestant social thought also defends the right to strike as necessary for a just society. The National Council of Churches proclaimed in 1969 that "the right to strike is ethically defensible as long as it is essential to the achievement of justice and freedom for workers; . . . the only ethical way to eliminate strikes is to develop alternative strategies for the protection of freedom and justice, which render strikes unnecessary."[16]

The right to strike, it contends, counterbalances the employer's power to hire and fire, and offers an instrument for extending democracy into industry.[17]

Social democratic theory also defends this right. T. H. Marshall, who analyzed the civil, political, and social components of citizenship, argued in 1950 that the right to strike helps to secure all three aspects of citizenship. By challenging the subordinate standing of servile labor, this right helps to establish the civil rights of free labor. By promoting collective bargaining, it extends political rights of participation and representation into industry. By providing the disfranchised with a means of demanding policies for economic security, it advances the social rights associated with the modern welfare state.[18]

The international human rights movement of the postwar era also affirms the right to strike. In 1948 The United Nations Declaration of Human Rights provided the foundation for this right, which Article 8(1)(d) of the 1966 International Covenant on Economic, Social and Cultural Rights specifically endorses.[19] Article 3 of the International Labor Organization's (ILO) Convention 87 on the Freedom of Association (1952) includes the right to strike as a corollary to the right of workers to organize.[20] Article 6(4) of the European Social Charter (1961), Article 27 of the Inter-American Charter of Social Guarantees (1948), and Article 8(1)(c) of the Additional Protocol to the American Convention on Human Rights in the Area of Economic, Social and Cultural Rights (1988) also acknowledge the right to strike.

Finally, modern democratic nations widely acclaim the right to strike, while totalitarian and authoritarian governments repudiate it. British law describes the right to strike as one of the "fundamental human liberties,"[21] and France, Germany, Spain, Italy, and Canada generally regard it as a basic human right. Canadian provincial laws protect the full reinstatement rights of strikers against permanent replacement, and Italy and Spain go so far as to specifically prohibit a struck employer from hiring *any* replacements, permanent or temporary.[22] The right to strike was not recognized by the former Soviet Union, Communist Poland, and apartheid South Africa, where, significantly, major strikes contributed to fundamental changes in their countries' regimes. In light of this association between the right to strike, movements for social justice, and democratic forms of government, the ambivalent status of the right to strike in the United States should be a matter of concern to all who revere democratic principles.

I argue that the equivocal standing of the right to strike in the United States emanates from the limitations of modern American liberalism as a public philosophy. As Michael Sandel argues, the modern American liberal conception of justice conflicts with those moral ties, loyalties, and allegiances we hold as members of a community, and the liberal conception of freedom "lacks the civic resources to sustain self-government."[23] Modern American liberalism overlooks the importance of work for strengthening and sustaining the institutions of civil society and, instead, treats it as a private concern. Modern American liberalism thus grudgingly regards the right to strike only as a commercial right instrumental for the collective bargaining process and denies its significance as a citizenship right fundamental for a democratic society. By constituting the right to strike only as a commercial right and ignoring it as a form of protest in civil society, modern American liberalism has constructed this right on an ambivalent and vulnerable foundation.

The Dual Character of Strikes

Modern American liberalism's grudging acceptance of the right to strike arises in part from the failure to appreciate the dual character of strikes. Policy makers and social scientists view strikes *instrumentally,* as a form of economic leverage or a political power resource. However, they frequently ignore the *expressive* character of the strike, which imparts meaning to collective action.

The Strike as an Instrument of Power

The conventional view considers the strike a legitimate instrument for wage earners to promote their common interests. According to this view, the right to strike levels the playing field between otherwise unequal employees and employers, and the threat of a strike forces the employer to the bargaining table. Milton Konvitz provides a succinct statement of this view:

> Without the right to strike, unions will lack the foundation for voluntary negotiation and agreement. If free labor agreement—free collective bargaining in a free enterprise system—is in the public interest, so is the right to strike, which makes the free labor agreement possible.[24]

The instrumental view of strikes is fundamental to bargaining theory, which represents the dominant paradigm in wage theory today. Bargaining theory assumes that agents in the collective bargaining process (management and labor unions) behave rationally in the economic sense: union negotiators pursue maximum wage gains for employees and management negotiators seek minimum wage costs.[25] Each party has means of applying economic pressures to compel the other to come to terms: wage earners may strike, boycott a struck employer's products, or encourage others to buy the union label; employers may stockpile inventory before a strike, shift production to another facility, lock out the workers, or replace strikers. Strikes, accordingly, are not spontaneous outbursts of worker dissatisfaction but carefully timed, well-planned measures to put pressure on employers in the wage-bargaining process.[26]

American labor law also presupposes an instrumental view of strikes. Justice Brandeis stated in *Duplex Printing Press Co. v. Deering* (1921):

> May not all with a common interest join in refusing to expend their labor upon articles whose very production constitutes an attack upon their standard of living and the institution which they are convinced supports it? Applying common-law principles the answer should, in my opinion, be: Yes, if as a matter of fact those who so cooperate have a common interest.[27]

The 1935 Wagner Act, which affirms the right to strike, justifies it on these grounds. In *NLRB v. Insurance Agents* (1960) the Supreme Court determined:

> The presence of economic weapons in reserve, and their actual exercise on occasion by the parties, is [therefore] part and parcel of the system that the Wagner and Taft-Hartley Acts have recognized. One writer recognizes this by describing economic force as "a prime motive power for agreements in free collective bargaining."[28]

Power resource mobilization theory similarly views strikes as instruments of power—not as instruments of bargaining power but rather as instruments of working class political power. Thus, Edward Shorter and Paul Tilly "portray the strike as an instrument of working-class political action. Workers, when they strike, are merely extending into the streets their normal process of political participation."[29] According to power resource mobilization theory, strikes arise from the competition between social classes over economic resources, and in particular over the distribution of national income. Strikers vote with their feet to pressure the state for a greater social wage. Labor organizations renounce their use of the strike weapon in exchange for stable and unified control of the government, which allows labor-based political parties to use their powers to redistribute income, reduce unemployment, and provide a variety of social benefits.[30]

Although political strikes have occurred on occasion in the United States, American labor law is generally hostile to strikes as an instrument of political power. Even as an instrument in the contest between employers and wage earners over the wage contract, however, strikes remain problematic for modern American liberalism, because strikes in the instrumental sense imply the private use of force. As Max Weber noted, "a state is a human community that (successfully) claims *the monopoly of the legitimate use of physical force* within a given territory."[31] Although no major American strikes have involved outright insurrection, mass strikes and employer strikebreaking have frequently overwhelmed the state's capacity to maintain law and order. The period of greatest industrial violence occurred between 1877 and 1940, during the emergence of the modern liberal American state; at a crucial point in the development of the modern American state, industrial warfare and civil disorders presented a serious, if indirect, challenge to the state itself. The modern liberal right to strike, which confines industrial conflict to narrow wage contract issues, emerged as a partial solution to this challenge.

The Strike as an Expression of Labor Liberty

Social theorists have long realized that models of economic rationality do not fully explain why workers strike. In 1932 British economist John Hicks concluded that strikes would never occur if negotiators for both employees and employers were rational and well informed, because both sides suffer losses in a strike. Excessive wage demands ultimately lead to job losses, so union negotiators would realize that it is counterproductive to demand more than the employer's ability to pay. Hicks surmised that strikes are either irrational or they occur when both sides do not share information equally. Lacking full information, labor organizations miscalculate the employer's concession curve, or employers miscalculate the union's resistance curve; one mistakenly calls the other party's bluff: "The majority of strikes are doubtless the result of faulty negotiation."[32] Likewise, Mancur Olson suggests that strikes defy the logic of collective action. Collective bargaining, as a collective good, generates a free-rider problem. Strikes, by limiting labor supply, drive up wages for those who choose to cross the picket line, while eliminating the wages of the strikers: "All of the economic incentives affecting *individuals* are on the side of those workers who do not respect the picket lines."[33]

Strikes, however, are more than instruments in the collective bargaining process; they are also expressive activities through which groups of workers voice their grievances and proclaim their allegiances. They are a form of protest, an expression of defiance, and one of the most powerful ways for wage earners to say they will not accept arbitrary treatment at work. According to Robert Blauner, strikes enable workers to express both dissent and dignity against the powerlessness, meaninglessness, and self-estrangement generated by mass-production work.[34] Strikes also give wage earners a voice in the firm and thus serve to extend democracy and justice into economic institutions.[35] To define a strike as simply a collective work stoppage to pressure an employer to accept new contract terms devalues this highly symbolic act.

Traditionally, strikes involved extremely rich symbolic displays. During the nineteenth century, strikers would don the traditional garb of their craft and display the symbols emblematic of their trades as they paraded through the streets, calling others to walk out.[36] Strikes have prompted a tradition of folk music, as strikers expressed their grievances and allegiances in song. Picketers display placards publicizing their grievances and often exhibit religious symbols. Mass strike rallies have frequently attracted the most famous orators of the day, such as Eugene Debs, Mary Jones, Elizabeth Gurley Flynn, and Martin Luther King Jr. La Causa's display of the Virgin of Guadalupe, Woody Guthrie's union songs, and the Memphis sanitation strikers' signs declaring "I AM A MAN" illustrate that strikes are not merely instruments in the wage bargaining process.

Claus Offe argues that this symbolic aspect of collective action is essential for strike activity. For less powerful groups, such as labor organizations, collective action involves more than just the aggregation and articulation of manifest interests; it requires the formation of collective identities and activities that facilitate the discovery, definition, and expression of the true interests of members. These "dialogic" patterns of collective action complement and facilitate instrumental forms of collective action.[37] Strikes are not merely mistakes in the collective bargaining process; they are expressive-symbolic activities with which wage earners develop an understanding of their shared interests and build organizational unity. The expressive character of strike activity thus helps to overcome the collective action dilemmas that Olson examined.

Some have argued that the expressivist view of strikes implies a right to strike based on the First Amendment.[38] For example, in *Thornhill v. Alabama* (1940) the Supreme Court overturned, as a violation of the freedom of speech, an Alabama law that banned all picketing at the site of a labor dispute, and extended to picketing the protections of the First and Fourteenth Amendments.[39] In general, however, modern American liberalism has rejected broadening the constitutional freedom of expression to include the right to strike. As constitutional law scholar Edward S. Corwin argued, "In many circumstances picketing, even when unaccompanied by actual violence or fraud, is coercive and intended so to be; and when it is, it is related to freedom of speech to about the same extent and in the same sense as the right to tote a gun is related to the right to move from place to place."[40] By 1942, in *Carpenters and Joiners Union v. Ritter's Café*, the Supreme Court had already begun to limit peaceful picketing by distinguishing between speech and conduct.[41] For the most part, the Supreme Court treats picketing and other forms of labor protest as conduct, and considers strikes to be a form of commercial activity, not a form of communication protected under the First Amendment.[42] Modern American liberalism does not apply civil libertarian discourse to strikers; it treats strikes as instrumental activities in-

volving economic coercion and creates a framework of permissible and for-
bidden conduct, considered as such.

Liberal discourse, however, has not always been the sole symbolic system through which working Americans have expressed their aspirations
and their dissent. Prior to the rise of pure-and-simple trade unionism,
which promotes labor's organizational and economic interests within the
existing social system, labor leaders and reformers adapted the discourse of
civic republicanism to the needs of working Americans, emphasizing in
particular the civic significance of free labor.[43] This ideology rejected the
view of labor as just a commodity and repudiated the claim that wage
labor and free labor are equivalent. Instead, nineteenth-century worker-
republican discourse conceived of free labor as a political condition necessary for full citizenship in the American republic. As such, it extended to
the free worker the Jeffersonian principle that political independence rests
on the economic independence of the citizen. Free labor itself was expressive, symbolic of self-realization and independence, and essential for self-
governance. Employment thus has deep historical significance for Americans, in establishing one's standing as a full member of the American
community.[44]

Prior to the rise of the modern labor movement, labor leaders and reformers declared that the principle of free labor supported labor protest—
the right to strike was one of the liberties that distinguished the free worker
from the slave and the bondsman. Strikes were not merely instruments for
improving wages and working conditions but affirmations of personal autonomy and dignity. Low wages mainly presented a concrete symbol to
protest; the underlying issues included the growing concentrations of private power, the declining standing of the citizen-worker, and the wage system itself. Nineteenth-century worker-republican discourse thus provided a
much more robust and less grudging defense of the right to strike, as one of
the rights of free labor. Nineteenth-century worker-republican discourse
thus suggests a constitutional basis for the right to strike as a citizenship
right, namely, the Free Labor Amendment, which protects workers in the
United States against involuntary servitude.[45] The right to strike is more
than a commercial right; it is a right of citizenship.

American Political Development and the Right to Strike

If civic republican discourse provided a more emphatic right to strike as
a citizenship right, why did the American labor movement abandon this
tradition? This transformation of the right to strike into a limited, commercial right based on liberal principles is inextricably linked to American
political development of the late nineteenth and early twentieth centuries.

During this period a new American state emerged amid the most intense industrial strife in U.S. history. Although labor leaders prior to the rise of pure-and-simple trade unionism justified the right to strike as necessary to defend republican institutions and free labor from the encroachment of the wage system, mass strikes threatened the emerging American state's claim to a monopoly of the legitimate use of force. Lacking the political, constitutional, and administrative resources to address the underlying causes of industrial unrest, federal and state officials by default relied on armed force to break strikes, in the process destroying the Knights of Labor; the Amalgamated Association of Iron, Steel, and Tin Workers; the American Railway Union (ARU); the Western Federation of Miners; and the Industrial Workers of the World (IWW). The mainstream labor movement, facing annihilation, eventually renounced labor republicanism and accepted a narrower right to strike based on pure-and-simple trade union principles. The state assented to a limited right to strike against individual employers when it became apparent that the state's use of force to break strikes was undermining the state's legitimacy, and when state officials realized that a limited right to strike would support the state's interest in industrial recovery.

American Exceptionalism and the Wisconsin School

My account here challenges the progressive interpretation of the evolution of the right to strike, which originated with John R. Commons. Commons and others in the Wisconsin school of American labor history traced the case law concerning strikes back to the early nineteenth century labor conspiracy cases, in which the courts treated strikes as illegal combinations under common law.[46] During the late nineteenth and early twentieth centuries, the courts added the labor injunction and the Sherman Anti-Trust Act to their arsenal of antistrike weapons.[47] According to these accounts, the emergence of the modern liberal American state during the early twentieth century eventually provided statutory grounds for a protected right to strike. The Wisconsin school of labor history regarded the repudiation of the common law conspiracy doctrine and the legalization of the right to strike as consistent with a progressive, evolutionary form of modern American liberalism.[48] Commons, Selig Perlman, and their students argued that a legally protected right to strike in the United States emerged within the unique framework of American liberal values and institutions.[49] In other words, the Wisconsin school argued that the development of the modern liberal American state supported the right to strike.

This progressive account of the legalization of the right to strike embraced the assumptions of "American exceptionalism" whose proponents argue that the American labor movement has always rejected socialism and instead has espoused the precepts of American liberalism.[50] American exceptionalism is one of the dominant frameworks for understanding the relationship between American political development and American working-class formation. Proponents of American exceptionalism, such as Louis Hartz and Seymour Martin Lipsitz, as well as Commons and Perlman, argue that American society lacks the social class antagonisms characteristic of modern European labor politics, that a broad liberal consensus exists in American society, and that this consensus frames all political discourse, including discussions of labor relations.[51] Unlike its European counterparts, American labor exhibits low levels of worker political mobilization, low levels of class consciousness, acceptance of capitalism, no working-class-based political party, and "wage consciousness" rather than class consciousness.[52] American wage earners accepted the system of private property and engaged in collective action mainly to advance their position within the existing social order.[53] In addition, the early extension of the right to vote to white male wage earners reduced the need for class-based political activity and integrated wage earners into the existing two-party system on a non-class basis.[54] The power of judicial review frustrated the labor movement's legislative strategy and compelled unions to turn to economic action to seek improvements in wages and working conditions.[55] The final emergence of a legal right to strike in the 1930s, following the passage of the Norris–La Guardia Anti-Injunction Act (1932) and the National Labor Relations Act (1935), represented the culmination of American liberalism.

More recent scholarship in the fields of American political development and social history criticizes many of the assumptions and conclusions of American exceptionalism. Karen Orren argues that a vestige of feudal employment relations law persisted in America well into the twentieth century, thus challenging Hartz's contention that a liberal consensus had existed from the time of the founding. Orren demonstrates that courts applied the common law doctrine of enticement, which is based on the feudal law of master and servant, against strikers during the late nineteenth century.[56] Unionization and concerted activity successfully challenged feudal employment relations laws and provided "the catalyst for modern liberal politics."[57] Thus, the organized labor movement is responsible for the elimination of feudalism and the rise of the modern liberal American state, rather than vice versa. Orren's provocative argument challenges the conventional view that American courts originally criminalized strikes under the common law of conspiracy. But in the final analysis, Orren accepts the Wisconsin school's progressive conclusions—that the coming of modern American liberalism emancipated the labor movement from an oppressive common law rooted in feudalism. With the Supreme Court's validation of the National Labor Relations Act in 1937, "the remnant of feudalism that was labor relations gave way to liberal government."[58] Orren, moreover, does not regard the right to strike as problematic for modern American liberalism, nor does she argue that the legalization of the right to strike constrained as well as liberated concerted activity.

American labor historians and comparative historians have also challenged American exceptionalism.[59] The Wisconsin school dismissed the early labor movement's endorsement of civic republican values as symptomatic of its failure to differentiate between wage earners' interests and middle-class interests; pure-and-simple unionism, the Wisconsin school claimed, articulated workers' interests independently of the middle class, and therefore represented the natural condition of the American labor movement. The "new" labor historians (namely, those inspired by E. P. Thompson's *The Making of the English Working Class* [1963]), however, have taken a fresh look at working-class culture and ideology of the nineteenth century and have discovered a rich, well-developed civic culture, which they describe as neither liberal nor socialist. This ideology, nineteenth-century worker republicanism, grew out of American workers' civic values, personal experiences in the workplace, and encounters with industrialization. As independent producers, artisans regarded themselves as critical for the commonwealth and considered their standing as self-governing workers to be crucial for citizenship in a self-governing political system. The right to strike for the early American labor movement was more than a right to engage in concerted commercial activity; it was a vital symbol of working Americans' status as self-governing citizens and an important instrument for defending republican institutions.[60]

The "Law Turn" and the Critical Legal Studies Movement

This account of the evolution of the right to strike and its relation to American political development also challenges the "law turn" in labor studies, which stresses the role of a hegemonic judiciary in defining the boundaries of industrial conflict. The "critical labor studies movement" today represents the most radical version of this interpretation. Their critique is rooted in the corporate liberal thesis associated with the New Left historians of the 1960s (e.g., James Weinstein, Gabriel Kolko, and Ronald Radosh)[61] who argued that the emergence of the modern liberal state was the product of forward-looking businessmen and their progressive supporters, who promoted a more active and powerful state to rationalize and organize advanced capitalism.[62] According to the corporate liberal view of American liberal development, pure-and-simple trade unionism emerged out of an accommodation among progressive political, business, academic, and labor leaders who realized that "government by injunction" only inflamed labor conflicts and threatened to radicalize the labor movement. Mark Hanna, John R. Commons, and Samuel Gompers—members of the National Civic Federation (NCF)—regarded the American Federation of Labor's (AFL's) pure-and-simple trade unionism as a less threatening alternative to the radical industrial unionism of labor leaders such as Eugene V. Debs, Big Bill Haywood, and William Z. Foster.[63] While protecting the rights of wage earners to engage in concerted activities, the New Deal labor policy later co-opted the more radical elements of the labor movement, never really challenged property rights or the privileged position of business, and subjected labor conflict to a tightening web of federal laws that frustrated militant unionism.[64]

The critical legal studies movement develops its analysis of American labor law from this perspective. Representatives of this group—Duncan Kennedy, Karl Klare, Catherine Stone, Staughton Lynd, Christopher Tomlins, and James Atleson—regard the law as a superstructural mystification and an ideological support for the unequal capitalist relations of production.[65] They argue that this is particularly the case with the dominant postwar framework of labor law, which they refer to as "industrial pluralism." The principal theoreticians of industrial pluralism—Archibald Cox, John Dunlop, and William Leiserson—promoted the policies of free collective bargaining, responsible unionism, limited worker participation in management, and a restricted right to strike.[66] Industrial pluralists regarded the state as a neutral party that treats organized labor fairly if it functions within this framework.

Critical legal scholars consider industrial pluralism as an ideology whose purpose is to deradicalize the labor movement and maintain the existing system of domination. Kennedy claims: "Labor law doctrinal discourse . . . is best understood as lies and errors. Furthermore, the lies and errors have a bias in favor of the status quo."[67] Klare argues that collective bargaining reinforces the authority system inherent in the capitalist workplace and only permits wage earners to participate in their own domination.[68] As he sees it, the judiciary has consistently reinterpreted the NLRA and its amendments in order to limit labor activism. Klare and Stone argue that the Supreme Court has steadily circumscribed the right to strike, such as it exists in industrial pluralism, by outlawing sit-down strikes, permitting permanent striker replacements, and requiring unions to waive the right to strike during a collective bargaining agreement.[69] Tomlins concludes that the goal of labor law is to get organized labor to "lie down like good dogs" and that "a counterfeit liberty is the most American workers and their organizations have been able to gain through the state."[70]

Critical labor law scholars characterize the state as epiphenomenal, reducing it to an instrument of propertied interests, and the modern liberal right to strike to a business deal. The history of the NLRA and postwar labor relations policies, however, indicates that most corporate elites vigorously opposed the labor act from the start, and that the legal boundaries of labor conflict remain contested terrain to this day. Moreover, the American state has played a more active role in the development of the modern liberal right to strike. The American state as such is an agent in its own right, with autonomous interests, apart from the social-class interests of corporate elites, in setting the boundaries of industrial conflict.[71] Industrial conflict directly concerns the interests of the state as such, in that strikes challenge the modern state's claim to a monopoly of the legitimate use of force and affect the state's functions of maintaining the nation's defense, securing domestic peace, promoting industrial recovery, and establishing political stability.

Critical legal scholars such as Klare, Stone, Atleson, and Tomlins have provided the basis for the law turn in labor studies, which regards the judiciary as the key state institution that shaped the American labor movement and constrained collective action at the workplace. These scholars, and others who are part of the law turn, thus reject the premises and the conclusions of American exceptionalism, seeing pure-and-simple trade unionism, including a limited right to strike for commercial purposes, as something the judiciary imposed on American labor, and consider the modern liberal framework of labor relations law as a constraint on collective action. Victoria Hattam and William Forbath present the clearest example of the law turn in labor studies as it relates to working-class formation and American political development.

Hattam and Forbath conclude that the American labor movement turned away from nineteenth-century republican discourse and toward voluntarism (or "business unionism"—what I call pure-and-simple trade unionism) in the late nineteenth century in response to the distinctive power of judicial review and judge-made law, which thwarted labor's legislative reform efforts. Forbath states that "AFL voluntarism and advocacy of a collective laissez-faire policy for labor were a constrained but canny response to the inescapable power of the courts and common law over labor's fortunes."[72] Hattam concurs that a strong judiciary accounts for this transformation from a republican conception of labor's rights to the modern American liberal conception. "Business unionism was the product of the distinctive structure of the American state . . . forged during [the AFL's] prolonged struggle with the courts over workers' rights."[73] They argue that the modern liberal right to strike emerged in the late nineteenth and early twentieth centuries as a strategic response to judicial limitations imposed on labor conflicts and to judicial nullification of labor legislation. Hattam and Forbath thus reject the American exceptionalism thesis and emphasize the role of the American state in the development of pure-and-simple trade unionism.

Like the Wisconsin school of labor historians and the critical labor law theorists, Hattam and Forbath treat as definitive the judiciary's interpretations of workers' rights. However, one gets little sense from Hattam's and Forbath's accounts of the degree to which the state employed armed force to impede the right to strike during these years, even though the period form 1877 to 1922 was the bloodiest era of industrial conflict in this nation's history, during which state and federal governments deployed armed troops in hundreds of strikes. The state determines the scope of rights not only through judicial discourse but also through those *actions* that protect or abrogate rights, notwithstanding what a judge may say. During that period, presidents and governors frequently sought injunctions to warrant their interventions, but they also used emergency powers and declarations of martial law—sources of executive authority that bypassed and sometimes overruled civil authority.

In order to understand fully the role of the state in the transformation of the right to strike, scholars need to address all dimensions of American political development and not just the role of the judiciary. The growth of national supremacy, the nature of party coalitions prior to the New Deal, congressional neglect of the labor question, the rudimentary character of administrative capacities prior to the New Deal, the late institutionalization of the Department of Labor, the formation of ad hoc strike commissions and industrial commissions, the rise of the modern presidency, the involvement in wars, and the role of the military all shaped the right to strike. In particular, as a consequence of the development of the modern concept of sovereignty during the late nineteenth and early twentieth centuries, what Stephen Skowronek calls the "new American state" treated mass strikes as insurrections to be subdued with force.[74] The state thus treated strikers, who viewed themselves as defenders of republican institutions against the incursions of the wage system, as enemies of the state. As a consequence of other aspects of American political development (particularly wartime exigencies and economic crisis), state officials realized that indiscriminate strikebreaking would further inflame industrial strife and undermine other state interests in national defense, economic recovery, and stability. It was within this broader context of American political development that mainstream labor leaders abandoned civic republican discourse and accepted the more limited and less threatening strategies of pure-and-simple trade unionism.

In this book I provide a new interpretation of the development of the modern liberal right to strike, one that considers the transformation of the right to strike from a citizenship right into a commercial right. I also criticize the modern liberal right to strike. Beginning with Adolphe Sasser and Samuel Gompers in the late nineteenth century, mainstream labor leaders and reformers have tied the interests of the organized labor movement to the development of modern American liberalism. The current decline of the organized labor movement and the erosion of the right to strike should lead scholars and activists to reevaluate this relationship and to reconsider the civic republican discourse that shaped the labor movement's conception of the right to strike prior to the rise of pure-and-simple trade unionism.

The organization of this book is largely historical. Chapter 2 addresses the right to strike prior to the rise of the modern labor movement; in it I argue that early labor leaders and reformers regarded the right to strike as linked to the citizenship rights of free workers. Chapter 3 considers the transformation of the right to strike during the late nineteenth century, when the emerging new American state increasingly turned to the use of force to quell mass strikes. Chapter 4 concerns the early emergence of the modern right to strike during the Progressive Era; in it I argue that regression to the default policy of strikebreaking after World War I was due to the failure to unify and consolidate the progressive state. Chapter 5 discusses the New Deal; in it I claim that the collective bargaining model became the dominant framework for the right to strike, rather than a civil libertarian or a compulsory arbitration model, because of the interests and the limits of the New Deal American state. Chapter 6 addresses the right to strike during and immediately after World War II, when collective bargaining became much more formalized and disengaged from broader social reforms. Chapter 7 considers the right to strike during the 1960s, when most social movements turned away from workplace-based forms of collective action, and turned, instead, to community action to further their collective goals. Chapter 8 concerns the rise of the permanent striker replacement issue; in it I contend that this strategy arose not just because of the 1938 *Mackay Radio* decision but because of modern American liberalism's ambivalent understanding of the right to strike. Chapter 9 explores several branches of modern American liberalism (industrial pluralism, Keynesianism, economic liberalism, and rights-based liberalism) and maintains that none of them provides a robust foundation for the right to strike. Chapter 10 concludes with a discussion of the possibility of retrieving the discourse of nineteenth century worker republicanism as a more stalwart foundation for the right to strike as a citizenship right.

2

"Something of freedom is yet to come"
The Early American Labor Movement
and the Right to Strike

Prior to the rise of the modern American labor movement in the late nine-teenth century, early labor leaders and social reformers sympathetic to the labor movement embraced a public philosophy, based on civic republican discourse, that regarded the rights of free labor as essential for a self-governing citizenry. Nineteenth-century worker-republican discourse re-flected early artisans' experience with self-directed work as a practical foun-dation for citizenship.[1] Among the citizenship rights they espoused was a robust right to strike, which they regarded as necessary for defending their standing as citizens.

In particular, early labor leaders and reformers regarded the right to strike as a right to protest the encroachments of the wage system of labor, which undermined their claims as self-governing citizens. The rise of the wage system between 1820 and 1870 transformed the worker-citizen into a hireling, which not only impoverished once-proud artisans but also sub-jected them to the authority of the employer and deprived their work of the moral and civic significance and autonomy requisite for citizenship. Unlike labor leaders at the end of the nineteenth century, who advocated the right to strike in order to obtain a larger share of income within the existing so-cial order, early labor leaders and reformers advocated the right to strike to protest these structural changes and to agitate for the creation of a cooper-ative commonwealth of worker-citizens.

This interpretation of the early right to strike challenges conventional analyses that focus on legal discourse and the common law. Beginning with John R. Commons and associates (volumes 3 and 4 of the *Documentary History of American Industrial Society*) and continuing up to the present, labor scholars have scrupulously dissected seventeen antebellum labor conspiracy cases, starting with *Commonwealth v. Pullis* (Pennsylvania, 1806) and ending with *Commonwealth v. Hunt* (Massachusetts, 1842), in order to divine from legal texts the changing boundaries of collective action during this era.[2] According to this perspective, judges initially applied the common law doctrine of conspiracy to criminalize work stoppages as illegal combinations in restraint of trade. In the first labor conspiracy case, *Commonwealth v. Pullis* (Pennsylvania, 1806), the court drew on *R. v. Journeymen Taylors* (England, 1721), which had ruled that "a conspiracy of any kind is illegal, although the matter which they conspired might have been lawful for them, or of any of them, to do, if they had not conspired to do it."[3] Conspiracies were illegal per se, not because of the ends sought or the means used but because they challenged the sovereignty of the state. Scholars generally point to *Commonwealth v. Hunt* (Massachusetts, 1842) as the Magna Carta of the U.S. labor movement, which overturned the per se doctrine and enunciated the "means-ends" test of conspiracy, namely, that if the ends sought and the means used are not themselves illegal, then the combination is not a conspiracy. Chief Justice Lemuel Shaw declared, "We cannot perceive, that it is criminal for men to agree together to exercise their own acknowledged rights, in such a manner as best to subserve their interests."[4] This provided the basis for the rise of pure-and-simple trade unionism, including a limited right to strike to obtain better wages and working conditions.

More recent scholars concur that the judiciary played the key role in regulating labor conflict during these years. Victoria Hattam asserts, "The conspiracy doctrine was the primary legal remedy for regulating industrial conflict between 1806 and 1896."[5] In a very detailed and thorough study of antebellum labor law, Christopher Tomlins argues that legal discourse during this period, and particularly judge-made law, played a pivotal role in re-ordering labor relations and subordinating labor to capital.[6]

Early case law, however, does not establish a definitive account of the right to strike during the early nineteenth century. The evidence that no right to strike existed consists of seventeen conspiracy convictions between 1806 and 1842; yet during this period hundreds of strikes took place in Boston, New York, Philadelphia, Baltimore, and elsewhere, most of which did not lead to indictments for conspiracy. Thus, a major strike wave promoting the ten-hour day erupted in Boston during 1836–37, but prosecutors did not indict a single striker.[7] A grand jury refused to prosecute leaders of the 1836 Philadelphia coal-heavers strike that had sparked a citywide sympathy strike by twenty thousand members of the General Trades

Union.[8] Likewise, the 1860 New England shoemakers strike, the largest antebellum strike, produced no indictments.[9] When prosecutors did bring charges, juries frequently refused to convict strike leaders. For example, in *People v. Cooper* (New York, 1836) the jury accepted the defense's argument that, because no coercion took place, strikers broke no laws. Massachusetts courts acquitted strike leaders in 1824, 1825, 1829, and again in 1832.[10] Moreover, before the Civil War, penalties for those convicted of labor conspiracy were negligible. In *Commonwealth v. Pullis* the court fined the strike leaders eight dollars. The fine in *People v. Melvin* (1809–10) was only one dollar. In only one case before the Civil War were strikers fined more than ten dollars (*People v. Faulkner,* New York, 1836), and in no case did strikers serve any jail time.[11]

In addition, authorities rarely resorted to force to subdue strikers before the 1870s. Federal authorities deployed troops during peacetime only once prior to 1877—in 1835, during a work stoppage in Maryland by canal builders. The show of force, however, was purely symbolic. The mayor of New York assembled a regiment of National Guardsmen once during the strike wave of 1836, against striking dockworkers. The militia never confronted the strikers, who quickly returned to work.[12] City officials again called on the police in 1850 to suppress the tailors' strike and to protect strikebreakers. During one engagement, police killed two and severely wounded several dozen striking tailors.[13] This appears to be the only occasion when public officials in any American city used lethal force before the 1870s.

Public officials in antebellum Philadelphia likewise seldom intervened in local work stoppages. Neither police nor militia apparently intervened during the 1836 strike wave, when thirty strikes (including the first citywide general strike in U.S. history) erupted in the city. Eighty strikes occurred in Philadelphia during the 1840s, but city officials deployed a *posse comitatus* and the militia only once, during a strike by hand-loom weavers in 1843. No bloodshed occurred in that incident.[14] Likewise, officials in smaller towns rarely intervened in strikes; Herbert Gutman conducted extensive research on industrial conflict in smaller American cities during the nineteenth century and concluded that local shopkeepers, small businessmen, and city officials in small industrial towns generally sided with striking workers, many of whom were their own family members, neighbors, and long-time customers. As late as the 1873 Pennsylvania Railroad strike, local officials in smaller cities throughout the Midwest and eastern United States refused to deploy local police and militias against the protestors, and bitterly criticized the power of the Pennsylvania Railroad in their refusals.[15]

None of the efforts to suppress strikes prior to 1877 compares to the American state's use of force afterward, such as during the railroad strikes of 1877, 1886, 1888, and 1894, the Homestead strike of 1892, the Coeur d'Alene strikes of 1892 and 1899, the coal wars of the early twentieth century, the Ludlow strike of 1914, the steel strike of 1919, or the "Little Steel" strike of 1937. Between 1885 and 1895, the states deployed the National Guard at least 118 times, compared to a mere handful prior to 1870.[16] As the next two chapters illustrate, the new American state's de facto strike policy during the late nineteenth and early twentieth centuries involved the repeated use of armed force to break strikes. By contrast, the state's infrequent use of force prior to 1870 to break strikes indicates that initially a benign early republican polity countenanced the rights of free workers to engage in work stoppages, notwithstanding seventeen court cases prior to the Civil War in which courts found strike leaders guilty of criminal conspiracy.

A more productive approach to evaluating the right to strike during the era of the early American republic must go beyond the legal conceptions and judicial discourse of the period and include the views of other participants, particularly the labor leaders and social reformers who were involved in these workplace struggles. This chapter draws on the writings and speeches of Seth Luther, Orestes Brownson, William Sylvis, George MacNeill, Ira Steward, and other early labor leaders and reformers who articulated the principles of nineteenth-century worker republicanism. Although working men with limited formal education, they presented a coherent critique of the structural changes that threatened American workers' standing as citizens, and pleaded passionately and eloquently for a principle of social justice that, unlike the modern American liberal conception of justice, promoted a vision of the common good and a harmonious society—namely, the cooperative commonwealth. For them, the American dream was not just the greatest possible individual liberty compatible with the equal liberty of others, but, as proclaimed in the 1868 platform of the National Labor Union (NLU), "the largest political and religious liberty compatible with the good order of society."

Nineteenth-Century Worker Republicanism and Free Labor

The citizenship claims of the early American labor movement rested on the premise that their free labor was not just a legal and economic condition but a requirement for republican self-government. Free labor signified more than the capacity to enter into labor contracts at will; it demonstrated that journeymen artisans were self-sufficient, productive individuals, capable of the self-directed activity necessary for self-rule. Unlike the indentured servant and the slave, free workers enjoyed the liberty, equality, and civic virtue necessary for full membership in the American republic; they regarded themselves, in Jefferson's phrase, as "the yeomanry of the city."[17]

Labor Liberty

> Our aim is to reach that standard in society which enables us to
> be recognized as intelligent free agents—a portion of the body
> politic—exercising a controlling power commensurate with the
> responsibilities devolving on us; and must convince the world
> that we merit exaltation.
> —William Sylvis, speech delivered in Boston, January 1867

Labor liberty constituted the first political principle on which the free
worker established his claim to American citizenship.[18] In a polity based on
the principle of popular sovereignty, liberty implied more than the personal
freedom to be the master of one's personal affairs. Instead, it was a condition of "a freeman, a sovereign possessing intelligence and capacity for self-
government."[19] Productive, self-directed work accorded the free worker the
same economic independence that British political philosopher James Harrington had ascribed to private property ownership; thus free labor became
the emblem of independence during the early nineteenth century.[20] This
close association between labor liberty and self-government became a principle of American democracy in the 1820s when every state (except Rhode
Island) removed all property qualifications from the right to vote and ad-
mitted all wage-earning white men into the polity.[21] Labor liberty thus accorded adult white males the mandate to govern collectively and the duty to
resist despotism through combination.

The free worker guarded his liberty jealously, because he lived in a world
in which the vast majority of the laboring classes toiled in bondage and
servitude. Indeed, many free workers had personal experiences with servitude. During the colonial era, approximately half of all white immigrants
arrived as bonded servants—as indentured workers, apprentices, redemp-
tioners, and paupers.[22] The auctioning of able-bodied paupers into bonded
servitude continued throughout the late eighteenth and early nineteenth
centuries. States enforced indented contracts into the 1820s, and remnants
of bonded servitude persisted into the 1840s.[23] After 1860, labor contractors imported thousands of Chinese to work on western railroads under
conditions reminiscent of bonded servitude, while the American Emigrant
Company brought in tens of thousands of eastern Europeans under contract to specific employers.

The southern slave system in particular presented a stark contrast to the
free labor system. Where the latter dignified work and promoted economic
development, the slave system degraded work and produced neglect and
decay. The slave system not only debased the slave but devalued all work
and degraded the southern free laborer as well. During the Iowa state constitutional convention, one lone Republican stated: "Slavery withers and
blights all it touches. . . . slavery is a foul political curse upon the institu-

tions of our country; it is a curse upon the poor, free, laboring white man."[24] It was an article of faith that the expansion of slavery into the western territories would drive free laborers from the territories and eventually subject free workers nationwide to the competition of slave labor.[25]

However, the most challenging question for the free labor ideology concerned the meaning and nature of labor liberty under the expanding wage system. Under the household system of craft production, young journeymen artisans hired themselves out for a few years in order to complete their vocational training and to amass enough capital to establish their own shops. The wage relationship was temporary, and journeymen looked forward to the day when they, too, would become self-employed masters training journeymen and apprentices. The moral economy that governed the household system of production, moreover, involved a set of rights and responsibilities beyond the wage contract. The spread of the wage system, however, altered the journeyman's opportunities and relationships. The greater size and capitalization of the new workplaces made it extremely difficult for wage earners to save enough to set up competitive shops. Greater division of labor also meant the deskilling of the labor process and the parceling of work to less skilled "green hands." In addition, the spread of the wage system transformed the role of the master from teacher, exemplar, and moral leader to entrepreneur and employer.

Middle-class supporters of the free labor ideology discerned no conflict between labor liberty and the wage system. Their view of free labor, which became the ideology of the Republican Party before the Civil War, affirmed that the wage contract preserved labor liberty and still provided ample opportunities for all hard-working men to become self-employed. The interests of capital and labor, accordingly, remained in harmony. "Let not him who is homeless," President Lincoln told a delegation of workingmen, "pull down the house of another; but let him labor diligently and build one for himself, thus by example assuring that his own shall be safe from violence when built."[26] After the Civil War, Republicans continued to support the wage contract as the guarantor of labor liberty, and broke with the labor reform movement when the latter demanded the expansion of Reconstruction into the North to liberate northern workers from the oppressions of the wage system.[27] This concept of labor liberty, which equated wage contracts with free labor, eventually became the modern American liberal view.

For most wage earners, however, the wage system created neither the opportunity to rise above the condition of wage labor nor the actual liberty to enter into free labor contracts. By the 1850s, most journeymen artisans remained wage earners, unable to save enough to compete as independent artisans with the emerging factory system.[28] Orestes Brownson asserted, "No man born poor has ever, by his wages, as a simple laborer, risen to the class of the wealthy."[29] George McNeill observed, "The laborer who is forced to sell his labor to-day, or starve to-morrow, is not in equitable relations with the employer, who can wait to buy labor until starvation fixes the rates of wages and hours of time."[30]

By the mid- to late-nineteenth century, labor leaders and reformers increasingly referred to the wage system as a system of wage slavery, in an attempt to find common cause with the emancipation of slaves.[31] "Wages is a cunning device of the devil, for the benefit of tender consciences, who would obtain all the advantages of the slave system, without the expense, trouble, and odium of being slave-holders," averred Brownson.[32] Mike Walsh, a New York newspaper editor in the 1850s and a candidate for Congress, asserted that the only difference between the wage system and the slave system was that the wage earner had to "beg for the privilege of becoming a slave."[33] Ira Steward chided the antislavery movement for its failure to support the aspirations of northern wage earners:

> The anti-slavery *idea* was, that every man had the right to come and go at will. The labor movement asks how much this abstract right is actually worth, without the power to exercise it. . . . [The wage earner] instinctively feels that something of slavery still remains, or that something of freedom is yet to come, and he is not much interested in the anti-slavery theory of liberty. He wants a fact, which the labor movement undertakes to supply.[34]

The wage system thus took on an increasingly compulsory character, while subjecting working Americans to a new system of authority and hierarchy. Many considered the wage system a regime of false liberty that trapped working Americans. "Republican institutions," declared the preamble to the constitution of the Knights of Labor, "are not safe under such conditions. . . . We declare an inevitable and irresistible conflict between the wage system of labor and republican system of government."[35]

Free Labor and Equality

> Let us be determined no longer to be deceived by the cry of those who produce *nothing* and who enjoy *all*, and who *insultingly* term us—the *farmers, the mechanics and laborers*, the LOWER ORDERS—and *exultingly* claim our homage for themselves as the HIGHER ORDERS while the DECLARATION OF INDEPENDENCE asserts that "ALL MEN ARE CREATED EQUAL."
> —Seth Luther, "An Address to the Workingmen of New England," 1832

The political and social equality of free labor composed the second political principle on which the free worker established his claim to American citizenship. This view of the equality of the free worker distinguished nineteenth-century worker republicanism from classic republican theory, which asserted that self-government requires freedom from toil in order to comprehend the good life. Aristotle had argued that physical labor debased the person and made him unfit for citizenship; employment placed the worker in servitude, subordinating him and rendering him incapable of self-government.[36] Nineteenth century labor leaders and reformers rejected this aristocratic outlook and instead argued that free labor ennobled the worker and established the conditions for political equality.

Nineteenth-century worker republicanism drew its inspiration for political equality from the American revolutionary tradition and the works of Tom Paine, whose *Common Sense* and *The Rights of Man* were among the most widely read political pamphlets of the early nineteenth century.[37] In his pamphlets, Paine expressed an abiding faith in self-rule and popular government, and support for urban working men as productive classes worthy of equal rights and liberty. Paine's use of the terms "republican" and "democratic" as terms of approbation, his denunciations of aristocracy as parasitic and predatory and political privilege as corrupt provided nineteenth-century worker republicanism with a political vocabulary to critique growing inequalities associated with the wage system.[38]

Their analysis of social inequality also incorporated Robert Dale Owen's, Frances Wright's, and Thomas Skidmore's neo-Ricardian conception of class. This analysis divided society into two opposing classes: the producers, made up of artisans, mechanics, small farmers, small manufacturers, and small proprietors, who were the source of all wealth and contributed to the overall well-being of society, and the nonproducers, who were parasitic on society and the producing classes. Producers controlled modest amounts of property and included nonindustrial classes such as small farmers. Nonproducers included a variety of occupations that derived their income in ways that did not produce anything deemed socially useful; landlords, speculators, bankers, lawyers, bond holders, as well as criminals and the dependent poor composed this class.[39]

Labor leaders and reformers argued that corruption within the political system had permitted passage of unequal laws—class legislation—that granted privileges, special advantages, and monopolies to segments of the nonproducing classes. Land grants provided land speculators with unequal access to real estate; bank charters permitted monied interests to speculate, control credit, and demand usurious interest rates; and corporate charters granted monopolistic privileges to wealthy employers. Critics throughout the nineteenth century denounced monopolies not simply because they violated the principles of the free market but because they encouraged political privilege, corrupted republican institutions, and undermined the free labor system. William Leggett, publisher of the New York *Plaindealer,* argued:

> The humble mechanic, who exhausts the fruit of many a day and night of toil in supplying his workshop with the implements of his craft, desires no charter. . . . They are content to stand on the broad basis of equal rights. They trust with honourable confidence, to their own talents, exercised with industry, not to special immunities, for success. . . . Why should the banker, the insurer, the bridge builder, the canal digger, be distinguished by peculiar privileges? Why should they be made a chartered order, and raised above the general level of their fellow-men?[40]

Abraham Lincoln asserted a similar view. He said, "I affirm it as my conviction that class laws, placing capital above labor, are more dangerous to the republic at this hour than chattel slavery in the days of its haughtiest supremacy. Labor is prior to and above capital and deserves a much higher consideration."[41]

The early labor movement's legislative agenda for national political economic reform—including antimonopoly regulation, worker lien laws, abolition of imprisonment for debt, abolition of the national bank, and monetary reform—was part of their program for promoting greater equality. Many labor leaders maintained that bankers' and financiers' control of the money supply, credit, and interest impeded the opportunities for self-employment and workers' cooperatives and gave bankers and financiers the power to determine the distribution of income between labor and capital. With interest rates exceeding the annual increase in the national income, labor leaders believed that the difference came out of the wage earner's paycheck.[42] Thus, the early labor movement's opposition to the Bank of the United States and its support for Greenbackism in the 1860s and 1870s and for bimetalism in the 1890s was part of its program for reforming the inequalities generated by the wage system.

Although advocates of nineteenth-century worker republicanism used the language of equal rights, their concept of equality stands apart from modern liberal and socialist notions. Equal rights referred not only to equal individual legal rights but also to the elimination of social-class distinctions and the elevation of the laboring classes. Moreover, "producers" and "nonproducers" cut across the class lines of proletariat and bourgeoisie and should not be equated with socialist class divisions of "labor" and "capital," or modern liberal categories of "employer" and "employee." None called for the overthrow of ruling classes or the elimination of capitalism, but instead they sought reforms to eliminate privileges that corrupted the republic and programs to prepare the laboring classes for equal citizenship. Labor leaders and reformers within the republican tradition, such as Sylvis, Steward, and McNeill, never advanced their critique of class inequality into a theory of exploitation, surplus value, and capitalist accumulation, nor did they propose the radical elimination of capitalism, at least not in the Marxist or syndicalist sense. Instead, they sought reforms that would elevate labor to an equal position to capital. Sylvis proclaimed:

> Labor always goes first, and capital follows after. We, however, have no objection to an equal division of the credit and honor, provided we get an equal share of the profits. But there is no equality about it. Capitalists not only appropriate to themselves all the profits, but all the honor and glory; while humble labor goes unrewarded but by the taunts and jeers of the usurper. We are perfectly willing the profits and honors should be equally divided between us.[43]

Civic Virtue

> The working classes are the bone and sinew of the land; and . . . upon their health, virtue and happiness depend the security and perpetuity of our glorious and free institutions.
> —Declaration of the Philadelphia General Trades Union in support of the "ten-hour strike" by coal haulers, 1836[44]

The civic virtue of the working classes was the third political principle on which they established their claim to American citizenship. Self-directed work, advocates of worker republicanism argued, established working Americans not only as worthy of equal respect but as a primary source of civic virtue. Sylvis declared that "the act of *producing* tends to develop the powers of the mind, while the luxury of *consuming*, blended with the vice of idleness, generally renders it inert and contracted."[45] The yeomanry of the city also claimed a greater capacity for self-sacrifice for the good of the republic. As William Leggett noted in 1837,

> It is to the farming and mechanick interests we must look, in these days of extraordinary delusion among mercantile men, for sound views as to the causes of evils which distract the country, and as to the proper means of bringing affairs back to their former prosperity. . . . While we may look to them for such a host of sound minds in sound bodies, for such a multitude of men who, like Roman Mutius, are not only able and willing to act, but to suffer for their country, we shall not lose our confidence in the stability of our democratick institutions.[46]

Nineteenth-century worker republicans, however, recognized that over-
work and lack of education interfered with the laboring classes' capacity for
self-government. As Sylvis eloquently stated:

> What would it profit us, as a nation, were we to preserve our institutions and
> destroy the morals of the people; save the constitution, and sink the masses
> into hopeless ignorance, poverty, and crime; all the forms of our republican in-
> stitutions to remain on the statute-books, and the great body of the people
> sunk so low as to be incapable of comprehending their most simple and essen-
> tial principles . . . ? Remember, too, that all popular governments must depend
> for their stability and success upon the virtue and intelligence of the masses;
> that tyranny is founded upon ignorance; and that while long hours, low wages,
> and few privileges are the strength and support of the one, they are entirely in-
> compatible with the other.[47]

Thus, early reformers advocated that common schools provide the children of the laboring classes with the capacity for active and thoughtful citizenship, so that working Americans could resist demagoguery and restore
American politics to its democratic foundations. Labor activists during the
1830s also supported greater leisure, not only to ensure relief from toil and
improve safety and efficiency at the workplace but also to enhance the civic
virtues of working Americans. "The overworked and under-paid are dangerous enough in any country," Steward averred, "but especially so in
America, where they have votes."[48]

The Just Society

> All free men are equal in political rights, and entitled to the
> largest political and religious liberty compatible with the good
> order of society, as also the use and enjoyment of their labor,
> and talents and no man or set of men are entitled to exclusive,
> separate emoluments, privileges or immunities from the govern-
> ment but in consideration of public service.
> —Preamble to the platform of the Labor Reform Party, an-
> nounced at the Philadelphia Congress of the National
> Labor Union, August 1869

Social justice for the laboring classes constituted the fourth principle of
nineteenth-century worker republicanism. Labor leaders and social reformers proposed a vision of the just society that transcended the wage system
and restored America to its civic republican foundations. According to their
outlook, justice between employers and employees is not simply a matter of
securing a better deal with the employer through a fair procedure; instead,

justice requires the formation of a new kind of economic enterprise that will eventually eliminate the oppression and inequalities of the wage system and restore civic virtue to worker citizens. Although this normative ideal lacks the analytic sophistication of the modern liberal theory of justice, it nonetheless presented an alternative worthy of our present serious consideration.

The nineteenth-century worker-republican conception of justice presupposed a vision of the good society as a foundation for their notion of right. Accordingly, William Sylvis and the National Labor Union believed that justice demanded "the greatest political and religious liberty compatible with the good order of society."[49] Workingmen and women during the nineteenth century had witnessed the great social progress brought by industrialization, but they had also experienced the economic dislocations and the increasing disparities in wealth between the producing and nonproducing classes, which undermined the good order of society. According to Sylvis, workers have a right to a just portion of the fruits of their labor, and to share in social progress:

> Shall he not dwell in palaces, who raises palaces? Shall she not go in rich attire, whose fingers wind the silk of the toiling worm? Shall the ruby, the diamond, and the red, red gold, not glitter on the miner's manly breast, or deck the fingers of his wife and child? Shall she not wear who spins; he eat who sows?[50]

The preamble to the constitution of the Knights of Labor called on "all who believe in securing 'the greatest good for the greatest number' to join and assist us."[51] In his address to the 1865 national convention of the Iron Molders International Union in Chicago, Sylvis stated: "There is, there can be, but one rule for estimating the true value of wealth; that rule is *human happiness.* General competence . . . can only be secured by an equitable distribution of the products of labor."[52] Many pointed to the Declaration of Independence and its guarantee of the right to the pursuit of happiness. What good was the material progress associated with industrialization, they asked, if those who helped to create the nation's wealth were miserable?

Other labor leaders and reformers turned to an early version of the social gospel for a vision of the good society. Thus, Orestes Brownson argued for altering social arrangements to embody Christian righteousness:

> According to the Christianity of Christ no man can enter the kingdom of God, who does not labor with all zeal to bring down the high, and bring up the low; to break the fetters of the bound and set the captive free; to destroy all oppres-

sion, establish the reign of justice, which is the reign of equality between man and man; to introduce new heavens and a new earth, wherein dwelleth righteousness, wherein all shall be as brothers, loving one another, and no one possessing what another lacketh.[53]

George McNeill proclaimed, "then the new Pentecost will come, when every man shall have according to his needs."[54]

The nineteenth-century worker-republican vision of the good society not only exhibited Christian and utilitarian ideals but also the civic ideal of self-government as necessary for a just society. The platform of the National Labor Union affirmed the inherent sovereignty of the people and argued that concentration of wealth was "subversive of the principles of justice upon which our Democratic Republican institutions are founded."[55] McNeill argued:

> Republican institutions are sustained by the ability of the people to rule. The government has the right, and is bound to self-defence to protect the ability of the people to rule. . . . It is the policy of the government to protect, not only her domain from monarchal interference, as set forth in the Monroe doctrine, but to protect her citizens from the influence of cheap labor and over-work.[56]

This civic conception of a just society distinguished the public philosophy of the early American labor movement from modern American liberalism. According to Michael Sandel, the public philosophy of contemporary liberalism "does not see political life as concerned with the highest human ends or with the moral excellence of citizens."[57] In other words, the liberal theory of justice endorses no particular ideal of the good society.[58] Only individuals can determine their own ends, and the most extensive personal liberty demands that the state remain neutral toward these ends. Human happiness, righteousness, self-government, the common good, or the well-ordered society may be laudable human goals, but they are the concerns of personal morality and not the liberal theory of justice.

Early labor leaders and reformers, however, regarded the existing conditions of the laboring classes as unjust not merely because these conditions unfairly limited individuals' capacity to chose their own ends freely, or simply because these conditions did not treat every individual with equal concern and respect. In the nineteenth-century worker-republican conception of it, justice is not entirely neutral toward ends but supports the institutions of self-government. Morally degraded and impoverished people, however, lack the capacity for self-rule. Unlike the discourse of modern American liberalism, in nineteenth-century worker-republican discourse the good preceded the right.

The contrast between the modern liberal theory of justice and the nineteenth-century republican conception of justice is also apparent in their respective evaluations of the labor market. Friedrich Hayek has made the case that *only* market systems (including the labor market) provide the most extensive personal liberty and justice:

> When we can no longer depend upon the impersonal determination of wages by the market, the only way we can retain a viable economic system is to have them determined authoritatively by government. Such determination must be arbitrary, because there are no objective standards of justice that could be applied.[59]

According to Hayek, the rule of law demands the enforcement of general rules "which do not seek particular aims."[60] For Hayek liberal justice demands that the state remain neutral toward the ends of both wage earners and employers. John Rawls also maintains that the free market, including the market for labor, is compatible with social justice: "A further and more significant advantage of a market system is that, given the requisite background institutions, it is consistent with equal liberties and fair equality of opportunity. Citizens have a free choice of careers and occupations."[61] Likewise, advocates of pure-and-simple unionism accept the labor market but promote labor organization as an antidote for the unequal market power of employees and as a means of securing "true liberty of contract."

Early labor leaders and reformers, by contrast, objected to the wage system in principle because it treated labor merely as a factor of production. This conception of labor as a market commodity subverted their presuppositions that labor was the source of all wealth and their normative belief that free labor established one's civic claim as a citizen with full standing in the polity. Under the market system for labor, McNeill claimed, "When [the worker] is at work, he belongs to the lower orders, and is continually under surveillance; when out of work, he is an outlaw, a tramp,—he is a man without the rights of manhood,—the pariah of society, homeless, in the deep significance of the term."[62]

As early as the 1830s, artisans associated with the General Trades Union claimed that work was not a market commodity but rather the wage earner's personal estate, and demanded the right to determine its value. Striking sailmakers proclaimed, "We hold that our labor is our property, and we have the inherent right to dispose of it in such parcels as any other species of property," and journeymen house carpenters asserted that "we, the working-men, consider that we are by far the most competent judges of the value of our labor."[63]

Sylvis observed, "A pound of butter has no control over itself; I have over my labor. A pound of butter cannot say that it will not be bought and sold for less or more than a given price. I can dispose of my labor as I please."[64] But, McNeill noted, "the laborer's commodity perishes every day beyond possibility of recovery. He must sell to-day's labor to-day, or never."[65] According to Steward, this subjects the wage earner to "the power of the cheaper over the dearer," driving wages down to the lowest common denominator.[66] As such, it was the source of the growing antagonism between employers and wage earners, in that the former regard wages as a cost to be minimized. The wage system thus undermines the "good order of society" by destroying any harmony of interest that once prevailed between employers and wage earners.[67] "This general antagonism," Sylvis averred, "is the source of all strikes."[68]

"The Good Order of Society"

It is to co-operation, then, as the lever of labor's emancipation, that the eyes of the workingmen and women are directed; upon co-operation their hopes are centered. . . . By co-operation alone can a system of colonization be established in which men may band together for the purpose of securing the greatest good for the greatest number.
—Grand Master Workman Terence Powderly, "Address to the Fourth Session of the General Assembly of the Knights of Labor," September 7–11, 1880, Pittsburgh

The Cooperative Commonwealth

Nineteenth-century worker republicanism involved more than complaints against the commodification, deskilling, and disenfranchisement of labor that accompanied the expansion of the wage system. Advocates also proposed the creation of a cooperative commonwealth to "engraft republican principles into our industrial system."[69] To accomplish this, they called for policies that would eventually lead to the dissolution of the wage system, transforming the working men and women into their own employers, and eliminating from the workplace those who lived off the productive labor of the working classes.

By the 1860s cooperative organizations had become the labor movement's principal long-term goal. "Cooperation is the great idea of the age," proclaimed Sylvis. "It is the only means by which we can fully control both labor and money, by which we have been so long creating for the use of others; for by it we secure a fair standard of wages, and a fair share of the profits arising from our industry."[70] Both the 1866 Baltimore Program of the National Labor Union and the 1879 constitution of the Knights of Labor declared cooperation as the ultimate aim of the labor movement.[71] Eugene Debs, before he turned to socialism, likewise advocated the substitution of the cooperative commonwealth for the wage system when he testified before the U.S. Strike Commission in 1894.[72]

According to Sylvis, cooperative enterprises would overcome the antagonism between the capitalist and the wage earner by transforming working people into their own employers, deposing from workplaces those who lived off the productive labor of working Americans, and making every employed person a capitalist.

> We cannot hope for an identity of interests until capital and labor become united in the same person. . . . This will forever destroy all antagonism, and prove a sure remedy for all the unpleasant and unprofitable struggles between capital and labor. . . .
>
> It is but equitable and just, because labor is the foundation of all wealth. I maintain that this division of profit will produce harmony in society.[73]

Eventually, the principle of cooperation would extend to other economic sectors, including retail trade, banking, farming, building associations and transportation, transforming the entire political economy.[74] The cooperative commonwealth, or "producers' republic," would guarantee the political and economic standing of the laboring classes, foster self-government, and encourage working Americans to contribute to the welfare of the community.[75] Thus, the cooperative commonwealth sought to extend the principles of republican self-government into industry.

This nineteenth-century worker-republican understanding of the just society, however, was unlike the modern liberal conception of the residual welfare state. The residual welfare state addresses injustices generated by the market system not by transforming the market system but by supplementing it with limited state interventions. Labor leaders and reformers, by contrast, rejected the use of a positive state to redistribute income and provide social services for the poor, advocating instead public policies that would foster the creation of self-governing producers' and consumers' cooperative enterprises, with the ultimate aim of establishing the cooperative commonwealth. The realization of the good order of society and human happiness would come through mutual aid and self-help. Advocates of the cooperative commonwealth realized that cooperative enterprises required supportive public policies but still looked to their own efforts, rather than the state, to construct the producers' republic.

In particular, they proposed a legislative agenda that would eliminate perceived privileges that benefited speculators, monopolists, and the moneyed interests, especially those that benefited private bankers.[76] For example, labor reformers supported Greenbackism, which attempted to make credit more available for cooperative enterprises by reducing interest on government bonds to 3 percent and by limiting the power to create money to the federal government. Advocates of the cooperative commonwealth also supported the eight-hour workday, but they turned to collective action, rather than legislation, to promote this central demand of the early labor movement.

Collective Action

> The strike of the trainmen on the Baltimore & Ohio Railroad was the serving of a notice upon the people of this nation that wages could not be further reduced,—a protest against robbery, a rebellion against starvation. The trainmen were under despotic control. To leave their employ was to become tramps, outlaws; to submit was to starve in serfdom.
> —George McNeill, *The Labor Movement*, 1877

Early labor leaders yearned for the creation of the cooperative commonwealth to realize their republican ideals. Such a society, they believed, would again dignify productive work, eliminate gross inequalities and poverty, restore the citizenship of working Americans, promote the good order of society, and reestablish popular sovereignty. The workers' republic would not come about through proclamations alone, however. Labor leaders and reformers believed that organization and strikes were appropriate interim measures to defend workers' rights and to precipitate the transition to the cooperative commonwealth. Once the cooperative commonwealth had superseded the wage system, none of the antagonisms and injustices that generated industrial conflict would exist. Few labor leaders ever entertained the notion that strikes alone could completely emancipate the laboring classes.[77] Nonetheless, throughout the era, labor leaders promoted a robust right to strike to defend the institutions of nineteenth-century worker republicanism and to advance the ideal of the cooperative commonwealth.

Throughout the nineteenth century the most compelling strike issue did not concern wages but the hours of labor. Shortening the workday (with no corresponding decrease in wages) would not merely alleviate toil, promote safety, and improve efficiency at the workplace, but, they asserted, it would safeguard the citizenship rights and civic virtues of working Americans. Workers first struck for the ten-hour day in the mid-1830s in Philadelphia, Boston, Baltimore, New York City, Salem, Hartford, Albany, and elsewhere, declaring that the long hours of toil interfered with the capacity of recently enfranchised workingmen to participate as informed and enlightened citizens. Philadelphia strikers protested:

Our institutions place all power in the hands of the very men who are now in a great measure debarred from mental improvement, and shut out from the mental cultivation which can render them capable of wielding their tremendous strength to the advantage of our common country. .·. . The working man asks time for improvement. Give it to him.[78]

After the Civil War, advocates for the eight-hour day argued that the reduction of the workday would gradually dissolve the wage system as a precondition for creating the cooperative commonwealth. Ira Steward, national leader of the Eight Hour Leagues during the 1860s, '70s, and '80s, declared that the reduction of the hours of work would, contrary to the arguments of his critics, *increase* the general level of wages and eventually lead to a redistribution of income from profits to wages.[79] Contrary to the wage-fund theory accepted by nineteenth-century political economists such as David Ricardo and John Stuart Mill, Steward and other labor leaders rejected the premise that entrepreneurs unilaterally determined the amount of money available for wages.[80] Instead, Steward argued that the level of wages depends on the habits and desires of the laboring classes: "Men who labor excessively are robbed of all ambition to ask for anything more than will satisfy their bodily necessities, while those who labor moderately have time to cultivate tastes and create wants in addition to mere physical comforts."[81] Additional leisure would increase the laboring classes' desires and give them an opportunity to cultivate their interests, Stewart maintained.

> The masses must be made discontented with their situation, by supplying them with the leisure necessary to go about and observe the dress, manners, surroundings, and influence of those whose wealth furnishes them with leisure. . . .
> Tempt every producer of wealth then, by theaters, concerts, fine clothes, stories; and the leisure to enjoy, and the higher wages necessary to support them, will, by wiser fellows, be used to study political economy, social science, the sanitary condition of the people, the prevention of crime, women's wages, war, and ten thousand schemes with which our age teems for the amelioration of the condition of man.[82]

Wage earners who worked less would demand higher wages to satisfy their desires, and the higher wages would come out of profits rather than higher prices. Just as increasing profits during the nineteenth century appeared to have driven down wages, higher wages would drive down profits. Eventually higher wages would absorb most profits and establish the conditions for the transition to the cooperative system. Agitation for the eight-hour day was the first step toward what Steward called "the republicanization of labor, as well as the republicanization of government."[83]

The eight-hour day first emerged as a national demand in 1866, when the National Labor Union enunciated it in its Baltimore Program as one of organized labor's primary demands.[84] Workers turned to massive strikes for the eight-hour day not only to call attention to the issue and to demand eight-hour day legislation but also, in the absence of regulatory agencies to enforce the law, as a principal means of enforcement.[85] Strikes in support of the eight-hour day first peaked in 1872, when upward of one hundred thousand tradesmen in New York City struck for nearly three months to enforce the state's eight-hour law. Strikes peaked again in 1886, when labor leaders called for workers nationwide to strike after May 1 to force the reduction in hours. This demand created a sensation among the laboring classes and led to spectacular growth in the Knights of Labor and the Federation of Organized Trades and Labor Unions, the predecessor of the AFL. The "great upheaval," as the strike wave was called, however, ended in tragedy following the May 3 bombing at the Haymarket demonstration in Chicago.[86] Widespread repression following the bombing marked the beginning of the end for the Knights of Labor, the largest labor organization that espoused nineteenth-century worker republicanism, and provided an object lesson to Samuel Gompers, who, as leader of the AFL, subsequently rejected the goals of nineteenth-century worker republicanism and adopted the ends and means of pure-and-simple trade unionism.

Of course, workers in the late nineteenth century also engaged in ordinary wage strikes, usually in reaction to pay reductions. The most spectacular of these included the great railroad strike of 1877 and the Pullman strike of 1894. Unlike the modern labor movement, however, they did not regard their concerted activities merely as attempts to improve their conditions within the existing order, but as part of the struggle against the wage system. Working Americans in the nineteenth century considered low wages, long hours, and degrading working conditions to be public issues, because they diminished the capacity of the laboring classes to exercise their civic duties as citizens. They recognized that economic arrangements have civic consequences and that the new employment relations eroded the independence and equality necessary for citizenship. As such, they regarded the right to strike as not simply an economic right but as a political right. Worker-republican principles, rather than pure-and-simple objectives, informed their actions.[87]

Criticisms and Responses

Some may object that the forgoing presents a very idealistic analysis, which glosses over certain realities. Critics may raise two obvious objections against this interpretation of nineteenth-century worker republicanism and the early right to strike. First, previous critics attempted to discredit the early American labor movement as immature, unable to articulate wage earners' distinct interests as such, and subject to the panaceas of middle-class reformers. They asked, didn't the American labor movement make progress only after workers abandoned nineteenth-century worker republicanism and turned to pure-and-simple trade unionism? Second, others might say this interpretation overlooks the fact that the early American state was a weak state. Instead of arguing that the early American republic failed to intervene in strikes out of benign toleration for those who shared its republican values, doesn't it make more sense to argue that it lacked the administrative capacities to suppress strikes?

The Early Labor Movement as Immature

Historians of the early labor movement John R. Commons and Selig Perlman regarded the early American labor movement as undeveloped and argued that its adherence to middle-class nostrums such as antimonopoly legislation, monetary reform, and cooperation retarded its development. Commons declared that the early labor movement lacked a well-developed "wage consciousness" and that wage earners had to differentiate their concerns from those of the middle class before they could adequately defend their own interests. Perlman likewise argued that the labor movement had to rid itself of intellectuals, by whom he meant middle-class reformers and radicals, before workers' natural "job consciousness" could emerge. Both insisted that the labor movement could flourish only after it turned away from political action and embraced pure-and-simple trade unionism. The labor movement had to accept the wage system and develop a pragmatic, opportunistic philosophy of improving the workers' position within the existing system through economic action before they could establish lasting and effective organizations.[88] The spectacular decline of the Knights of Labor and the longevity of the American Federation of Labor support their claim that pure-and-simple unionism has better served wage earners' interests.

The claim of Commons and Perlman that the early labor movement lacked its own advocates, however, exaggerated the influence of middle-class writers. True, throughout the nineteenth century middle-class intellectuals such as Robert Dale Owen, Frances Wright, Orestes Brownson, Horace Greeley, Henry George, and Jane Addams frequently addressed the concerns of the laboring classes and met with their organizations. However, there were others who were undeniably of the laboring classes, and who directly addressed wage earners through their speeches and journal articles.

Seth Luther, one of the foremost labor reformers of the 1830s and 1840s, worked as a carpenter. William Sylvis, the president of the Iron Molders International Union and a leader of the National Labor Union, was an iron worker with only one year of formal education. Ira Steward was a machinist, and George McNeill was a shoemaker. Their inspiration was Thomas Paine, who had been a corset maker's apprentice. The ideas and programs that energized the labor movement during these years were largely their own, and their views of free labor as a component of American citizenship and their critique of the wage system grew out of free workers' daily experience with self-directed work and self-government.[89]

Their claim that a successful workers' movement emerged only after labor organizations turned toward pure-and-simple unionism is also dubious. *Some* workers clearly benefited—those in skilled trades and railroad occupations in particular—but the majority of working Americans in industry, on farms, and in offices did not.[90] At most, only five million workers belonged to unions before 1920—less than 20 percent of the workforce. After 1920, labor union membership went into a free fall, declining to about three million members before the resurgence of the 1930s. The modern labor movement may have embraced the wage system, but, as the open shop movement of the early twentieth century illustrates, most businessmen did not share the enthusiasm for pure-and-simple unionism. Finally, the recent decline of the labor movement to barely 10 percent of the private sector workforce casts further doubts on claims that a successful workers' movement emerged in the United States only after labor organizations abandoned the worker-republican philosophy.

The Early Republic as a Weak State

Earlier in this chapter I argued that the common law doctrine of labor conspiracy did not provide a definitive account of the right to strike during the early nineteenth century, given the small number of prosecutions and military interventions prior to the 1870s. But perhaps the early American state's restraint toward the labor movement revealed not the forbearance of a republican polity toward citizen-workers attempting to defend republican institutions against the encroachments of the wage system but rather a weak state that lacked the institutional capacities to intervene in industrial disputes. According to Stephen Skowronek, the early American state exhibited low levels of stateness and manifested evanescent, diffuse, and unassuming institutional capacities, in contrast to the strong European states that evolved out of absolutism.[91] The federal Constitution, he argues, established a state that lacked the specialized institutions that characterize strong states. Others have described the early American state as "elusive and embryonic."[92] Thus, no state bureaus of labor statistics existed until the late 1860s, and no federal bureau of labor statistics until 1882. Federal officials did not authorize an arbitration commission until the late 1880s, and only in 1913 did the federal government establish a separate department of labor. The modern army, moreover, developed slowly after the Civil War, and did not fully emerge until the Spanish-American War. Consequently, the state lacked the capacities to suppress strikes until the late nineteenth century.

The weakness of the early American state, moreover, provided few reasons for the labor movement to mobilize; there just was not much that the federal government could do for them. The reduction of the hours of work, public education, antimonopoly regulation, worker lien laws, abolition of imprisonment for debt, and so on were policies that were under state and local control throughout the nineteenth century, so most labor organizations had little cause to direct work-based protests against the nation-state. Those national issues that did concern the early workers' movement, such as federal subsidies, access to land, tariffs, internal improvements, and the bank issue, generally did not divide wage earners and employers.[93] The widely dispersed nature of the early labor movement, combined with the rural bias in congressional representation, further limited the movement's capacity to mobilize work stoppages to influence national politics.[94]

Granted, the development of the new American state during the period of industrial upheaval between 1877 and 1922 was decisive for the emergence of pure-and-simple unionism. As I argue in chapter 3, the new American state turned to the de facto policy of strikebreaking partly because it lacked the administrative capacities to mediate, arbitrate, and investigate the underlying causes of industrial conflict. In the absence of an institutional framework for resolving labor disputes, industrial conflicts after 1876 quickly surged out of control, and the state responded with the only power it had—armed force.

However, characterizing the early American republic as a weak state is not a completely objective observation. Implicit in the weak state/strong state distinction is a Weberian notion of the state, which abstracts functions and powers away from civil society and reifies them into legal-bureaucratic institutions—an anachronism when applied to the early republican polity. Republican theory, by contrast, proposes an organic relation between civil society and the state. For example, the early republic relied on the institutions of the *posse comitatus* and the citizens' militia to preserve the peace, whereas the modern state claims a monopoly of the legitimate use of force, and depends on the institutions of the professional police department and the army. The right to strike threatens the sovereignty of the modern state more directly than it challenged the sovereignty of the early republic.

The principle of popular sovereignty in the early American republic blurred the distinction between the people and the state. As Alexis de Tocqueville observed, the principle of the sovereignty of the people dominated the whole society; popular sovereignty "took possession of the state. . . . It became the law of laws."[95] The early American republic was a part of people's daily lives, in their civic rituals as well as in their voting behavior. This strong relationship between the people and their state generated electoral participation rates of about 80 percent that persisted from the 1840s until 1896. Working Americans also demonstrated their identification with the state in a variety of civic displays: parades, orations, holiday rituals, and the like.[96] Free workers believed that they had a vested interest in the republic and struck to protest against the wage system because it not only subverted the self-rule they once enjoyed at work but also undermined their standing as full-fledged citizens of the republic.[97]

Popular sovereignty in the modern American state, by contrast, has become an abstraction, rooted in constitutionalism rather than self-rule. With the emergence of the modern American state, voter participation plummeted and now averages only 50 percent in presidential elections.[98] The state seems distant, and trust in government remains low.[99] The early American republic may have lacked the institutional characteristics we identify with the strong state, but it had distinctive institutions with their own characteristic strengths. It was the *transformation* of the American state during the late nineteenth century from a republican polity into a modern liberal state, rather than the emergence of a stronger state where once there had been a weak state, that led the American labor movement to abandon nineteenth-century worker republicanism and embrace pure-and-simple trade unionism.

3

"A nation of mock citizens"

The New American State and the Right to

Strike, 1877–1895

From 1877 to 1895 the American labor movement suffered a series of stunning defeats that destroyed working Americans' aspirations of creating a cooperative commonwealth of worker-citizens. During this era, recurrent labor strife at times escalated into industrial war, as great industrial armies confronted one another in Pittsburgh, Baltimore, Milwaukee, Homestead, Chicago, and elsewhere. Although strikers directed their collective protests against employers, these strikes brought them into direct conflict with a newly emerging state that brooked no challenge to its autonomous interests. Presidents and governors authorized military force to break mass strikes, in the process crushing the unorganized railway workers, the Knights of Labor, the Amalgamated Association of Iron, Steel, and Tin Workers, the American Railway Union, and others. Once-proud worker-citizens fighting for the republicanization of labor became pariahs and enemies of the state. By the mid-1890s, mainstream trade unionists like Adolphe Sasser and Samuel Gompers concluded that, within the new political system, the cooperative commonwealth was an unattainable illusion and that it was folly for a new social movement to come into conflict with the new American state.[1] Instead, they advocated a narrower, more instrumental right to strike for pure-and-simple union goals, such as better wages and working conditions, union recognition, and the closed shop.

Conspiracy convictions under the Sherman Anti-Trust Act and "government by injunction" during this era were among the most potent weapons officials used to suppress labor conflicts. Consequently, many scholars now credit a hegemonic judiciary for the rise of pure-and-simple unionism and the transformation of the right to strike. Thus, legal historian William Forbath argues that "AFL voluntarism and advocacy of collective laissez-faire policy were a constrained and canny response to the inescapable power of the courts and common law over labor's fortunes."[2] Likewise, sociologist Holly McCammon concludes that "because labor law around the turn of the century tended to define the more radical and inclusionary action of workers (such as sympathy strikes and citywide boycotts) as illegal, the law contributed to the growing exclusionary nature of the U.S. labor movement with goals and tactics often limited to 'pure and simple unionism.' "[3] Victoria Hattam concurs:

> Voluntarism . . . was the AFL's strategic response to the unusual configuration of state power in the United States. The separation of powers and the dominance of the courts within the divided state made political action less rewarding for American workers than it was for their counterparts across the Atlantic. When faced repeatedly with an obstructionist court from 1865–1895, the AFL eventually devised other means of advancing workers' interests at the turn of the century.[4]

Challenging this view, I argue that the emergence of pure-and-simple unionism and the transformation of the right to strike were a reaction to the state's use of force to suppress strikes. Officials within the executive branch during this era had little trouble finding compliant judges to sign formulaic strike injunction orders. If none were available, they could declare martial law and suspend the authority of the civil courts. Between 1877 and 1900 presidents dispatched the U.S. regular army in eleven strikes, governors deployed their National Guard units in 118 to 160 labor disputes (nearly half of all deployments of the Guard during that period), and mayors called on their police departments in countless more industrial conflicts.[5] The frequency with which public officials resorted to military force to break strikes indicates that judges were not the prime movers in the abandonment of nineteenth-century worker republicanism and the rise of pure-and-simple trade unionism. To call the turn to pure-and-simple concerted activity "a constrained and canny response" to the judiciary belies the violent nature of this conflict.

Accounts that focus exclusively on the role of the judiciary overlook the broad changes in American political development that Stephen Skowronek describes as the rise of the new American state. Amid burgeoning industrial unrest, a qualitatively different state was emerging, one that initially lacked the administrative capacities to address this conflict with any means other than military force. Two fundamental political developments particularly predisposed the new American state to engage in strikebreaking. First, a modern conception of sovereignty emerged, which abstracted authority from its early republican basis in the citizens' daily experience of self-government and reified it in specific state institutions. This disengagement of civil society and the state distinguishes the modern polity.

Second, national political institutions became more articulated and established their supremacy over the states. The distinctive ways in which these national political institutions developed had a profound impact on the regulation of conflict in civil society. In particular, the failure to incorporate the labor movement into the national party system after the Civil War, congressional neglect of the labor question, and the lack of administrative capacities to regulate industrial conflict relegated to political executives the responsibility to intervene in labor disputes on an ad hoc basis, usually after the strike had degenerated into civil disorder. Political executives exercised their emergency powers, calling on the National Guard and the regular army to suppress the work stoppage, and leading authorities to treat mass strikes as civil insurrections. The new American state no longer treated working Americans who exercised their right to strike as citizens but as public enemies.

The Emergence of the Modern Conception of Sovereignty

The modern conception of sovereignty that emerged during the late nineteenth century constituted one of the most significant qualitative changes in American state development and fundamentally restructured relations between citizens and the polity. Previously, American sovereignty had embodied a distinctly republican view of the relationship between civil society and the state. Tocqueville had observed that "in the United States, society governs itself for itself. . . . It may also be said to govern itself, so feeble and so restricted is the share left to administrators, so little do the authorities forget their popular origin and the power from which they emanate."[6] During the early nineteenth century, free white men's daily experience of self-directed work formed the basis for self-government, giving substance to this conception of popular sovereignty.[7]

Accordingly, citizens' use of force had not, in principle, been illegitimate. The right to bear arms and serve in the militia conveyed deep significance for the citizens of the early republic, in that this right distinguished the republican polity from feudal systems. Likewise, strikers justified their collective action as necessary for the redemption of republican institutions and the defense of their standing as free, self-governing citizens.[8] As long as strikes did not serve private interests, they were legitimate. "It is our duty as American citizens," proclaimed the 1892 Homestead, Pennsylvania, strikers, "to resist by every legal and ordinary means the unconstitutional, anarchic and revolutionary policy of the Carnegie Company, which seems to evince a contempt of public and private interests and a disdain of the public conscience."[9]

Citizens' collectively taking the law into their own hands, however, is untenable for the modern state. At the turn of the century, two otherwise dissimilar social scientists made remarkably similar observations about the modern state and the modern form of sovereignty. John R. Commons noted that

> the state is the coercive institution in society. . . . Every statute, legal decision, or executive ordinance newly enforced is a new differentiation and transference of coercion from its original private control to that of social organization, and every such fact is an increment of growth in the state.[10]

Commons argued that the modern state has evolved as the primary institution employing force to create social order and to establish a framework of rights. Max Weber made a similar observation about sovereignty: "A state is a human community that (successfully) claims a *monopoly of the legitimate use of physical force* within a given territory."[11] Sovereignty in its modern form rests not on the idea of justice but on the state's capacity to exercise and control force, *and* to do so legitimately.

The modern state thus has an autonomous interest (that is, an interest not reducible to the interests of a social group) in asserting its claim to a monopoly of the legitimate use of force. As industrial strife intensified after 1872, however, the nascent state faced direct threats to its sovereign claims. With the emergence of the modern American state after 1877, state officials turned to strikebreaking to suppress the unauthorized use of force and to reassert the state's autonomous, sovereign interests. Although strikers never directly challenged the authority of the new American state, governors and presidents relied on armed force to quell the great railroad strike of 1877, the great upheaval of 1885–86, the Coeur d'Alene strike of 1891, the Homestead strike of 1892, the Pullman strike of 1894, and dozens of other smaller work stoppages throughout the late nineteenth century.

Force, however, is a blunt instrument of policy, and strikebreaking as a de facto industrial relations policy raises fundamental difficulties for the modern state. Weber asserted that the modern state claims a monopoly of the *legitimate* use of force, but the persistent use of coercion to suppress collective action erodes the legitimacy of the modern liberal state. The legitimacy of such a state demands the subordination of military power to civilian control, so utilization of the military as a gendarmerie raises basic concerns.

The legitimacy of the modern liberal state also necessitates the rule of law, but, as Lt. William Wallace noted in his famous 1895 essay, "The Army and the Civil Power," "soldiers are soldiers, not lawyers."[12] Military officers are trained to defend against invasion, not to restore civil order, so violations of constitutional rights frequently accompanied strikebreaking. For example, in the 1891 Coeur d'Alene strike military officials arrested, without warrant, over one hundred strikers and sympathizers, including public officials, and incarcerated them in a bull pen. Rule of law, moreover, means that the state strives for neutrality in its enforcement, but there are no recorded cases in which state officials deployed the military to protect strikers from employer aggression. The repeated use of the National Guard and regular army to break strikes thus undermined the new American state's legitimacy.

Employers' widespread use of force raised a related problem for the modern American state's sovereign claims. During the 1877 railroad strike and the great upheaval of 1885–86, businessmen in many cities sponsored and subsidized their own National Guard units.[13] Throughout this period, firms employed industrial armies of Pinkerton Agency detectives, Baldwin-Felts agents, and their own armed guards. Thus, at the time of the Homestead strike, the Pinkerton Agency alone had more men in reserve than the entire U.S. regular army.[14] As late as 1937, the La Follette Civil Liberties Committee documented the widespread stockpiling of industrial munitions and determined that Republic Steel, U.S. Steel, Bethlehem Steel, and Youngstown Sheet and Tube each purchased more tear gas equipment than any law enforcement agency in the country.[15] The committee reported: "During strikes company police and hired guards constantly usurped the public police power by venturing from company property, weapons in hand, to maintain 'law and order.' "[16] Eventually, to secure its claim to a monopoly of the legitimate use of force, the modern American state had to suppress *all* private uses of force in industrial disputes.

Nation-State Building and the Right to Strike

The emergence of the modern concept of sovereignty helps to explain why the new American state sought to suppress widespread industrial unrest. But why did the state use force to suppress strikes, rather than arbitration or mediation of industrial disputes? Why did the state fail to investigate the underlying sources of worker dissatisfaction and address the root causes of industrial strife?

Strikebreaking revealed the rudimentary development of national administrative capacities during this period. The federal government in the 1870s included departments of justice, treasury, state, post office, interior, navy, and war, but when the great railroad strike of 1877 plunged the nation into a commercial and industrial crisis, the federal bureaucracy included no agencies committed to labor, commerce, or industry. Labor unionists first championed the creation of a federal department of labor with the power of compulsory arbitration in their first nationwide conference in Baltimore in 1868 and continually called for such an agency throughout the rest of the nineteenth century. Congress eventually created the Labor Bureau within the Department of Interior in 1882, but Congress only authorized it to gather labor statistics and did not authorize it to adjust labor disputes, to compel arbitration, to safeguard employee rights, or even to investigate the causes of industrial strife.[17] Although the labor question loomed as one of the most urgent domestic issues of the period, the new American state remained unprepared for the great upheaval of 1885–86, the 1892 Homestead strike, and the 1894 Pullman strike.

Constitutional Impediments to Administrative Intervention in Labor Disputes

This delay in the creation of new administrative capacities to address the labor question partly manifested the legacy of the federal constitutional framework, which reflected the needs and concerns of an agrarian society. With no experience of major industrial conflicts, the framers made no provisions for the adjustment of labor disputes, much less for affirming a constitutional right to strike. Moreover, most labor disputes before 1877 were local conflicts and thus came under the jurisdiction of state and local authorities. After 1877, only railroad strikes unquestionably fell within federal jurisdiction, because they interfered with interstate commerce and the mail. This limited the federal government's authority to intervene in other work stoppages until 1937, when the Supreme Court validated the National Labor Relations Act, recognizing that strikes in manufacturing interfered with interstate commerce. To this day, the federal government's authority to regulate labor disputes largely rests upon the weak foundation of the interstate commerce clause.

Even in railway labor disputes, the federal government had limited authority to intervene throughout the late nineteenth century. The 1887 Interstate Commerce Act authorized the Interstate Commerce Commission (ICC) to regulate railroad rates, services, and operations but not to regulate wages or adjust wage disputes, even though wages were the primary variable costs affecting rates and wage cuts were the immediate causes of most major railroad strikes during this period.[18] ICC chairman Thomas M. Cooley had attempted to intervene in the 1888 Burlington strike, but other commissioners insisted that the ICC lacked the authority even to investigate railway labor disputes.[19] In response to the strike, Congress passed the 1888 Arbitration Act, which provided for the creation of an ad hoc, three-person U.S. Strike Commission on the request of the disputants, or, in the case of an emergency, by the president. Congress did not, however, authorize compulsory arbitration. The federal government only appointed one such U.S. Strike Commission, which investigated (but did not arbitrate) the 1894 Pullman strike after the regular army had broken the strike. The commission recommended the creation of a permanent strike commission and legal protections for unions but, again, only supported voluntary arbitration.[20]

Although the U.S. Strike Commission's specific policy proposals went unheeded, Congress did pass the 1898 Erdman Act, which established a board of arbitration for the railroad industry. However, arbitration remained voluntary, and the board lacked the authority to initiate any procedures for adjusting railway labor disputes; hence, no case came before the board until 1906. The Supreme Court subsequently weakened the Erdman Act in *Adair v. United States* (1908), declaring the clause outlawing contracts prohibiting union membership (so-called "yellow dog" contracts) a violation of employees' liberty of contract under the Fourteenth Amendment. Congress replaced the Erdman Act with the Newlands Act in 1913, permitting the Board of Arbitration and Conciliation to initiate proceedings but not to compel arbitration. Likewise, the Department of Labor's Mediation Service, created in 1913, lacked the authority to compel arbitration. On the eve of World War I, the new American state still had no authority to prevent industrial disputes from escalating into violence.

Party Alliances of the Nascent Labor Movement

Congressional failure to authorize administrative intervention in labor disputes also reflected the weak political incorporation of the working classes at the national level. Although wage earners had exercised the right to vote since the 1820s, throughout the nineteenth century the American labor movement failed to forge lasting alliances with political parties at the national level. Labor organizations tended to be isolated and dispersed, with their political influence concentrated in larger cities. Representation in Congress, by contrast, favored rural constituencies, especially after the entry of midwestern and western states into the union. City machine politics, moreover, dictated that city labor federations form alliances with whatever party dominated at that level, which varied from city to city.[21] This further limited the early labor movement's capacity to form a nationwide party alliance.

Between 1866 and 1872, labor reformers attempted to forge a national coalition with Radical Republicans, hoping to nationalize Reconstruction and address inequalities generated by the wage system in the North. Labor reformers and Radical Republicans, however, never reached consensus over the meaning of free labor—a key issue for labor leaders who challenged the emerging wage system.[22] Labor leaders regarded eight-hour legislation as essential, but Radical Republicans like E. L. Godkin considered such proposals as infringements on workers' liberty of contract.[23] Moreover, the most important nationwide labor organization at the time, the National Labor Union, did not survive the depression of the mid-1870s. The "bargain of 1877" subsequently left the labor movement out of the Republican Party's national coalition and opened the way for the deployment of U.S. regulars against the railroad strikers later that summer.[24]

The American labor movement remained poorly integrated into the national party system for the rest of the nineteenth century. During the late 1870s, labor leaders briefly aligned with the Greenback-Labor Party, but it was basically a one-issue party that did not appeal to the rank and file. Following the Pullman strike, trade unions allied with the Democratic Party to oppose President Cleveland in 1896. The party platform, which Illinois governor John Altgeld penned, denounced "government by injunction," and proclaimed a right to strike. The Democratic Party, however, failed to solidify the alliance between prairie populists and urban workers; most urban workers did not vote for William Jennings Bryan, whose loss to William McKinley secured Republican domination of the federal government for the next thirty-six years.[25] The 1896 Democratic Party alliance, moreover, split the labor movement, because it excluded new immigrant industrial labor.[26]

Without the labor movement's political incorporation at the national level, the labor question remained off the legislative agenda. Thus, Congress neglected to investigate the great railroad strike of 1877, which brought interstate traffic to a halt for two weeks. With the return of industrial discord in the early 1880s, the Senate authorized the Blair Committee to investigate the causes of strikes and propose reforms. For nearly two years the committee traveled around the country, and collected four volumes of testimony from workers, labor leaders, reformers, and businessmen. But the committee never published a final report and proposed no legislation to promote the peaceful adjustment of labor disputes or to improve workers' living and working conditions.[27] Subsequent strikes also generated volumes of testimony, which remained unnoticed by a heedless Congress.[28]

The Militarization of Federal Strike Policy

The neglect of Congress, the limited capacities of administrative agencies, and the tenuous alliances between the labor movement and national political parties meant that the responsibility for dealing with widespread industrial conflict fell, by default, on the executive branch. Strike policy during the late nineteenth century developed erratically, as presidents, governors, and military officers responded ad hoc to crises and improvised state responses to mass work stoppages. With no institutionalized means of peacefully adjusting labor disputes, presidents drew on their war powers to intervene. This redefined the work stoppage as an insurrection and invariably broke the strike. It also led to an expansion of presidential authority and the reordering of the presidency's role in the American political system.

The Constitution, to repeat, does not grant specific powers to the federal government to intervene in industrial disputes; nonetheless, it does authorize the federal government to suspend civil law and declare martial law during a domestic insurrection. Article I, Section 8 specifies that "the Congress shall have the Power . . . to provide for calling the militia to execute the Laws of the Union, suppress insurrections and repel invasions." In addition, Article IV, Section 4 asserts that "the United States shall guarantee to every State in the Union a Republican Form of Government, and shall protect each of them against Invasion; and on Application of the Legislature, or of the Executive (when the Legislature cannot be convened) against domestic violence." As the practice of martial law developed, civil disorder alone did not justify federal intervention; the state must first exhaust its own resources before the governor may petition for federal troops. Constitutional requirements thus inclined public officials to characterize mass strikes as uncontrollable civil insurrections, justifying the suspension of the rule of law and its replacement with the rule of force.[29] Strikers became enemies of the state and lost their standing as citizens with constitutional rights.

During the period extending from the late eighteenth century through the nineteenth, Congress expanded this authority and established more specific rules of involvement in civil matters.[30] Following the first insurrectionary challenge to the new nation, the Whiskey Rebellion in 1794, Congress authorized the federal government to intervene without the governor's request, whenever insurrections or conspiracies interfered with civil court proceedings or prevented the execution of federal laws. In Ex parte Milligan (1866), the Supreme Court ruled that, outside the actual theater of war, no one may suspend the right of habeas corpus and try civilians in military tribunals, as long as civil courts remained in operation.[31] In the Revised Statutes of the United States (1875), Section 5297, Congress delegated to the president the authority to call forth the militia or the regular army to suppress insurrections, permitting governors to appeal directly to the president, rather than Congress, for assistance. Finally, in response to abuses of military power by local civil authorities during Reconstruction, Congress passed the 1878 Posse Comitatus Act, which prohibited military officers from taking orders from state officials or acting to enforce state laws. U.S. army officers must follow the chain of command through the White House and the Department of War.[32]

These laws provided only minimal guidelines for political executives and commanding officers and left many important questions unanswered. For example, just when did a local civil disturbance overwhelm local authorities and demand federal intervention? Magistrates and justices of the peace, especially in smaller industrial cities and towns, frequently resisted employing force to subdue strikers, who often included family members, friends, neighbors, and customers.[33] In addition, local party organizations with political ties to labor organizations often held zealous local officials in check.[34] Employers, on the other hand, frequently regarded local law enforcement agencies as unreliable and cultivated closer political ties with state capitals and Washington, D.C. Consequently, employers would represent strikes as uncontrolled civil disorders requiring a declaration of martial law by outside authorities.

In addition, these laws did not address issues that frequently arose in the field. For example, what were the rules of engagement in civil disorders, and when might troops wield deadly force? Did the army have the authority to detain picketers and strike leaders? Might the army escort strikebreakers? In the absence of presidential supervision, might commanding officers take orders from state authorities? What constituted the restoration of order—the cessation of violence, or the reopening of a railroad line or workplace? How long might military occupations last, and who decided when the military was no longer needed? U.S. army officers recognized that they took orders from federal civil authorities and that their purpose was to assist in the restoration of order, to protect federal property, and to enforce federal laws. In principle, they should act as a neutral peacekeeping force rather than as strikebreakers. Thus, in his prizewinning essay on the military and civil authority, Lt. William Wallace declared:

> That the army is on the side of the constituted authority and is in all things merely a reflection of that power, which is essential to its existence, is an assertion too apparent to be in need of demonstration. In view of this fact, the oft heard charge that the Army is an ally of capital as opposed to labor must be regarded as somewhat singular.[35]

In practice, however, army officers faced unprecedented and rapidly changing conditions in the field, and often they had to act without explicit direction from Washington. Before the Spanish-American War, the military bureaucracy remained undeveloped, even chaotic. Moreover, army officers generally came from the same class as employers and tended to look upon the strikers, who often included numbers of foreign-born workers and tramps, as a lawless mob. "There is a certain class that require force to make them keep the law," noted Lieutenant Wallace.[36] Army officers naturally took orders from local officials and employers, who represented law and order and social respectability. Consequently, military intervention invariably led to the defeat of the strikers.

The Great Railroad Strike of 1877

The first significant suppression of a strike by the federal government took place in the summer of 1877. The great railroad strike of 1877, occurring only weeks after the withdrawal of the last federal troops from the South, came at a significant moment in American political development and initiated an era of industrial unrest that persisted for nearly seventy years. Railroads represented a new form of industrial organization in the United States, and their rapid growth had led to pent-up anger and frustration among the workforce. Four years of depression had reduced wages and increased unemployment, producing tens of thousands of tramps along the rail lines, so when employees of the Baltimore & Ohio Railroad and the Pennsylvania Railroad walked out in the summer of 1877, the work stoppage quickly spread along the rail lines, stopping all rail traffic in the eastern two-thirds of the country and reaching as far west as San Francisco. The strike erupted into one of the largest civil disturbances in American history, and it quickly overwhelmed local law enforcement officials.[37]

Governors of Maryland, Pennsylvania, Ohio, Indiana, Illinois, Missouri, and West Virginia summoned their state militias, but the strike revealed the inadequacy of the old militia system. Some states had no militias whatsoever; in other states, militias served as fraternal lodges rather than as military organizations. Only five states had enough troops to subdue strikers, and existing militias lacked adjutant generals, professional training programs, contingency plans for deployments, and even the firearms necessary for crowd control.[38] In addition, most troops came from working-class backgrounds themselves and were loath to charge fellow citizens with bayonets affixed. Explained one militia officer:

> Meeting an enemy on the field of battle, you go there to kill, the more you kill, and the quicker you do it, the better. But here you had men with fathers and brothers and relatives mingled in the crowd of rioters. The sympathy of the people, the sympathy of the troops, my own sympathy, was with the strikers proper. We all felt that those men were not receiving enough wages.[39]

Open fraternization between troops and strikers in Martinsburg, West Virginia, prompted the governor to request federal troops. The governor of Pennsylvania had to call upon the Philadelphia militia to control Pittsburgh crowds when the local militia refused to use artillery to clear a railroad crossing. The untrained Philadelphia militia fired upon a crowd, killing twenty rioters and bystanders. The action so inflamed the mob that they destroyed several roundhouses, 104 locomotives, and 2,152 railroad cars.[40] Rioters in Baltimore seized the Baltimore & Ohio Railroad depot and burned it down. Mobs in several cities broke into poorly defended armories and absconded with rifles and artillery. President Hayes eventually had to dispatch U.S. regular army troops to subdue the rioters in Pennsylvania, West Virginia, Maryland, and Indiana.

The introduction of the U.S. army finally broke the strike.[41] The army ejected strikers from the rail lines, dispersed picketers, arrested strike leaders, and escorted replacement workers. The arrival of the Second U.S. Artillery under the command of William H. French in Martinsburg, West Virginia, permitted strikebreakers to enter the train yards and clear all blocked freight.[42] Gen. Winfield Scott Hancock, commander of the Military Division of the Atlantic, placed troops on trains to restore railroad traffic through Pennsylvania, Maryland, and West Virginia.[43] In Indiana, army regulars assisted U.S. marshals in opening bankrupt railroads in receivership, and remained on duty for another month to insure that no more strikes occurred.

The railroad strike of 1877 represented a milestone in state development and the relationship between the state and civil society. For one, it became clear that the regular army needed to modernize in order to handle future civil disorders. The War Department's 1877 annual report declared:

> As our country increases in population and wealth, and as great cities become numerous it must be clearly seen that there may be great danger of uprisings of large masses of people for the redress of grievances, real or fancied. It is a well-known fact that such uprisings enlist in greater or lesser degrees the sympathies of the communities in which they occur. This fact alone renders the militia unreliable in such an emergency.[44]

Generals William Sherman and Emory Upton also urged the expansion of the army into a gendarmerie, and until World War I, strike duty was the regular army's principal function.

The 1877 strike had a greater impact on the militia, as most states, expressing "fear of violence by 'anarchists, internationalists, and nihilists,' " reorganized their militias.[45] William Riker notes a strong positive correlation between the number of strikers in each state in 1877 and the subsequent state appropriations for their militias, which they expanded and professionalized.[46] States centralized control under adjutants general, provided riot training, developed contingency plans and rules of engagement for civil disorders, and allocated more funds. Many cities built fortress-like armories to defend against future raids on armaments.[47] Supporters established the National Guard Association to promote professionalization and to represent the militias' interests in Washington.[48]

The 1877 strike also transformed relations between the state and civil society. President Hayes's insistence that others justify their requests for federal assistance on the grounds that the industrial unrest had escalated into an uncontrollable insurrection prompted governors, railroad officials, the secretary of war, National Guard officers, and others to characterize mass strikes as rebellions. Journalists and politicians frequently compared labor unrest to the Paris Commune of 1871, generating the first American Red scare. "The volcano of Communism burns angrily beneath the thin crust of civil law which holds it in subjection, ready to break forth into fiercer flames than ever," one writer reported.[49] The *Philadelphia Inquirer* stated that the strikers "have declared war against society. . . . They have practically raised the standard of the Commune in free America."[50] In a famous editorial entitled "The American Commune," the *National Republican* of Washington, D.C., asserted:

> The fact is clearly manifest that communistic ideas are very widely entertained in America by the workmen employed in mines and factories and by the railroads. The poison was introduced into our social system by European laborers. . . . [The Great Strike] is nothing less than communism in its worst form . . . not only unlawful and revolutionary, but [also] anti-American.[51]

Lt. William Wallace later proclaimed, "When the laborer is guilty of [interfering with strikebreakers] either by overt acts or encouragement given to others, he places himself as much outside the protection of the law as if he were a foreign adversary. In fact he becomes a public enemy."[52]

Nineteenth-century worker-republican discourse had celebrated free workers as the yeomanry of the city and had emphasized free labor as a condition for full membership in American society. The railroad strikers protested a wage system that undermined their standing as citizens. Although the strike escalated into a major civil disorder, strikers never sought to overthrow the state. Under the emerging regime, however, the state treated the strike as an insurrection, and strikers as outcasts and pariahs of society.

The Great Upheaval of 1885–1886

The emergence of the Holy and Noble Order of the Knights of Labor, the largest labor organization of the late nineteenth century, constituted one of the most spectacular insurgencies in American political development. Founded in 1869 as a secret society, the Knights of Labor declared "an inevitable and irresistible conflict between the wage system of labor and the republican form of government" and proposed the creation of the coopera-

tive commonwealth.[53] As such, it represented the most important labor organization that espoused nineteenth-century worker-republican precepts.
The leaders of the Knights had witnessed the spontaneous eruption and
rapid collapse of the 1877 strike and surmised that one of the primary reasons that it had failed was that strikers had lacked organization, leadership,
strategy, and goals. Consequently, in 1878 the Knights of Labor decided to
remove their veil of secrecy and extend membership to all wage earners,
skilled and unskilled alike.

After affiliates of the Knights participated in a series of successful railroad
strikes in 1885 against "Southwest System" railroads, the organization's
membership skyrocketed from about one hundred thousand to nearly one
million the following year.[54] The explosive growth in the Knights and their
success in the 1885 strike against Jay Gould, one of the most powerful financiers in the United States, ignited one of the largest strike waves in American history. According to the *Third Annual Report of the Commissioner of
Labor*, the number of workers striking tripled in 1886 compared to the average annual rate for the preceding five years, and the number of firms
struck quadrupled.[55] These work stoppages included another strike against
the Southwest System railroads and, beginning on May 1, 1886, a coordinated series of strikes in support of the eight-hour workday.

The great upheaval of 1885–86 was especially significant, in that establishing the eight-hour workday was, according to nineteenth-century
worker republicanism, a decisive step toward establishing a cooperative
commonwealth of worker-citizens. Rather than relying on legislation,
which had failed to secure the new hours of labor even when the bills
passed, labor leaders in the Federation of Organized Trades and Labor
Unions and the Knights of Labor turned to direct mass action to try to obtain a shorter workday from all employers.[56] The demand invigorated the
new movement and provided a galvanizing symbol of their struggle, but
leaders of the Knights of Labor lost control over the swelling movement.
Turbulence swept through Chicago, Milwaukee, New York, Cincinnati,
Detroit, Baltimore, Boston, Pittsburgh, St. Louis, and other cities. In all, between 190,000 and 340,000 strikers participated in the May Day strikes,
with another 150,000 joining the demonstrations.[57]

Due to the localized nature of these protests and the capacity of state and
local officials to subdue the strikers, governors did not call upon the federal
government to intervene. Instead, state and local governments relied on
their recently reformed National Guard units and police departments to
quell the railroad and May Day strikes. Governors dispatched National
Guard units to Fort Worth and East St. Louis to suppress railroad strikers
who had rioted after sheriff's deputies shot and killed some of the strikers.
The governor of Ohio directed National Guard troops to pacify strikers in
Cincinnati. Parsons, Kansas, was placed under martial law. Wisconsin gov-

ernor Jeremiah Rusk ordered National Guard units into the south side of Milwaukee, against the advice of the mayor and law enforcement officials; on May 5, the militia fired on an angry crowd of eight-hour day strikers in Bay View, killing five.[58]

The most infamous violence erupted in Chicago, on May 4, in an incident that devastated the Knights of Labor and the May Day insurgency.[59] On May 1, thirty thousand Chicagoans participated in the eight-hour strike, and another thirty to sixty thousand joined the demonstration. Militia units and police were readied for civil unrest. On May 3, police fired upon strikers outside the McCormick factory, killing two strikers. Anarchists then issued a call to arms, and announced a series of protests on May 4. When police attempted to disperse one such rally at the Haymarket, a bomb exploded, killing one police officer and wounding seventy others. The police then fired upon the crowd, killing one and wounding several more.

Despite the inflammatory rhetoric of fringe groups associated with German socialists and syndicalists, such as Johann Most and the eight convicted Haymarket bombers, no labor leaders or labor organizations had advocated taking up arms against the state. The Knights of Labor promoted working within the political system and directed the eight-hour strikes against employers, rather than the state. Nevertheless, the 1886 strikes spurred a second nationwide Red scare and public officials once again defined these strikes as uncontrollable insurrections. In Chicago, law enforcement officials arrested eight anarchist leaders, who were summarily convicted of murder and sentenced to die.[60] In the aftermath of the Bay View incident, Milwaukee officials arrested all radicals and labor leaders, including all members of the executive board of the local Knights of Labor; Governor Rusk subsequently ran for reelection on an antiradicalism platform.[61] Labor leaders and their followers faced the charge that they represented radical, foreign, and un-American ideals. The *New York Times* asserted that the strikers were "entirely un-American . . . [with] no real conception of what American citizenship is or implies."[62] Increasingly, the discourse of nineteenth-century worker republicanism seemed out of step with the political development of the United States. "Under the guise of republican freedom," claimed social reformer Florence Kelley in 1889, "we have degenerated into a nation of mock citizens."[63]

Despite their affirmations of support for American republican institutions, the Knights of Labor were tarred with the brush of radicalism and went into rapid decline; by 1893 membership had dropped to only 80,000 from a high of 750,000.[64] The collapse of the Knights provided an object lesson to pure-and-simple trade unionists like Samuel Gompers, who recognized the power of the state and the futility of the workers' republic, and who promoted the shift toward pure-and-simple trade unionism. The final blow to nineteenth-century worker-republican discourse, however, was the breaking of the American Railway Union strike against the Pullman company in 1894.

Eugene Debs's Revolution

Many labor scholars regard the defeat of the 1894 Pullman strike as the paradigmatic case of the judiciary's hegemony over the labor movement.[65] Exercising equity powers first employed in the 1877 railroad strike and extended under the Sherman Anti-Trust Act, federal marshals blanketed Chicago with over one hundred strike injunctions. Although Illinois governor Peter Altgeld condemned "government by injunction" in the 1896 Democratic Party platform, for the next thirty-six years federal judges enjoined thousands more strikes. According to these labor scholars, federal court injunctions not only broke the ARU but they also destroyed the movement toward inclusive industrial unionism, and sent the labor movement down the path of exclusive, business-oriented craft unionism.

Government by injunction, however, would have failed without the deployment of thousands of federal troops who enforced these injunctions and broke the Pullman strike. This intervention represented the high point in the regular army's suppression of strikes, as well as a pivotal moment in the emergence of national supremacy.[66] Previous interventions, by treating strikes as insurrections, had reordered relations between the state and civil society. Federal strikebreaking in the Pullman case, by contrast, also reordered authority relations between the national and subnational levels of government, affirming national supremacy to intervene in industrial conflicts that affect interstate commerce, and anticipating the expansion in national government power in the twentieth century. Thus, the rise of the new American state, and not a hegemonic judiciary, precipitated the demise of nineteenth-century worker republicanism and hastened the mainstream labor movement's turn to pure-and-simple trade unionism.

Prior to the Pullman strike, federal intervention had been ancillary to state authority, assisting governors in the restoration of civil peace when strikes overwhelmed state and local control. Notwithstanding the 1878 Posse Comitatus Act, earlier presidents had permitted federal forces to take orders from state authorities. For example, in 1892 President Benjamin Harrison had deployed federal troops at the governor of Idaho's request, when the Coeur d'Alene mining district erupted into labor unrest. Due to the remoteness of the region, state officials exercised complete authority over the federal troops. The inspector general of the Idaho National Guard assumed control of the regular army and employed them to arrest strikers and sympathizers, and to escort strikebreakers. Gen. J. M. Schofield and his troops then remained in the region for four months after they had subdued strikers.[67]

As Skowronek notes, however, the rise of the new American state called for the centralization of authority within the national government and the penetration of that authority throughout the territory.[68] Accordingly, in order to develop a national strike policy, the federal government had to assert its authority to intervene in labor disputes without the invitation of the state and local governments. The Pullman strike provided this opportunity.

Unlike the great railroad strike of 1877 and the Coeur d'Alene strike, during the Pullman strike state and local authorities opposed federal government intervention. Governor Peter Altgeld declared that the American Railway Union maintained an orderly, if tense, work stoppage in Chicago and that state troops had the situation under control. The introduction of federal troops, he feared, would inflame the situation.[69] Mayor John Hopkins, a former Pullman employee, hoped that local authorities could arbitrate the dispute, but the General Managers Association (GMA), which represented the employers, refused. The GMA realized that federal authorities were more sympathetic to the railroads and that federal intervention would break the strike.[70] The GMA consequently urged President Cleveland to intervene.

Under the Constitution, the federal government could not deploy the regular army to restore law and order—that was the responsibility of local civil authorities, and only they could request federal assistance for that purpose. However, Sections 5298–5299 of the Revised Statutes authorize the president to deploy the military to execute federal law.[71] The U.S. attorney for Chicago, Thomas Milchrist, subsequently obtained a sweeping federal court injunction under the Sherman Anti-Trust Act, forbidding anybody from promoting the strike. According to the *Chicago Times*, "The object of the injunction is not so much to prevent interference with trains as to lay a foundation for calling out the United States troops."[72] U.S. Attorney General Richard Olney requested federal troops to execute the injunction, and on July 4 the Department of War sent nearly two thousand troops to Chicago; the federal Marshals Service deputized five thousand more agents in Chicago.

The imposition of federal forces instigated a constitutional crisis. Altgeld telegraphed President Cleveland, charging that federal intervention was an unconstitutional usurpation of state authority:

> The assumption as to the power of the Executive is certainly new, and I respectfully submit that it is not the law of the land. . . . The autocrat of Russia could certainly not possess or claim to possess greater power than is possessed by the Executive of the United States, if your assumption is correct.[73]

In response, Olney asserted the federal government's authority over the state of Illinois:

> The soil of Illinois is the soil of the United States . . . , and the United States is there . . . not by license or comity, but as of *right*. . . . The notion that the territory of any State is too sacred to permit the exercise thereon, by the United States government, of any of its legitimate functions never had any legal existence, and, as a rule of conduct became practically extinct with the close of the Civil War.[74]

The *New York World* noted the unprecedented expansion of federal power: "So outrageous a stretch of federal power was not attempted during the Civil War, when amid the tumult of arms laws were silent."[75]

The U.S. Supreme Court confirmed the federal government's authority under the commerce clause, the Interstate Commerce Act, and federal mail statutes, when it reviewed ARU president Eugene Debs's convictions for contempt of court:

> The entire strength of the nation may be used to enforce in any part of the land the full and free exercise of all national powers and the security of all rights entrusted by the Constitution to its care. The strong arm of the national government may be put forth to brush away all obstructions to the freedom of interstate commerce or the transportation of the mails. If the emergency arises, the army of the Nation, and all its militia, are at the service of the Nation to compel obedience to its law.[76]

Thus, the executive branch and the Supreme Court asserted the supremacy of the federal government throughout the United States, and the federal government's claim of the monopoly of the legitimate use of force—definitive characteristics of the modern state.

As Governor Altgeld had predicted, federal intervention fomented civil disorder. Increasing violence in Chicago permitted others to recast the disorder as an insurrection by the ARU against the federal government and to demonize strikers as enemies of the state. Gen. Nelson Miles, commander of federal forces in Chicago, proclaimed that "men must take sides either for anarchy, secret conclaves, unwritten law, mob violence, and universal chaos under the red or white flag of socialism on the one hand; or on the side of the established government."[77] Olney declared: "We have been brought to the ragged edge of anarchy and it is time to see whether the law is sufficiently strong to prevent this condition of affairs."[78]

Eugene Debs pleaded with Samuel Gompers to call a general strike in Chicago, but Gompers, who had witnessed the defeat of the railroad strikers in 1877 and the demise of the Knights of Labor after 1886, refused to defy the armed forces of the new American state. Federal authorities would treat any broad-based industrial conflict as an insurrection and quash it by force, he realized. "Against this array of armed force and brutal monied aristocracy," responded the AFL executive council, "would it not be worse than folly to call men out on a general or local strike in these days of stagnant trade and commercial depression?"[79]

The collapse of the strike followed shortly. On July 10, federal attorneys arrested the strike leaders for conspiracy to obstruct interstate commerce and the mails. That day, the military removed blockades and the first trains began to move. By July 13, federal troops had quelled all resistance, and trains were moving on schedule. Authorities again arrested Debs and the strike leaders three days later on charges of contempt, and on July 18 the Pullman company began to rehire the strikers, conditional on their quitting the ARU.

The AFL executive board's refusal to support the strike revealed a widening breach in the labor movement between those who sought the acceptance of the labor movement and those who promoted the cooperative commonwealth. Throughout the confrontation, Debs remained committed to republican ideals; while testifying before the U.S. Strike Commission in September 1894, Debs again called for the creation of the cooperative commonwealth to replace the wage system.[80] On his release from prison in November 1895, Debs once more enunciated nineteenth-century worker-republican themes:

> Manifestly the spirit of '76 survives. The fires of liberty and noble aspirations are not yet extinguished. I greet you tonight as lovers of liberty and despisers of despotism. . . . I comprehend the significance of this demonstration and appreciate the honor that makes it possible for me to be your guest on such an occasion. The vindication and glorification of American principles of government, as proclaimed to the world in the Declaration of Independence, is the high purpose of this convocation.[81]

Working Americans, he asserted, are not hereditary bondsmen, but self-governing sovereigns, with the capacity to redeem the promise of the republic.

The destruction of the ARU, however, marked the demise of nineteenth-century worker republicanism and the dream of the cooperative commonwealth. The Pullman strike demonstrated to Debs the limits of economic action alone and convinced him of the need to engage in political activity as well. The outcome of the 1896 election revealed to him that working Americans could not establish the cooperative commonwealth by working within the existing two-party system. Debs subsequently established a nonrevolutionary, Americanized brand of socialism, which Norman Thomas, Irving

Howe, and Michael Harrington later came to represent. Eventually, the radical branch of the labor movement disintegrated, due to the controversy over the use of violence by groups like the Industrial Workers of the World, and the new American state's increasing suppression during and after World War I.[82]

The other branch of the American labor movement that emerged after the early labor movement's defeats of 1877–1894 fared much better. The American Federation of Labor, founded in 1886 following the Haymarket debacle, abandoned the ideals of worker republicanism in favor of opportunistic, pure-and-simple trade unionism. The modern American labor movement accepted the wage system, proclaimed its fealty to the modern American state, and abandoned any transformational objectives in its concerted activities. "We are living under the wage system," Gompers declared, "and so long as that lasts it is our purpose to secure a continually larger share for labor, for the wealth producers."[83]

> What is to be remedied—the economic or social or political life? If it is the economic life that is to be remedied, then it should be done through the economic life and no other medium. Some tell us that the solution of this question is the cooperative commonwealth. But is that the final solution to everything? You tell us.[84]

Mainstream labor leaders no longer justified the right to strike as necessary to defend free workers' standing as citizens or to usher in the cooperative commonwealth. Instead, trade unionists like Samuel Gompers justified the right to strike as an instrument for promoting the organizational and economic interests of wage earners within the existing social system. This engendered the modern liberal conception of the right to strike as an instrument of private collective bargaining.[85] Trade unions shunned political activity and instead engaged in more measured, limited, and strategic forms of concerted action, which did not directly challenge the modern American state's claim to a monopoly of the legitimate use of force. Reciprocally, the mainstream labor movement supported a policy of industrial laissez faire, namely, that the state would not intervene in labor disputes through court injunctions, compulsory arbitration, or the force of arms. According to Gompers, "[Labor] asks no special privileges, no favors from the state. It wants to be left alone and to be allowed to exercise its rights and use its great economic power. Workmen must rely on their own strength, the strength resulting from mutualism and organization."[86]

The mainstream labor movement's adoption of pure-and-simple unionism was not simply a product of working Americans' inherent wage-consciousness, as Commons and Perlman have argued, nor was it merely a canny response to the autonomous power of judicial review and judge-made law, as Hattam and Forbath contend. It was also a realistic reaction to the stunning defeats the labor movement sustained at the hands of the emerging modern American state. True, the courts gave Olney and President Cleveland the pretext to intervene, but the executive branch had initially sought these injunctions. Court orders were plastered onto every railroad car in Chicago, but the presence of thousands of armed troops, not these pieces of paper, terminated the strike. Against the power of this emerging modern American state, citizen-workers could no longer champion the right to strike to defend worker-republican ideals and to promote the creation of a cooperative commonwealth.

In the aftermath of the Pullman strike, some federal officials began to express a more conciliatory attitude toward Gompers's pure-and-simple form of concerted activity. On the request of the Knights of Labor, President Cleveland established an ad hoc strike commission.[87] Composed of U.S. Commissioner of Labor Carroll D. Wright, Nicholas Worthington of Illinois, and John D. Keernan of New York, the U.S. Strike Commission's 1894 investigation was the first serious attempt by the federal government to study the labor question. In place of the law of the jungle, the commission recommended union recognition, workers' rights to join unions, a permanent strike commission, and voluntary arbitration. Following its advice, Congress passed the 1898 Erdman Act, which established the permanent Board of Arbitration and Conciliation to address railway labor disputes. More importantly, although the commission denounced strikes, lockouts, and boycotts as "barbarism unfit for the intelligence of this age," it presented a sympathetic portrayal of the strikers and an unfavorable view of the federal government's role in suppressing the strike.[88] Their implied criticism of the use of force, their support for a strong labor movement, and their endorsement of workers' rights to organize and bargain collectively foreshadowed a sea change in the federal government's strike policy. However, the development of a new strike policy based on these principles was delayed for another forty years.

4

"The very instruments of democracy are often used to oppress them"
The Right to Strike during the Progressive Era

Despite the mainstream labor movement's acceptance of pure-and-simple unionism after 1894, the right to strike remained elusive throughout the Progressive Era. The early twentieth century represented the height of the open shop movement, during which employers in basic industry presented a united front against unionization. Open shop employers refused to recognize their employees' representatives; forced workers to sign "yellow dog" contracts disavowing union membership, as a condition of employment; and routinely fired and blacklisted labor unionists. This era was also the bloodiest in American labor history, with such notorious events as the bombing of the *Los Angeles Times* building, the massacre at the Ludlow, Colorado strikers' camp, near civil war in the West Virginia coalfields, and police brutality in Pennsylvania steel towns.

Advocates of the law turn in labor studies attribute the weakness of the right to strike during this era to the power of the judiciary, and particularly to "government by injunction." Following the Supreme Court's affirmation of the constitutionality of injunctions obtained under the Sherman Anti-Trust Act in 1895, injunctions became one of the most frequently used anti-strike weapons. Employers could obtain injunctions even before a strike simply through ex parte proceedings and affidavits alleging an immediate and irremediable harm.[1] Strike injunctions became more restrictive, prohibiting not only picketing but also strike rallies, private meetings, telephone conversations, strike announcements, boycotts, and the like, and they became more extensive, blanketing entire communities and applying to "all persons whomsoever." Moreover, if the strike continued, judges had the power to cite strike leaders for contempt and to unilaterally determine the penalty.[2] At the peak of "government by injunction" in the 1920s, the courts enjoined 2,130 strikes—about one-fourth of all strikes.[3] Advocates of the law turn also point to the *Lochner*-era Court's overruling of prolabor legislation, especially Section 20 of the 1916 Clayton Act, which exempted labor organizations from court injunctions under the antitrust acts "unless necessary to prevent irreparable injury to property, or to property right." The Supreme Court ruled that this phrase only codified case law and that Section 20 of the Clayton Act did not immunize trade unions from injunctions for engaging in conspiracies in restraint of trade.[4]

American political development, however, reveals a much more complex and equivocal picture of the development of the right to strike during the Progressive Era, particularly with regard to the role of executive powers. On the one hand, executive power frequently trumped judicial authority through declarations of martial law. Political executives often acted without the imprimatur of the courts, and military authority overruled the courts when judicial decisions favored strikers. On the other hand, this default strike policy increasingly placed the new American state in an equivocal position, particularly with regard to its sovereign interests and national security interests. Strikes may have challenged the state's claim to a monopoly of the legitimate use of force, but strikebreaking, which entailed the suppression of civil liberties and the suspension of the rule of law, undermined the state's claim to legitimacy. Strikebreaking during wartime created additional dilemmas. Strikes interfered with war production, weakened morale, and signified disloyalty during World War I, but strikebreaking threatened to undermine working-class support for the war. These dilemmas drove state officials to seek a more moderate strike policy. In addition, the rise of presidential power permitted Progressive Era presidents to intervene personally in labor disputes and to pursue a strike policy consistent with pure-and-simple unionism, anticipating the New Deal's revolution in federal strike policy.

Ultimately, however, the new American state failed to resolve these dilemmas and develop a consistent and coherent strike policy. Even after the creation of the Department of Labor and the Federal Conciliation and Mediation Service in 1913, the United States Commission on Industrial Relations in 1915, and the National War Labor Board (NWLB) in 1918, the new American state's capacity to intervene in industrial disputes remained undeveloped and ad hoc, contingent on the personal intervention of the president or the exigencies of war, and easily subverted by governors and local officials. The progressive alliance between trade unionists and reformers, who supported conciliation of labor disputes, failed to solidify into a governing coalition, splitting in the 1912 presidential election, and suffering a devastating blow when President Wilson collapsed from a stroke in 1919. Soon after Wilson's breakdown, the new American state reverted to its default strike policy, breaking the 1919 steel strike, the 1922 coal miners' strike, and the 1922 railway shopmen's strike. Thus, the emerging liberal American state continued to display an unreconciled and equivocal position toward the right to strike, an ambivalence that it continues to display today.

Strikebreaking in Progressive Era Miners' Strikes

Miners' strikes during the early twentieth century involved some of the bloodiest civil strife in American history, when, by declarations of martial law and force of arms, governors and the military often overruled local courts. These cases illustrate the limited power of the judiciary when judges intervened to protect strikers from overreaching military power. Such strikebreaking not only abridged the right to strike narrowly defined but also infringed on basic civil liberties of strikers and sympathizers, indicating that safeguarding the right to strike would also serve to protect civil liberties. In addition, these cases also demonstrate that a more restrained strike policy would require greater presidential leadership and power.

The first example involves the 1899 Coeur d'Alene, Idaho, miners' strike. Following the 1892 miners' strike, the mine operators in the region decided to rid themselves of the Western Federation of Miners (WFM), the most radical union of the day. The labor dispute escalated into violence, and, following the bombing of a mine processing plant, Governor Frank Steunenberg declared that the state of Idaho faced an uncontrollable insurrection, even though the civil courts remained open and functioning. On the governor's insistence, President McKinley dispatched regular U.S. Army troops to northern Idaho. In violation of the 1878 Posse Comitatus Act, State Auditor Bartlett Sinclair assumed command of the troops, who assisted the state police in arresting approximately one thousand union members and sympathizers as well as executing the blacklisting of WFM members.[5] Union attorneys obtained writs of habeas corpus from local judges, but military officials refused to release the strikers, in violation of Ex parte Milligan (1866).[6] After the restoration of civil order, the U.S. Army remained in Idaho for two years at Steunenberg's request, but against Secretary of War Elihu Root's instructions.[7] The Idaho Supreme Court subsequently affirmed the governor's power to suspend civil law and ruled that local courts may not challenge the facts cited in his proclamation when petitioning for writs of habeas corpus.[8]

The Coeur d'Alene strike revealed the continuing feebleness of federal authority in remote areas and led to widespread criticism of the abuse of federal military authority. Consequently, when the WFM instigated another work stoppage in 1903 in Cripple Creek and Telluride, Colorado, President Theodore Roosevelt denied Governor James Peabody's request for federal troops.[9] Local officials insisted that they could enforce the law and maintain order without military intervention, and Roosevelt determined that the state of Colorado had not exhausted its own resources.[10]

Peabody's subsequent declaration of martial law and deployment of the National Guard transformed the labor dispute into a virtual civil war. The Guard arrested WFM members and sympathizers en masse, held them without the right of habeas corpus and without bail, and banished them from the region. When a district judge authorized four writs of habeas corpus, the commanding officer resisted; instead, National Guardsmen surrounded the county courthouse and marched into the courtroom armed with bayonets. Against the protestations of the attorney general, Adjutant General Sherman Bell maintained that Peabody's proclamation had given the Colorado National Guard the authority to intervene in court proceedings and to suspend the right of habeas corpus.[11] The commanders subsequently defied a court injunction forbidding the Guard from deporting WFM strikers. The governor's office instead instructed the commanding officer "to pay no attention to [court] orders, neither by permitting service or to obey the mandate of the court if such order is issued."[12]

The conflict between the local civil courts and the National Guard culminated with the Guard's arrest of Charles H. Moyer, president of the WFM. Moyer's attorneys obtained a writ of habeas corpus, arguing that no insurrection existed because civil courts remained in session. When the adjutant general and the commanding officer ignored the writ, the judge found the adjutant general in contempt and fined him five hundred dollars. Moyer eventually appealed to the Colorado Supreme Court, which held that only the governor could determine whether an insurrection existed, and that the governor had the authority to use all necessary means to restore order, including the suspension of the right of habeas corpus.[13] Moyer then brought a federal civil suit against Peabody and the two officers. On appeal, the U.S. Supreme Court determined that Peabody had acted to suppress a rebellion and therefore could not be sued. "Public dangers warrant the substitution of executive process for judicial process," the Court declared.[14]

Governors not only broke strikes by radical unions such as the WFM but also suppressed work stoppages by pure-and-simple trade unions such as the United Mine Workers. During a contract dispute in Paint Creek and Cabin Creek, West Virginia, in 1912, coal operators withdrew recognition of the union, evicted strikers from company housing, and hired replacement workers and Baldwin-Felts detectives to break the strike. Although the strike intensified into one of the bloodiest and most prolonged industrial conflicts in American history, civil courts remained in session, and civil authorities still arrested and prosecuted strikers who had taken the law into their own hands. Nonetheless, the governor declared martial law and suspended the right of habeas corpus. National Guardsmen then arrested two hundred strikers without warrants and held them without bail. In violation of Ex parte Milligan, the Guard tried more than one hundred civilians in military tribunals, without defense attorneys and without juries.[15] A Senate investigation concluded "the military tribunal deemed itself bound by the orders of the commander-in-chief, the governor of the State, and in no respect bound to observe the Constitution of the United States or the constitution of the State of West Virginia."[16] Constitutional historian Robert Rankin noted, "In the history of the United States, martial law has never been used on such a broad scale, in so drastic a manner, nor upon such sweeping principles as in West Virginia in 1912–1913."[17]

Despite the creation of the Department of Labor and the Federal Conciliation and Mediation Service in 1913, the federal government still lacked sufficient administrative capacities and authority to intervene peacefully in an industrial dispute. Thus, violent strikebreaking continued in 1913–1914 during the momentous UMW strike against the Colorado Fuel and Iron Company.[18] John D. Rockefeller Jr. treated the dispute as a struggle over the principle of the individual's liberty of contract, but the miners regarded it as a conflict over pure-and-simple trade union issues: union recognition, a 10 percent wage increase, and the enforcement of Colorado labor laws. After the coal operators rejected private conciliation, they evicted ten thousand families from company housing. In late 1913 coal operators also rebuffed federal mediation, refusing to meet with union representatives when Labor Secretary William Wilson traveled to Colorado to mediate the conflict.[19] Instead, Colorado Fuel and Iron recruited thousands of armed guards and imported machine guns, armored vehicles, and searchlights. After sporadic gun battles claimed the lives of several strikers and guards, Governor Elias Ammons called out the National Guard.

Although Governor Ammons had not declared martial law, and specifically prohibited the Guard from escorting replacement workers, the mine operators pressured the governor to give free rein to the militia. The Guard, now largely composed of company guards, followed the employers' direction, arresting strikers and strike supporters without warrant and holding them without right of habeas corpus.[20] The Guard's harassment of the strikers peaked on April 20, 1914, in Ludlow, when a twelve-hour gun battle ended with a fire that consumed the strikers' tent colony. Twenty strikers lost their lives in this battle, including thirteen women and children, who suffocated in the blaze.[21] According to a military commission report, "Beyond a doubt it was seen to intentionally that the fire should destroy the whole of the colony."[22]

Civil disorder shattered the Colorado mining regions as the Colorado Federation of Labor issued a call to arms:

> Organize the men in your community in companies to protect the workers of Colorado against the murder and cremation of men, women and children by armed assassins in the employ of coal corporations, serving under the guise of state militiamen. Gather together for defensive purposes all arms and ammunition legally available. . . . The state is furnishing us no protection and we must protect ourselves, our wives and children from these murderous assassins.[23]

Hundreds of miners attacked mines and dynamited property in a four-day battle, and armed strikers occupied Trinidad, Colorado. The United States Commission on Industrial Relations stated: "This rebellion constituted perhaps one of the nearest approaches to civil war and revolution ever known in this country in connection with an industrial conflict."[24]

Ammons requested federal assistance, and on April 28 President Wilson ordered U.S. Army regulars to restore peace. The army functioned as an impartial peacekeeping force, disarming both sets of combatants and prohibiting the importation of out-of-state strikebreakers. The coal operators, however, employed in-state replacement workers, again rebuffed state and federal efforts to arbitrate the dispute, and ultimately defeated the UMW.

The Ludlow massacre underscored the failure of U.S. strike policies and the need for more restrained approaches that acknowledged the right to strike. The default policy of strikebreaking had failed to abate the overall level of industrial violence and strike activity, and weakened the state's legitimacy among working Americans. Indeed, according to Phillip Taft and Philip Ross, only the Civil War surpassed the level of domestic violence that erupted during industrial conflicts between 1911 and 1916.[25] The U.S. strike rate reached all-time records, averaging 162 strikes per million nonagricultural workers annually between 1901 and 1910, and 143 strikes per million between 1911 and 1920. During the 1919–1920 strike wave, 22 percent of the nonagricultural workforce went on strike. By comparison, during "the turbulent years" of the 1930s, the annual strike rate was 79.6 strikes per million.[26]

State-sponsored strikebreaking instead inflamed strikers and radicalized some labor organizations. Thus, an assassin killed Governor Steunenberg soon after he broke the 1899 Couer d'Alene strike. After the 1903 Colorado miners' strike, Charles Moyer, William Haywood, and other WFM officials founded the Industrial Workers of the World, arguably the most notorious radical labor organization in U.S. history. The IWW defiantly rejected pure-and-simple trade unionism, eschewed both collective bargaining and conventional political action, and instead advocated the general strike.[27] In Los Angeles, less radical pure-and-simple trade unionists blew up the antiunion *Los Angeles Times* building and Llewellyn Iron-Works, following the passage of an anti-picketing ordinance and the arrest of four hundred picketers.[28]

The new American state's use of force to suppress strikes had not only failed to reduce industrial conflict, but also had weakened its claims of legitimacy when the use of force to break strikes repeatedly overstepped constitutional limits. Whether the right to strike is a citizenship right may be open to debate, but peaceful strikers still retain rights of habeas corpus, due process, freedom of association, assembly, speech, press, and so on. Both the 1915 Commission on Industrial Relations, which investigated industrial conflict generally, and the Commission of Inquiry of the Interchurch World Movement, which investigated the 1919 steel strike, reached this conclusion. The *Final Report of the United States Commission on Industrial Relations* observed that

> in the majority of cases [the suppression of personal rights] undoubtedly is the result of a belief by the police, or their superiors, that they were "supporting and defending the Government" by such an invasion of personal rights. Such action strikes at the very foundation of Government. It is axiomatic that a Government which can be maintained only by the suppression of criticism should not be maintained.[29]

The Seeds of a New Strike Policy

The development of a new, more restrained strike policy is closely associated with the early rise of the modern presidency, and particularly the presidencies of Theodore Roosevelt and Woodrow Wilson. Before 1902, presidential interventions in industrial conflicts had been ad hoc and reactive, in response to emergencies and civil disorder. Presidents Roosevelt and Wilson, however, advocated a more active and energetic presidency. Both consequently endorsed more measured responses to labor disputes involving pure-and-simple trade unions and personally intervened to conciliate major labor disputes that threatened national interests.

The National Civic Federation

This new strike policy of moderation and conciliation originated with the National Civic Federation, a private, voluntary association that championed progressive social, economic, and municipal reforms. The NCF emerged out of the 1894 Pullman strike, during which Ralph Easely, a progressive journalist, established the Chicago Civic Federation's Industrial

Commission to mediate the strike. Although his attempt failed to end the strike, Easely recognized the need for a national organization dedicated to finding peaceful solutions to mounting industrial conflicts. These efforts attracted progressive social reformers in the labor movement, business, academe, and politics, including Samuel Gompers, UMW president John Mitchell, Republican Party chairman Marcus Hanna, labor historian John R. Commons, Theodore Roosevelt, New York City mayor Seth Low, financier August Belmont, and Harvard University president Charles Elliot.

The NCF's primary contribution to modern liberal strike policy involved a redefinition of the labor question. For earlier reformers such as Richard Ely and George McNeill, the labor question concerned a broad array of social issues: What role should wage earners play in the emerging social order? What should be the relationship between labor and capital? How can one improve the working *and* living conditions of the laboring classes?[30] The NCF, however, emphasized the narrower and more urgent issue of how to promote industrial peace.[31] Thus, when the NCF held its historic Conference on Industrial Conciliation in December 1912, newspapers hailed it as a "tribunal of peace."[32] The bylaws of the Industrial Department of the NCF declared, "The scope and province of the Department shall be to do what may seem best to promote industrial peace and prosperity." The NCF advocated collective labor contracts as industrial peace treaties, rather than as a means of protecting the constitutional rights of wage earners.[33] This conception of the labor question, as a practical problem of promoting industrial peace, rather than as safeguarding the constitutional rights of strikers, eventually became one of the primary goals of the 1935 National Labor Relations Act.[34]

The NCF espoused pure-and-simple unionism as the best way to foster industrial peace. Pure-and-simple unionism, unlike nineteenth-century worker republicanism, accepts the wage system and promotes labor's basic organizational and economic goals, including the right to organize, union recognition, collective labor contracts, and better wages and working conditions. Among the rights it espouses is the right to strike for these purposes. Unlike earlier labor leaders and reformers, the NCF accepted the legitimacy of business corporations; unlike open shop employers, the NCF regarded the rise of unionism as a legitimate response to the growing concentration of capital.[35] Easely, Gompers, Mitchell, Hanna, and others promoted the negotiation of trade agreements between employers and wage earners—what we call collective bargaining—as a new form of industrial governance.

The NCF also promoted voluntarism, that is, noncompulsory measures for adjusting labor disputes. Since the 1860s, labor reformers had endorsed compulsory arbitration as an alternative to strikes, but NCF vice president Samuel Gompers adamantly rejected this reform as a violation of the voluntaristic principles of pure-and-simple unionism.[36] Throughout the 1880s and 1890s Gompers had witnessed the new American state's interventions in labor disputes, and he doubted that the state would arbitrate labor disputes fairly. Instead, the NCF espoused voluntary conciliation of labor disputes, a position that established a limited right to strike free from state compulsion. Reformers in the NCF, such as John R. Commons, who conciliated dozens of labor disputes, regarded labor disputes as technical problems, which experts trained in employment relations, industrial sociology, and negotiation could solve.[37] The NCF consequently established a department of conciliation, which, on the request of both parties, provided tripartite boards, with representatives of labor, business, and the public, to investigate and propose solutions to labor disputes. The boards expected the employer and the union to suspend hostilities, present their cases, and submit to a trade agreement mediated by the board. During its heyday, from 1900 to 1907, the National Civic Federation's Department of Conciliation helped to adjust as many as five hundred labor disputes.[38] Although today's principal labor court, the National Labor Relations Board, does not conciliate, the principle of voluntarism remains one of the foundations of national labor relations policy.[39]

Radicals have dismissed the NCF's efforts as class collaboration that strengthened the corporate status quo and subverted the radical industrial union movement. New Left critics regard the NCF's encouragement of pure-and-simple unionism as part of the Progressive movement's support for a rationalized, organized capitalism and its subversion of socialism. Gabriel Kolko's and James Weinstein's critiques of corporate liberalism offer well-known interpretations of the NCF from this perspective, although IWW leaders had made similar arguments during the early 1900s.[40] NCF leaders, however, were not personally motivated by the desire to rationalize business or thwart radical unionism. Easely, Commons, Gompers, Hanna, and others had witnessed the devastation of industrial conflicts and the futility of state suppression. Throughout his career, Commons rejected the principles of competitive capitalism, formulated an institutional economics to warrant collective action and the positive state, and insisted that a "new equity is needed" for wage earners.[41] Hanna also rejected those aspects of competitive capitalism that dehumanized working people.[42] Leaders of the NCF were not apologists for corporate capitalism but pragmatic liberals who rejected both revolution and unregulated capitalism.

Pure-and-simple unions, moreover, could be quite disruptive of business rationalization. David Montgomery argues that the scientific management movement, which sought to extend employer control over the shop floor, ignited control strikes by skilled workers throughout the Progressive Era. Although not wage issues, worker control issues—such as union recognition, enforcement of union work rules, discharge of unpopular foremen, and control over layoffs—are, nonetheless, pure-and-simple trade union concerns. The record is incomplete, but the ratio of control strikes to wage strikes appears to have peaked between 1900 and 1920.[43]

In addition, many employers vigorously opposed the NCF's conciliatory strike policy, and developed alternative strategies that did not entail union recognition, collective bargaining, or a limited right to strike. For example, John D. Rockefeller Jr.'s Colorado Industrial Plan, developed following the Ludlow massacre, promoted a company-supervised employee representation program and introduced significant improvements in employee housing, sanitation, and community organizations.[44] Coupled with these reforms, however, was a rejection of the UMW and the right to strike. This became the model for the corporate welfare and company union programs popularized during the 1920s as union avoidance strategies. Other business leaders simply rejected all forms of employee representation, supporting the brutal employment policies of the open shop movement.

The weakness of the NCF's conciliation efforts was not class collaboration but rather its tenuous affirmations of the right to strike and the civil liberties of strikers. Conciliation and restraint marked advances over the default policy of suppression, but they were a far cry from respecting strikers as citizens of the republic. In this way, as well, they foreshadowed the modern liberal right to strike.

The Roosevelt Presidency

The NCF's new policy of moderation and support for pure-and-simple trade unionism first influenced federal strike policy during the presidency of Theodore Roosevelt, whose application of the NCF's principles and methods of conciliation helped to expand the power of the presidency. In 1902, 120,000 anthracite coal miners in eastern Pennsylvania struck to gain union recognition, a nine-hour day, a 20 percent wage increase, a standardized pay scale, and union checkweighmen, whose duties are to make sure that miners are properly paid. After the coal operators rejected Marcus Hanna's effort to conciliate, the UMW prepared for a nationwide sympathy strike. The dispute threatened to erupt into violence, as the coal operators deployed the Pennsylvania Coal and Iron Police and the governor dispatched one thousand National Guard troops. President Roosevelt personally intervened, persuading J. P. Morgan, whose bank was reorganizing the railroads that owned most of the coal mines, to urge coal operators to submit to a tripartite strike commission.[45] The coal operators accepted the commission's recommendation for the creation of regional boards of conciliation to handle future disputes, and the UMW agreed to strike only as a last resort.[46] Roosevelt later commented, "There was no duty whatever laid upon me by the Constitution in the matter, and I had in theory no power to act directly unless the Governor of Pennsylvania could not keep order."[47] Thus, in the absence of national administrative capacities to adjust labor disputes, the threat of mass civil unrest called for the expansion of presidential power.

Expansion of presidential power also demanded repudiating governors' requests for federal troops. President McKinley's deployment of U.S. regular army troops in the 1899 Coeur d'Alene miners' strike had drawn considerable criticism because the president had relinquished authority over the military to Idaho authorities. By contrast, Roosevelt insisted on independent reports of uncontrollable labor unrest, and demanded direct presidential control if federal troops were deployed. As a result, he rejected governors' requests to dispatch federal troops in the 1903 Colorado miners' strike and the 1907 miners' strike in Goldfield, Nevada, after his envoys determined that civil unrest had not overwhelmed the states' powers. "Better twenty-four hours of riot, damage, and disorder than illegal use of troops," Roosevelt declared.[48]

Roosevelt's intervention in the 1902 anthracite coal strike and his restraint in the western miners' strikes demonstrated that a protected right to strike based on pure-and-simple trade union principles required expansion of the president's powers. However, despite Roosevelt's restraint, his interventions remained ad hoc, depending largely on his personal involvement. Furthermore, as the Colorado Western Federation of Miners strike demonstrates, presidential restraint alone does not protect the right to strike. The institutional framework and administrative capacities for peacefully adjusting industrial disputes thus remained rudimentary.

The Wilson Presidency and the Commission on Industrial Relations

The National Civic Federation's new strike policy of moderation and conciliation had a more decisive influence on the Wilson administration, which further enhanced the power of the presidency. Thus, the creation of the Department of Labor in 1913 authorized the secretary of labor "to act as mediator and to appoint commissions of conciliation in labor disputes whenever in his judgment the interests of industrial peace shall require it to be done." Likewise, President Wilson's personal intervention in a railroad labor dispute in 1916 averted a nationwide strike and culminated in the passage of the Adamson Act, which mandated the eight-hour day for railroad workers. Congress also passed the Clayton Act in 1916 to try to immunize labor unions from court injunctions under the Sherman Act.

The NCF, however, had its greatest influence when Wilson appointed eight NCF members to the Commission on Industrial Relations. The nine-member commission, established in 1914 in the aftermath of the Los Angeles bombings to "discover the underlying causes of dissatisfaction in the industrial situation," held hearings for more than two years and issued an eleven-volume report of its findings. Its chairman, Frank P. Walsh, a Kansas City lawyer with strong prolabor views, wielded his position to turn the commission into a tribunal for the American labor movement. Walsh presided over public testimony by prominent industrialists, financiers, reformers, labor activists, and working people, culminating in early 1915 with the interrogation of John D. Rockefeller Jr., whose testimony concerning the Ludlow massacre dominated the front pages of national newspapers during the early battles of World War I.

With the creation of the Commission on Industrial Relations, officials of the new American state for the first time conducted a comprehensive investigation into the underlying causes of industrial strife, and issued a comprehensive report that was sympathetic to strikers.[49] Unlike previous strike investigations, which looked for immediate causes of disorder in particular strikes and recommended a patchwork approach to reform, Walsh's *Report of the United States Commission on Industrial Relations* declared that industrial discord arose from actual grievances rooted in oppressive living and working conditions, autocratic management, the unequal distribution of wealth, and the unavailability of collective bargaining. Walsh argued that these findings demonstrated the need for positive state action to check corporate resistance to labor unions. According to David Montgomery, these recommendations "were nothing less than a platform for an American labor party."[50] To address the underlying sources of industrial unrest, the report recommended a highly progressive tax rate structure; social programs to protect the unemployed, the disabled, and the elderly; public works programs for the unemployed; equal pay for women; and protection of the rights to organize and to bargain collectively. Among these rights was a limited right to strike for improved working conditions. Thus, the *Report of the United States Commission on Industrial Relations* first presented the objectives and the legislative program of the modern liberal American state and became a model for the New Deal.[51]

The Wilson Presidency and World War I

Equally important for the development of a more measured strike policy during the Wilson administration was the involvement of the United States in World War I. Wartime generally creates favorable economic conditions for unions to press for organizational gains and improvements in wages and working conditions. Thus, soon after the outbreak of World War I, increased European demand for U.S. goods, combined with wartime restrictions on immigration, caused the unemployment rate to plummet to 1.4 percent.[52] Meanwhile, inflation soared to its highest rate in years, with the cost of living doubling between August 1915 and December 1919.[53] A tight labor market combined with rising consumer prices characteristically prompts rational, pure-and-simple trade unions to strike.[54] Strike rates consequently intensified throughout the war, exceeding all previous strike waves. Over one million workers struck yearly in 1916, 1917, 1918, and 1919, peaking at over four million in 1919. Of the workforce, 9.2 percent participated in strikes in 1916, 6.9 percent in 1917, 6.8 percent in 1918, and 22.5 percent in 1919. Despite Gompers's public statement that "neither employers nor employees shall endeavor to take advantage of the country's necessities to change existing standards," over sixty-two hundred strikes erupted between April 1917 and November 1918.[55] From April 6 until October 5, 1917, strikes consumed more than six million workdays, "a figure that dwarfed even the record militancy of 1912–13 and 1915–16."[56]

Wartime strikes, however, present a dilemma for the state. On the one hand, they interfere with defense industry production, create social unrest, weaken the national unity necessary for war, and drain resources from the war effort.[57] Strikes may also represent a challenge to the state and signal to the enemy that there is opposition to the war. On the other hand, modern war demands working-class support in order to endure the sacrifices on the battlefield and at home, and strikebreaking may undermine that support. The new American state consequently had to develop a more restrained and discriminating policy for dealing with wartime labor disputes. The result was a dual strike policy of suppression of strikes by outlawed labor organizations and mediation of strikes by pure-and-simple unions.

The new American state directed its greatest suppression against the radical Industrial Workers of the World. Although the IWW seldom engaged in violence and represented at most only one hundred thousand workers, its advocacy of mass direct action, and denunciation of capitalism and the state, placed it beyond the pale.[58] Wartime, moreover, intensifies the state's sovereign interests, and under such conditions the state regarded the IWW's syndicalism as treason and IWW strikes as treachery. Twenty states consequently passed antisyndicalism laws aimed specifically at the IWW, which made advocacy of sabotage and terrorism for the purpose of overthrowing the state a crime. Based on the assumption that the IWW advocated revolution, hundreds of IWW members were imprisoned in California, Washington, and Idaho, although none actually committed any violent acts.[59] The U.S. Supreme Court validated these antisyndicalism laws in 1927.[60]

Federal authorities directly suppressed at least two wartime IWW strikes, in the spruce lumber industry in the Northwest and in the western copper mines. Spruce and copper were crucial raw materials for the war industries, and authorities regarded these strikes as efforts to subvert war production. The Department of War assigned federal troops to the western lumber and copper industries to quash the strikes, arrest leaders, and organize workers into patriotic organizations such as the Loyal Legion of Loggers and Lumbermen. The Justice Department, assisted by the Department of Labor and the Post Office, subsequently raided every IWW office in the country, and arrested several thousand Wobblies, including the entire executive board, for violating the Espionage and Sedition Acts. The Justice Department deported hundreds more as undesirable aliens under the new immigration law.[61] State and federal authorities recognized no right to strike for groups that advocated radical alternatives to the new American state, even when they posed no real threat to the state.

On the other hand, the new American state displayed unprecedented restraint toward pure-and-simple unions that pledged their support for the war effort. During the war, the Wilson administration implemented many of the recommendations of the Commission on Industrial Relations and employed as presidential advisors labor reformers such as Frank Walsh, Felix Frankfurter, William Wilson, and Samuel Gompers. Labor dispute adjustment boards, wage commissions, and labor advisory boards in coal mining, shipbuilding, railroad, war production, and other industries encouraged peaceful adjustments of labor disputes.

As the 1917 strike wave intensified and U.S. entry into the war became imminent, the administration established the War Labor Conference Board to formalize the wartime labor disputes policy. The cochairs of the board could not have been more dissimilar: they were Frank Walsh and Howard Taft, father of the labor injunction. Nonetheless, both supporters of pure-and-simple unionism and advocates of the open shop on the board quickly agreed on the principles of a wartime labor policy: no strikes or lockouts for the duration of the war; and no discriminatory discharge of union members or employees engaged in concerted activities. Although the board permitted the open shop, it required employers to bargain with shop committees, and it agreed on the eight-hour day, pay equity for women, the maintenance of current safety standards, and a living wage for all workers.[62] Finally, the board proposed a war labor board to mediate all unresolved labor disputes in war industries and primary industries where no labor adjustment boards existed, and to advise the administration on labor issues. Thus emerged the outlines of a national labor disputes policy, which eighteen years later became the New Deal labor policy.

In the spring of 1918 the Wilson administration implemented these recommendations by executive order and reconstituted the board under the same cochairs as the National War Labor Board.[63] From April 1918 to August 1919 the NWLB investigated over 1,250 disputes and directly mediated nearly five hundred cases. Little dissension occurred in the handling of most cases, despite the differences between the cochairs. Under these favorable wartime conditions, unions flourished—from about three million members in 1914 to about five million, or about 20 percent of the nonagricultural workforce, by the end of the war.[64]

Although voluntary mediation was successful during the brief U.S. involvement in World War I, ultimately the wartime strike policy rested on the president's powers of compulsion. Such was the case in an unresolved labor dispute in the munitions industry in Bridgeport, Connecticut.[65] Radical leaders of the local machinists union led a strike in sympathy with the metal polishers at Remington Arms in July 1917, demanding the eight-hour workday, nondiscrimination toward union members, recognition of shop committees, and the elimination of the company's piece-rate system. In June 1918, the Ordnance Department's Labor Adjustment Board mediated the dispute and accepted the union's standard rate pay plan. When one of the major arms manufacturers rejected the decision, all of the machinists in Bridgeport struck. The dispute then advanced to the NWLB, which called for continuation of the piece-rate system, raises for unskilled workers, government supervision of shop committee elections, and a city-wide labor disputes arbitration committee. Against the orders of the International Association of Machinists president, the local went back on strike. Wilson subsequently outlawed the strike, threatening to blacklist the strikers and to remove their draft deferments. In September 1918, the president sent to Bridgeport the director of the Committee of Public Information and his daughter, Margaret Wilson, to oversee shop committee and arbitration board elections, and to establish community organizations.

Despite the implicit threat behind Wilson's war labor disputes policy, many labor leaders regarded the president's wartime appeal to make the world safe for democracy as a promise to tackle industrial autocracy at home.[66] Presidential advisors such as Felix Frankfurter, Louis Brandeis, and Frank Walsh endorsed the collective action rights of workers and urged workers to support the war, not only to defeat autocracy abroad but also to promote industrial justice at home. Their support for workers' rights to organize and bargain collectively and for protections against discriminatory discharge, however, earned employers' contempt for the various war labor adjustment boards and the NWLB.[67] Moreover, the IWW and machinists' strikes illustrate the extent to which the emerging federal strike policy had adopted the NCF's primary aim in conciliation, namely, the maintenance of industrial peace, rather than the promotion of constitutional rights, social justice, or industrial democracy. The administration never challenged the principles of the open shop, and, when the war ended, many business leaders were determined to roll back federal controls and restore the open shop.[68]

Postwar Regression in Federal Strike Policy

Labor leaders, on the other hand, considered the constructive policies of the Wilson administration as signs that the new American state had developed a more tolerant policy toward strikes over limited pure-and-simple union goals, and, consequently, viewed the end of World War I as an opportune time to mobilize for the expansion of the labor movement and for improvements in wages and working conditions. Wilson bolstered this perception in his May 1919 special message to Congress in which he said, "The object of all reform in this essential matter must be the genuine democratization of industry, based upon a full recognition of those who work, to participate in some organic way in every decision which directly affects their welfare or the part they are to play in industry."[69] With the end of hostilities, moreover, many workers no longer supported the no-strike pledge, and the most massive strike wave in U.S. history erupted, with four million workers participating in work stoppages. However, in one of the most dramatic reversals in American political development, authorities renounced the policy of restraint and reverted to the default policy of armed suppression.

The largest and most significant strike of the postwar insurgency was the 1919 steel strike.[70] Organizing the steel industry was essential for extending unionism beyond the trades into basic industry, and a supportive administration was necessary for success. Strikebreaking had thwarted previous attempts by the Knights of Labor, the Amalgamated Association of Iron, Steel, and Tin Workers, the American Railway Union, and the Industrial Workers of the World to establish industrial organizations. Ever since 1892, when the Pennsylvania National Guard had suppressed the Homestead strike, the steel industry had remained nonunion, and U.S. Steel, headed by Judge Elbert H. Gary (a former Illinois county judge who presided over the Haymarket trial), was one of the leaders in the open shop movement.

In 1919, the AFL formed the National Committee for Organizing Iron and Steel Workers, and demanded union recognition and the eight-hour day for the steelworkers. Judge Gary rejected the demands. During the summer of 1919, a delegation from the organizing committee, including Samuel Gompers, asked Wilson to intervene, as he had in several major wartime strikes.

The president's capacity to mediate wartime labor disputes, however, had ultimately rested on his war powers, and the armistice had diminished his power to intervene. Officials in the steel industry, determined to thwart any further advances of organized labor, rebuffed the president's efforts. On September 22, 250,000 steelworkers—half of the workforce in that industry—went on strike. A second opportunity to intervene peacefully arose in October, when Wilson convened a nationwide industrial conference to develop postwar labor policies. Gompers and Gary both attended, so the conference provided an excellent opportunity to confront the steel strike. Wilson, however, suffered a stroke just before the conference, preventing him from exercising any personal influence. The conference ended in stalemate after labor representatives offered resolutions supporting the principles of pure-and-simple unionism and Gary proclaimed his allegiance to open shop principles.[71]

The work stoppage eventually degenerated into violence and civil disorder, as authorities reverted to the default strike policy of suppression. In Gary, Indiana, strikers rioted when U.S. Steel attempted to transport strikebreakers into a plant, and the mayor sought military intervention. Federal troops subsequently prohibited all picketing and strike rallies and arrested union officials in other trades who threatened to strike in sympathy. Justice Department agents declared the strike a Bolshevik conspiracy, and federal troops raided strike headquarters.[72] The Interchurch World Movement, which at the time conducted an exhaustive investigation of the strike, noted that sporadic striker violence throughout western Pennsylvania did not demand the suspension of civil liberties.[73] Nevertheless, the state, among other things, prohibited all meetings of three or more persons, denied freedom of speech and the press, imprisoned strikers without the right of habeas corpus, and conducted warrantless searches. According to the Interchurch World Movement's official report, "The policy of the State police was to club men off the street and drive them into their homes."[74] Under the protection of state and federal forces, steel companies throughout Pennsylvania and the Midwest installed strikebreakers, dispersed picket lines, and, within six weeks, broke the strike. The Interchurch World Movement observed that "the steel strike made tens of thousands of citizens believe that our American institutions are not democratic."[75] Following this defeat, workers in the steel industry remained unorganized until the late 1930s.

The second conflict that illustrates the failure of the new American state to establish enduring procedures for peacefully resolving labor disputes occurred in southern West Virginia in 1920–21, when an ongoing dispute over union recognition escalated into the largest domestic insurrection in American history. Samuel Gompers described this region as "the last remains of industrial autocracy in America," where coal miners subsisted in company towns and labored in mines under the surveillance of armed guards.[76] Since the 1890s, cutthroat competition in the region had disrupted the UMW's attempts to stabilize prices under the Central Competitive Field agreement, which regulated UMW contracts from western Pennsylvania to Illinois, and forced mine operators to resist unionization in order to control labor costs.

Labor conflicts in the coalfields eased during World War I after Congress passed the Lever Act, which authorized the administration to control the production and distribution of food and fuel during the war. The Fuel Administration, established under this act, brokered the Washington Agreement, which compelled the coal operators to permit the organization of the workforce. In return, the UMW accepted a no-strike pledge for the duration of the war.[77] After the war, however, in defiance of President Wilson's orders, the mine operators in southern West Virginia declared their mines nonunion and proceeded to evict union supporters from the company towns.[78]

Before the UMW could respond, coal operators obtained several preemptive labor injunctions, whose scope and breadth are legendary. The most comprehensive court order, which led to the landmark *Red Jacket Consolidated Coal & Coke Company v. Lewis* (1922) decision, forbade the UMW from defending evicted members in court, banned the UMW from nonunion company towns, and, as a practical matter, forbade the UMW from attempting to organize nonunion mines in West Virginia.[79] After the UMW disregarded the injunction, the coal operators imported several hundred armed Baldwin-Felts agents to evict union miners from company-owned houses. The miners' armed resistance became increasingly violent and provoked the governor to declare martial law.[80] The governor's decree proved to be more sweeping than the court injunctions, evicting miners from the strike camp, forbidding union supporters from talking to one another, permitting mass arrests, eliminating bail, and suspending the right of habeas corpus.

After the state legislature passed a bill that allowed judges to assemble juries from other parts of the state—an act aimed at the union sympathizers accused of killing agents Albert and Lee Felts in the famous Matewan shootout—the strike exploded into the largest domestic insurrection in American history. UMW officials issued the *Manifesto of Labor in West Virginia on Constitutional Liberty and the Bill of Rights,* denouncing the state's actions and summoning strikers "to resist any further encroachment upon our civil liberties and constitutional rights with intelligent coordinated use of their economic power in every instance where the constitution and bill of rights are infringed."[81] Twenty thousand miners took up arms and defeated the combined forces of the state and the coal operators after a weeklong battle. President Harding, who had resisted deploying federal troops, placed all of West Virginia under martial law on August 30, 1921, and dispatched twenty-five hundred troops, armed with machine guns and backed with air power.[82] Federal intervention broke the strike, paving the way for West Virginia to prosecute 550 strikers for treason.

Despite President Warren Harding's claim that he supported a moderate and impartial stance toward organized labor, he continued to retreat from the policy of restraint during the summer of 1922, when four hundred thousand railroad shop craft workers struck to protest wage reductions and unequal treatment by the Railroad Labor Board.[83] During the war, the Wilson administration had nationalized the railroad industry; and the Office of Railway Administration had authorized unionization and raises, in effect creating a nationwide bargaining structure for shop craft workers. After the war, however, railroad executives persuaded Congress to return the railroads to private ownership, and, following the passage of the 1920 Railway Act, sought to roll back the power of the shop craft unions. The 1920 act reconstituted the Railroad Labor Board, to which Harding appointed pro-management members, who subsequently reversed the previous board's wage decisions, triggering a strike of a quarter of a million workers that began on July 1, 1922.

Initially, Harding showed restraint toward the strikers, but after the railroads rejected Secretary of Commerce Herbert Hoover's mediated settlement, Harding instructed Attorney General Harry Daugherty to break the strike: "At any time you have an intolerant situation, where it is desirable for the federal government to intervene with armed force please let me know so that the matter may be immediately taken up."[84] Daugherty deployed over twenty-two hundred federal marshals to escort strikebreakers and arrest strikers, but the widespread nature of the strike made it impossible to keep all lines operating nationwide. In early September, frustrated by the continuing work stoppages, Harding ordered Daugherty to obtain an injunction against the strikers. The Daugherty-Wilkerson injunction, the most sweeping ever granted, covered the entire nation and ordered all persons to stop "picketing or in any manner by letters, circulars, telephone messages, word of mouth, or interviews . . . [encouraging any person] to abandon the employment of said railroad." Several unions quickly reached a negotiated settlement with the railroads, but the strike was not resolved in all sectors until 1925. In the meantime, the shop craft workers' unions were effectively broken, thousands lost their jobs, and several their lives. Thus ended the largest railroad strike in U.S. history.

The regression in federal strike policy had severe consequences for labor organizations and strike activity. Some employers engaged in an aggressive open shop campaign, while others organized their employees into employer-dominated company unions. Union membership plunged from 5,047,000 in 1920 to 3,622,000 in 1923, and the unionization rate plummeted from 19.5 percent in 1920 to only 10 percent in 1930. UMW membership dwindled from six hundred thousand to eighty thousand.[85] Less than one-fifth as many work stoppages occurred in 1926–1930 as in 1916–1921, and less than one-ninth as many workers engaged in work stoppages.[86] By 1930, the right to strike was as remote as it had been in 1894.

The regression in federal strike policy following World War I reveals more than the independent power of the judiciary over the labor movement. From the perspective of American political development, it also demonstrates the nature of national party coalitions, the limitations of federal administrative capacities, and the provisional character of presidential power prior to the New Deal. Thus, during the early twentieth century, a progressive alliance between reformers and unionists failed to crystallize into a unified governing party coalition. The alliance was split during the 1912 presidential campaign, when Theodore Roosevelt ran as a third-party candidate against Woodrow Wilson.[87] As had been the case during the late nineteenth century, organized labor remained outside of the national party coalitions and was limited to an ineffectual, nonpartisan political strategy of rewarding friends and punishing enemies.

In addition, the return to the default policy of strikebreaking displayed the meager development of the federal government's administrative capacities to intervene in industrial disputes. Notwithstanding the creation of the Department of Labor in 1913, the federal government lacked the power of compulsory arbitration during peacetime, and most conciliation took place through the private efforts of the National Civic Federation. Without peaceful administrative means of adjusting labor disputes, the new American state naturally turned to the blunt instrument of military force when labor conflicts erupted into violence. True, World War I provided unprecedented federal involvement in industrial relations and labor participation in administration, but the wartime adjustment of labor disputes lasted less than two years—far too brief to institutionalize new practices.

Furthermore, the nascent policy of restraint ultimately rested on transitory presidential war powers. Wartime enhanced presidential power and warranted the public management of wartime labor disputes, but after the armistice, the president's wartime authority evaporated, including his authority to extend the wartime labor relations regime into peacetime. President Wilson instead directed his energies toward creating a lasting peace abroad and building public support for the Treaty of Versailles at home. Wilson's physical collapse in 1919 and President Harding's ineptitude permitted employers to push back the encroachment of state planning and to reassert the policy of the open shop. Not until the Great Depression weakened the business community would the American state acquire the institutions and capacities to protect the right to strike.

The rise of the new American state had forced the early labor movement to abandon worker-republican principles and embrace pure-and-simple unionism, but the new American state failed to develop the policies and administrative capacities to uphold a limited right to strike, protect basic civil liberties, and uphold the legitimacy of the state. A limited right to strike for pure-and-simple union purposes called for an affirmative and restrained executive intervention that Progressive presidents like Theodore Roosevelt and Woodrow Wilson had experimented with, but had not institutionalized. It would have to await the further expansion of federal authority, presidential power, and administrative capacities associated with the New Deal, but even then the right to strike would remain qualified and ambivalent.

5

"Let the toilers assemble"
The New Deal and the Modern Liberal
Right to Strike

The 1935 National Labor Relations Act represents one of the most significant achievements in American political development. Hailed as the Magna Carta of the American labor movement, the NLRA promoted independent labor organizations and free collective bargaining in industry by affirming and protecting the rights of employees to engage in collective action. Among these rights was the right to strike. The right to strike for pure-and-simple union objectives replaced the default policy of strikebreaking, and the rule of law superseded the law of the jungle in labor disputes. Authorities no longer treated major strikes as insurrections calling for military intervention. Federal affirmation and protection of this and other rights encouraged the spread of collective bargaining from the skilled trades into basic industry, spawned the creation of a new labor federation, and over the next decade fostered a fivefold expansion in labor union membership. The passage of the National Labor Relations Act, and its validation in *Jones and Laughlin vs. NLRB* (1937), constitutes the most important development in the emergence of the modern liberal right to strike.

Despite the early success engendered by the NLRA, however, the New Deal labor policy failed to establish an unequivocal and robust foundation for the right to strike. Unlike their nineteenth-century predecessors, labor leaders and their political allies during and since the New Deal era no longer conceived of the right to strike as a citizenship right, but as a commercial right—as the liberty to engage in certain concerted activities for commercial purposes. This constituted the right to strike more narrowly as an instrument of free collective bargaining over wages and working conditions and abandoned the nineteenth-century view that the free laborer is not simply a factor of production but also a self-governing citizen with rights and duties beyond those enumerated in the labor contract. Furthermore, constructing the right to strike as a commercial right bound it to a vulnerable constitutional foundation, based not on any firm constitutional rights but on the interstate commerce clause of the Constitution. The New Deal labor policy thus accorded only a grudging acceptance of this right.

Constituting the right to strike as a commercial right was not a foregone conclusion, however. Instead, policy makers considered two other possibilities for constructing a vigorous and decisive right to strike—the civil libertarian model and the compulsory arbitration model. Initially, the New Deal labor policy contained elements of all three approaches to federal strike policy. The right to strike as a commercial right prevailed because it best managed the conflict between the state's interest in fostering economic recovery and constitutional, institutional, and social restrictions on state activism. Any new strike policy would have involved a reordering of authority relationships within the American political system, but the right to strike as a commercial right was the least disruptive. Moreover, constructing the right to strike as a commercial right proved to be more compatible with the values of, and required fewer alterations in, modern American liberalism than did the compulsory arbitration model or the civil libertarian model of the right to strike. Modern American liberal support for the right to strike, however, remained ambivalent and conditional and without a stalwart commitment to the right to strike.

The Right to Strike as a Civil Liberty

One of the hallmarks of the modern liberal American state has been the increasing protection of civil liberties. With *Twining v. New Jersey* (1925) and *Near V. Minnesota* (1931), the Supreme Court began the partial incorporation of the Bill of Rights under the Fourteenth Amendment.[1] During the New Deal the Justice Department also developed a more expansive conception of civil liberties as a positive liberty, calling on the federal government to protect citizens from private forms of oppression, rather than merely constraining the government itself. The Supreme Court and others have further broadened our civil liberties to encompass a penumbra of rights only suggested in the Bill of Rights, including the right to privacy and the right to abortion. Civil liberties thus provided one model for establishing a robust right to strike during the New Deal. Despite advances in protecting the civil liberties of strikers, however, advocates of workers' rights never succeeded in constituting the right to strike per se as a civil liberty, because doing so would have required a more radical reformulation of the traditional concept of civil liberty.

The troubled history of industrial relations between 1877 and 1932 provides a dismal testimony to the affinity between strikebreaking and violations of civil liberties. The U.S. Strike Commission's report on the Pullman strike, the Commission on Industrial Relation's report on the Ludlow strike massacre, the Interchurch World Committee's report on the 1919 steel strike, and the writings of Edwin Witte, Felix Frankfurter, and Nathan Greene all corroborate the repeated denial of strikers' basic civil liberties. Employers routinely resorted to labor espionage, yellow dog contracts, discriminatory discharge, blacklists, and private armed forces to suppress strikes during this era. Governors and presidents declared martial law, permitting mass arrests, suspension of habeas corpus and civil court proceedings, and the use of military force to quash strikes. Courts blanketed entire communities with labor injunctions, denying strikers' due process rights and the freedoms of assembly, expression, and movement.

Throughout the 1920s, a broad array of liberals denounced these judicial infringements on strikers' civil liberties. Senator George Wharton Pepper declared that "the growing bitterness of organized labor toward the federal courts" would have extraordinary consequences.[2] Senator William E. Borah asserted that "the Supreme Court [has] become . . . the economic dictator of the United States."[3] Justice Louis Brandeis, in his dissent in the *Bedford Stonecutters* case, noted that "if, on the undisputed facts of this case, refusal to work can be enjoined, Congress created by the Sherman Law and the Clayton Act an instrument for imposing restraints upon labor which reminds of involuntary servitude."[4] Frankfurter and Greene concluded that "the injunction includes more than the lawless; . . . it leaves the lawless undefined and thus terrorizes innocent conduct; . . . it employs the most powerful resources of the law on one side of a bitter social struggle."[5]

Congress had attempted to immunize strikers from labor injunctions with the passage of the 1916 Clayton Act, but Section 20 failed to withstand judicial review.[6] Consequently, in 1932 Congress enacted the Norris–La Guardia Anti-Injunction Act, which eliminated the lower courts' jurisdiction to hear cases regarding strikes.[7] Since Congress has, under Article III of the Constitution, the authority to determine the jurisdiction of lower federal courts, the Supreme Court could not rule the Norris–La Guardia Act unconstitutional. Henceforth, courts could only issue temporary restraining orders, and only after specifying who and what activities were restrained and providing strikers with the opportunity to respond to an employer's charges. Finally, the act specifically advocated the self-organization of workers and collective bargaining, thus linking federal labor relations policy with the protection of strikers' civil liberties.

By restricting the federal courts' equity powers, the Norris–La Guardia Act secured the Progressive Era goal of judicial noninterference in strikes, or "industrial laissez-faire," but the act hardly represented a radically new conception of civil liberties or the right to strike. A modern conception of civil liberties involves the constructive use of state authority to protect civil liberties against private forms of oppression. An affirmative right to strike thus requires more than legal immunity from court injunctions; it also compels the state to intervene to protect strikers' civil liberties from the oppressive practices of open shop employers and local governments. However, as things stood, employers still could discharge strikers, employ industrial armies and labor spies, blacklist strikers, and demand that employees sign yellow dog contracts; state and local officials still could prohibit picketing and strike rallies, and could wield excessive force against picketers and strike leaders; governors and presidents still could declare martial law and deploy National Guardsmen and the regular army against strikers. The Norris–La Guardia Act thus did not affirm the right to strike per se as a civil liberty.

The 1935 National Labor Relations Act, by contrast, provided additional federal protections of workers' rights, authorizing the federal government to defend the rights to organize into independent labor organizations, to engage in collective bargaining, and to participate in collective action. The act "[protects] the exercise by workers of full freedom of association," employees' right to bargain through "representatives of their own choosing," and specifically affirms the right to strike:

> Employees shall have the right to self-organization, to form, join, or assist labor organizations, to bargain collectively through representatives of their own choosing, and to engage in concerted activities, for the purpose of collective bargaining or other mutual aid or protection. (Section 7)
>
> Nothing in this Act shall be construed so as to interfere with or impede or diminish in any way the right to strike. (Section 13)[8]

The NLRA also prohibited specific unfair labor practices such as blacklisting, employment discrimination against union members, labor espionage, company-dominated employee organizations, and the like, and authorized the National Labor Relations Board to investigate charges of unfair labor practices and to supervise representation elections. Nevertheless, despite the NLRA's more constructive approach to workers' rights, nowhere does it declare a constitutional right to strike or that the right to strike rests on the Bill of Rights, or even (with the exception of the brief reference to freedom of association) that strikers' rights of habeas corpus, due process, freedom of expression, and so forth, call for special consideration.

The La Follette Civil Liberties Committee investigations forged a more explicit link between the New Deal strike policy and the civil libertarian

tradition of rights. In June 1936, on the requests of NLRB chairman Lloyd
Garrison and the American Civil Liberties Union, the Senate authorized a
special subcommittee to investigate "the full extent to which the rights of
labor to organize . . . [are] being denied and the extent to which civil liberties are interfered with."[9] Conducted between 1936 and 1940, this federal
investigation into employers' oppressive labor practices was the most thorough ever into organized industrial violence, even surpassing those conducted in 1914–15 by the Commission on Industrial Relations. Using its
contacts with radicals within the Economic Research Division of the National Labor Relations Board, the Civil Liberties Committee exposed employers who violently attacked strikers, in defiance of the new federal labor
relations law. Labor spies, massive stockpiles of private munitions, company police, private armed strikebreaking mercenaries, agents provocateurs, vigilante committees, and employers' associations provided grist for
the investigation. The exposure of strikebreaking practices by coal operators, automobile manufacturers, and steel producers paved the way for historic collective bargaining agreements between the United Mine Workers
and the coal operators in Harlan County, Kentucky; the United Automobile
Workers and General Motors; and the Steel Workers Organizing Committee and U.S. Steel. Although the stated purpose of the investigation was to
eliminate obstacles to the enforcement of the NLRA, its hidden agenda was
to build the legal and popular case for the NLRA at a time when the constitutionality of the act was still in question and to promote the cause of the
fledgling industrial union movement.

The La Follette Committee investigations revealed how the extensive use
of organized private force to break strikes not only violated the civil liberties of employees but also subverted the state's claim to a monopoly of the
legitimate use of force. According to the committee's reports, private police
forces comprised "an autocracy within a democracy. . . . It is an offense
against duly constituted authority." Citizens' committees, organized by employers during a strike to mobilize community support, had become "an invisible super-government" in many communities, whose vigilantism circum-
vented law enforcement agencies. The existence of an estimated forty
thousand labor spies "set at naught the powers of government itself."
Armed guards arrogated the police power of the state when they ventured
off company premises to attack strikers.[10] As former National Recovery Act
general counsel Donald Richberg noted, "If force must be the final arbiter
of any dispute, then the underlying principle of a civilized society compels
us to establish a public force controlled by public law as the arbiter and to
prohibit the use of any private law to dictate that decision."[11] Protecting the
right to strike as a civil liberty thus appeared to be consistent with the modern America state's sovereign interest in protecting its claim to a monopoly
of the legitimate use of force.

Jerold Auerbach observes that growing federal government protection of workers' rights was also a crucial step toward greater federal protection of civil liberties generally. The committee reports, for example, drew a direct connection between strikebreaking and interferences with civil liberties: "The most spectacular violations of civil liberty . . . proved upon investigation to have their roots in economic conflicts of interest . . . [A]ny concerted and prolonged rejection of the principles of collective bargaining leads to the invasion of constitutional liberty."[12] As a consequence of the investigation, Attorney General Frank Murphy established the civil liberties unit within the Department of Justice, and proposed using this unit to defend the NLRA's collective action rights. Justice Murphy later authored the majority opinion in *Thornhill v. Alabama* (1940), which overturned an Alabama antipicketing law as a violation of strikers' rights under the First Amendment. Labor historian Sidney Fine characterized this as "the high water mark in the constitutional rights of labor."[13]

The La Follette Civil Liberties Committee investigations exposed civil liberties violations that accompanied strikebreaking and helped to build support for the new national strike policy, but the committee failed to produce new legislation protecting the right to strike as a civil liberty. In 1940 Senator La Follette introduced a bill to "eliminate oppressive labor practices" and to establish a permanent federal agency to investigate future abuses. The bill, however, never came to the floor for a vote.

Two political developments undermined political support for legislation that might have established the right to strike as a civil liberty. First, a conservative coalition of Republicans and southern Democrats, much less sympathetic to workers' rights, emerged in Congress. The 1937 Court-packing fight, Roosevelt's failed attempt to purge conservative southern Democrats in the 1938 Senate elections, and the Democrats' losses of thirty-one seats in the House and six in the Senate solidified this coalition, which successfully resisted all future New Deal domestic reforms. The La Follette Committee's prolabor hearings provoked a backlash among the nascent conservative coalition, which realized that it could turn the tables and mount its own investigations of the NLRB, the labor movement, and even the La Follette Civil Liberties Committee investigators. Following its creation in 1939, the Special Committee on Un-American Activities, chaired by Representative Martin Dies of Texas, immediately launched attacks against the staff of the La Follette Committee and the NLRB; charges of Communist influence dogged the La Follette Committee investigators for more than a decade.[14]

Representative Howard Smith of Virginia, the leader of the conservative coalition in the House, followed up the investigations of the Dies Committee by chairing the newly created Special Committee to Investigate the National Labor Relations Board, which assailed the NLRB for its pro-CIO stance and its alleged Communist staff members.[15] The investigation forced out NLRB chairman J. Warren Madden and ushered in the more conservative Harry Millis, who initiated "an orderly retreat" from the controversial policies of the previous chairman, "so orderly as to escape all but limited attention."[16] On the recommendation of the Smith Committee, Congress slashed the budgets of the NLRB's Technical Service Division and the Division of Economic Research, which had supplied research assistance to the La Follette Committee.[17] The NLRB subsequently shifted away from the promotion of industrial unionism and workers' rights, toward more procedural tasks as a neutral arbiter of industrial relations law. Representative Smith also proposed new legislation in 1940 restricting the authority of the NLRB and curbing the power of labor unions. Although the Smith Act died in the Senate, it became a model for the 1947 Taft-Hartley amendments.

The second political development involved the outbreak of war in Europe. Defense mobilization stimulated the lowest unemployment rate and best wage increases in more than ten years, so domestic issues seemed less pressing. The administration instead needed Congress and industry to support its military plans and diplomacy, which limited progress on divisive domestic issues.[18] Unpatriotic defense industry strikers disturbed members of Congress far more than oppressive labor practices; fears of industrial sabotage and foreign infiltration of the labor force led to floor amendments to investigate the labor movement, which scuttled the La Follette bill. Following the massive wartime growth in union membership and the postwar strike wave, Congress was more concerned with reining in big labor than affirming the civil liberties of strikers.

Even if the La Follette oppressive labor practices bill had passed, grounding the right to strike in civil liberties still raised fundamental conceptual difficulties. That law-abiding strikers have the same constitutional rights as all Americans is undeniable. Wage earners who strike should not lose their rights of habeas corpus, due process, association, assembly, expression, petition, and so forth, and they should expect the state to protect them against physical coercion, espionage, and other private forms of oppression. The La Follette oppressive labor practices bill would have defended the civil liberties of strikers, but not necessarily the right to strike per se. To argue that the right to strike per se is a civil liberty requires a reformulation of the traditional concept of civil liberty. Modern civil liberties may incorporate the modern liberal concept of positive liberty, but they still rest on the classic liberal principle of individual rights. The right to strike, by contrast, is a right to suspend all work collectively, a group right that may conflict with individual rights. The right to strike, furthermore, guarantees to workers the right to return to their jobs after they have engaged in a temporary collective work stoppage. This restricts the individual rights of employers, who may want to resist the strike in order to maintain business operations, and obstructs the individual rights of potential replacement workers and fellow employees, who may want to work for the struck employer despite the on-going labor dispute. Should the state protect strikers against such nonviolent forms of strikebreaking? Should the state prohibit employers from hiring replacement workers? Should the state permit picket lines that block customers and other personnel and force the employer to suspend all business operations until they settle the dispute? Should the state force employers to discharge strikebreakers and rehire strikers when the labor dispute has been settled? If not, may employers demand police protection for replacement workers when they cross the picket line? The right to strike as a civil liberty would not only demand that the state defend strikers' civil liberties, but that it also defend strikes as a civil liberty, which amounts to taking sides in a rancorous social conflict.

The Right to Strike and Compulsory Arbitration

Compulsory arbitration offered a second model for constructing a robust right to strike during the New Deal. Under this model, labor and management submit unresolved disputes to an impartial board, which characteristically includes representatives of labor, industry, and the public. The board investigates the dispute, considers the demands of both sides, and decides based upon the substantive merits of the case; the board's decision is binding. The state resolves the impasse by determining the wages, hours, working conditions, work rules, and other terms of employment. In theory, compulsory arbitration abridges the right to strike, because strikers must return to work as a condition of adjusting the labor dispute.[19] However, compulsory arbitration involves an exchange of one form of power—economic coercion—for another—state coercion—in that the board's decision is also binding on the employer. In practice, wage earners initially retain the right to strike and only suspend it after an unresolved labor dispute goes to arbitration.

Labor leaders now regard compulsory arbitration in the private sector as anathema to our system of collective bargaining, but it is not alien to American labor relations policy. Prior to the rise of pure-and-simple unionism, early labor leaders supported compulsory arbitration in the private sector as an alternative to the bloody labor wars of the late nineteenth century. The National Labor Union first endorsed a federal department of labor with the power of compulsory arbitration in 1868.[20] Due to the essential nature of the railroad industry, reformers likewise sought federal arbitration of railway labor disputes in the 1888 Arbitration Act, the 1898 Erdman Act, and the 1913 Newlands Act, although the railway arbitration boards could not compel employers to submit. The most successful experiment occurred during World War I, when mainstream labor leaders suspended the right to strike and accepted mediation by the National War Labor Board and industry-level labor adjustment boards. Although these boards only exercised moral suasion, President Wilson exercised his wartime powers of compulsion when mediation failed.

During the early New Deal, associationalists within the administration promoted compulsory arbitration as part of their strategy of national industrial recovery. Associationalists such as Adolf Berle and Gerard Swope argued that market competition—once regarded as the motive force behind economic growth and spontaneous social order—had a detrimental effect on the mature American industrial economy. In a mature industrial economy, they argued, cutthroat competition forced businesses to undercut one another's prices, to overproduce, and to force down wages and profits, leading to low wages and widespread bankruptcies.[21] Associationalists consequently rejected the federal government's antitrust policies as counterproductive and, instead, under the 1933 National Industrial Recovery Act (NIRA), proposed codes of fair competition to fix prices and output. The National Recovery Administration (NRA) established industry-level boards to develop and enforce these codes.[22] Because industry codes of fair competition included labor standards, associationalists also supported labor organizations and collective bargaining, which they believed would stabilize prices as well as wages.[23] In fact, during the 1910s and 1920s the United Mine Workers had struggled to extend regional bargaining agreements throughout the highly decentralized and competitive coal industry for these reasons. Strikebreaking, however, destroyed the basis for this cooperation. Associationalists consequently supported Section 7(a) of the National Industrial Recovery Act, which asserted the rights of workers to organize in autonomous unions and to bargain collectively—key provisions of the New Deal labor policy[24]—and established industry-level labor adjustment boards.

Compulsory arbitration by industry-level labor adjustment boards failed to dampen industrial conflict, however, and instead sparked an upsurge in organizational and protest strikes. Labor activists like UMW President John L. Lewis realized that the current political climate presented the best opportunity to organize since World War I.[25] The strike rate doubled the first month after passage of the NIRA, and redoubled the following month. In 1933, six times as many workers struck as had in 1930, and the number of strikes during the last six months of 1933 exceeded the annual rates for every year since 1921.[26] One observer noted that "the country is full of spontaneous strikes. Everywhere one goes one sees picket lines."[27] John L. Lewis harnessed the insurgency in the coal regions, and, a few weeks after passage of the NIRA, had organized 80 percent of all miners in Ohio, Kentucky, and West Virginia.[28] Sidney Hillman and David Dubinsky revived the nearly defunct clothing and garment workers unions with massive recognition strikes in New York City. Because they were not organized along craft lines, these unions provided the organizational base and the leadership for the new industrial union movement of the 1930s; Lewis eventually helped to establish the Congress of Industrial Organizations (CIO) and the Steel Workers Organizing Committee.[29] Where the AFL during the time of Gompers had demanded state noninterference in labor union activities, advocates of the new industrial union movement sought federal protection for wage earners' rights to organize, to bargain collectively, and to strike.

The NIRA's purpose, however, was not to promote a new union movement, but to foster economic recovery; the NRA Industry and Labor Advisory Boards lacked the capacity to handle the hundreds of disputes, and by late summer 1933 NRA officials feared that the burgeoning strikes would undermine the recovery program. Consequently, in August the NRA advisory boards established a temporary National Labor Board to "further industrial peace through the adjudication of disputes."[30] Like the tripartite National War Labor Board, the National Labor Board (NLB) relied on informal, cooperative, and nonlegalistic methods of strike intervention. Although not authorized specifically to support the right to organize and bargain collectively, the labor board soon promoted those goals as consistent with industrial peace. Congress endorsed these functions in 1934 when it refashioned the NLB into the National Labor Relations Board (NLRB), authorizing it to intervene in disputes, to promote independent labor unions, and to supervise union representation elections. Public Resolution 44 proclaimed: "Nothing in this resolution shall prevent or impede or diminish in any way the right of employees to strike or engage in other concerted activities."

Unlike the current NLRB, which may only rule on the procedural fairness of the collective bargaining process, these early labor boards initially promoted the adjudication of labor disputes on the substantive merits of the cases. NRA general counsel Donald Richberg, one of the principal advocates of arbitration, argued that "the proposition that economic justice cannot be obtained except by leaving men free to coerce and intimidate one another is absurd on its mere statement."[31] As the railroad employees' representative before a railroad board of arbitration in 1927, he had asserted that "the conclusions reached by any arbitrator must be based, to some extent, upon economic theories which consciously or unconsciously shape the opinion of the arbitrator regarding economic justice."[32]

Despite the associationalists' attempts to establish a more just and cooperative alternative, however, board members soon turned away from arbitration toward more formal, quasi-judicial procedures to establish a common law of collective bargaining.[33] The labor board had the daunting assignment of intervening in the most volatile and immense social conflicts of the day. The board, moreover, was an improvised, ad hoc agency without firm statutory authority and only a vague mandate to do something about the industrial unrest that crippled the industrial recovery. Its powers were merely facilitative and depended on the cooperation of employers and labor organizations and the support of other federal administrators. Throughout 1934 and 1935, it became apparent that the labor board lacked the administrative capacities and the political legitimacy to carry out the overwhelming responsibility of adjudicating labor disputes throughout the American economy. Employers consequently turned to more sympathetic regional and industry-level labor adjustment boards, where employees often had no representation.

National Recovery Administration officials, who needed the cooperation of industry, displayed little support for the labor board when an employer challenged a decision. Because the NRA had created the NLB as an afterthought, there was no clear chain of command within the NRA. The NLB consequently lacked the authority to order the NRA's Enforcement Division to back up its decisions. The NLB could ask the Justice Department to charge an employer with violating the NIRA, but Justice Department officials had little interest in pursuing cases that might lead to a constitutional test of the administration's central legislative program.[34] Administration officials thus overruled the NLB whenever large employers disregarded its decisions, promoting the proximate goal of industrial peace, rather than defending employee rights under Section 7(a).

For example, struggles over union recognition ignited many of the bitterest and most disruptive strikes in 1934–35. Although the NRA had not authorized the NLB to do so, the labor board intervened in recognition strikes by supervising union representation elections. When Budd Manufacturing, Weirton Steel, and automobile manufacturers resisted, however, NRA administrators Hugh Johnson and Donald Richberg publicly denounced these election procedures because they awarded exclusive jurisdiction to a single union. Administration officials, including the president, favored a system of proportional representation that permitted employer representation plans, which labor board officials, including NLB chair Senator Robert Wagner, believed undermined independent labor organizations. After intervening in several major disputes, President Roosevelt established independent labor adjustment boards in the automobile, steel, and textile industries, circumventing the NLB's jurisdiction and repudiating its exclusive representation election rule. This discredited the early labor boards and further encouraged employers to defy the labor board's decisions.[35]

The final blow to compulsory arbitration came in early 1935. In February a lower federal court ruled in the *United States v. Weirton Steel* case that the federal government had no authority to regulate labor relations in manufacturing, which falls outside the flow of interstate commerce.[36] Then, in May the Supreme Court ruled that the entire Title I of the NIRA, including

Section 7(a), violated the Constitution. *Schechter Poultry Corp. v. U.S.* (1935) reaffirmed that economic activities' indirect influence on interstate commerce does not warrant federal intrusion. "The authority of the federal government," proclaimed the Court, "may not be pushed to such an extreme as to destroy the distinction, which the commerce clause itself establishes, between commerce 'among the several States' and the internal concerns of a State."[37] This invalidated the associationalist approach to national economic recovery and the compulsory arbitration of labor disputes; whether wage earners had a protected right to strike under U.S. law remained an unanswered question.

The rejection of compulsory arbitration denoted the renunciation of the planning model of state economic regulation that characterized the early New Deal. Critics of compulsory arbitration charge that it is rigid and bureaucratic, that an outsider could never fully appreciate all the complexities of the employment relationships within an industry, that the arbitration awards create administrative burdens on the employer, that it is difficult to obtain compliance for unpopular decisions, that it undermines the voluntary nature of the employment relationship, and that it weakens incentives for employers and employees to settle their differences privately.[38] These criticisms express broader concerns about state regulation and administration of an industrial economy, and present common criticisms of state planning. Compulsory arbitration also involves the state in broader macroeconomic policies, such as wage and price controls. Wage contracts typically include cost-of-living adjustments and often establish industrywide wage guidelines, both of which have a direct impact on inflation and unemployment. Hence, national economic policy considerations would have to be taken into account. The experience of the National War Labor Board during World War II illustrates how national economic policies easily subvert compulsory arbitration of labor disputes, and how that can provoke increasing labor conflict.[39]

Finally, because arbitrators have to justify their decisions, state adjustment of the content of the employment contract necessitates the development of standards of substantive justice. Compulsory arbitration inevitably draws the state into questions of fairness as they relate to wage rates, hours, working conditions, discharge, promotion, layoffs, and the full gamut of employment relations issues. In the absence of clear and widely accepted standards of substantive justice, such determinations would be highly subjective.[40] Senator Wagner recognized the danger that this creates for the modern liberal state:

> The outlawry of the right to strike is a natural concomitant of authoritarian governments. It occurs only when a government is willing to assume the definitive responsibility for prescribing every element in the industrial relation-

ship—the length of the day, the size of the wage, the terms and conditions of work.[41]

Policy makers who supported the labor movement had to develop an alternative approach to the right to strike.

The Right to Strike as a Commercial Right

The rejection of the civil libertarian and compulsory arbitration models set the stage for defining the right to strike as a commercial right for the purposes of free collective bargaining over wages and working conditions. Under the system of free collective bargaining, the labor contract is a private, voluntary agreement between labor and management; the state facilitates the private negotiation process by enforcing procedural rules of fairness. Unlike compulsory arbitration, the state may not determine the content of the labor agreement or even demand that both sides settle. Thus, the Senate report on the 1935 National Labor Relations Act states:

> Disputes about wages, hours of work and other working conditions should continue to be resolved by the play of competitive forces, so far as the provisions of the codes of fair competition are not controlling. The bill in no respect regulates or even provides for supervision of wages or hours, nor does it establish any form of compulsory arbitration.[42]

Senator David I. Walsh expressed this principle during the floor debate:

> When the employees have chosen their organization, when they have selected their representative, all the bill proposes to do is to escort them to the door of the employer, and say "Here they are, the legal representatives of your employees." What happens behind those doors is not inquired into, and the bill does not seek to inquire into it.[43]

The Supreme Court's majority opinion in *NLRB v. Jones and Laughlin* (1937), which upheld the law, agreed: "The theory of the Act is that free opportunity for negotiation with accredited representatives of employees is likely to promote industrial peace and may bring about the adjustments and agreements which the Act itself does not attempt to compel."[44] Former AFL president William Green also concurred: "To compel men to arbitrate violates a fundamental principle of a free enterprise economic system because it violates the principle of freedom of contract."[45]

Advocates of free collective bargaining argue that it preserves the voluntary character of the labor agreement and promotes the institutions of a free society. Free collective bargaining settles the terms of employment by private agreement rather than by administrative fiat, and depends on employers and employees settling their differences privately, with a minimum of state intervention. The state merely acts as a neutral referee, administering rules of procedural fairness. The terms of the negotiated wage settlements are, by definition, fair. Free collective bargaining establishes the workplace rule of law and a set of contractual rights, based on the voluntary consent of the employer and employees.[46] In this way, the NLRA provides a model for the modern liberal American state in its relations with the private sector.[47]

To promote free collective bargaining, the NLRA established administrative procedures to curtail industrial conflicts that would otherwise impede collective bargaining. During the 1930s, the primary obstacles to stable collective bargaining were employers' refusal to recognize their employees' labor organizations and their interference with their employees' rights to form independent labor organizations.[48] Hence, the NLRA authorized the NLRB to supervise representation elections, to guarantee employees' free choice, and to provide an alternative to disruptive representational strikes. In addition, the NLRA prohibited specific unfair labor practices, including firing a worker for engaging in concerted activities, coercion, espionage, promotion of company unions, and refusal to bargain.[49] Finally, the act empowered the NLRB to investigate unfair labor practice complaints and to order remedial action to restore employees' statutory rights, such as by ordering the reinstatement of employees dismissed for union activities and ordering a recalcitrant employer to bargain in good faith.[50]

Both advocates and critics of the labor movement consider the right to strike as an essential element within the system of free collective bargaining.[51] "Effective collective bargaining is impossible," according to Otto Kahn-Freund, "where the workers do not have the freedom to stop work collectively, and trade unionism cannot exist and function if effective collective bargaining is impossible."[52] Senator Robert A. Taft, coauthor of the 1947 Taft-Hartley Act, declared that "the right to strike is . . . an essential element of collective bargaining in a free society."[53] Strikes represent organized labor's principal form of leverage in the wage negotiation process; employer strikebreaking arose from employers' refusal to bargain with labor organizations, which heightened industrial unrest. Thus, Section 7 of the NLRA declares: "Employees shall have the right to self-organization, to form, to join, or assist labor organizations, to bargain collectively through representatives of their own choosing, and to engage in concerted activities, for the purpose of collective bargaining or other mutual aid or protection." According to this view, the threat of a strike or a lockout keeps both parties at the bargaining table, creates an inducement to reach an agreement, and forces both to face the consequences if they do not. An occasional strike provides a necessary test of wills and allows the contestants to ascertain their relative bargaining strengths.[54] A limited right to strike thus is instrumental for the system of free collective bargaining.

The NLRA, however, did not affirm free collective bargaining and the right to strike in order to promote industrial justice or industrial democracy or workers' citizenship rights. Instead, it affirmed these rights for the state's purpose of economic recovery. True, Senator Wagner frequently expressed his principled support for industrial democracy in numerous radio addresses and magazine articles: "The struggle for a voice in industry through the process of collective bargaining is at the heart of the struggle for the preservation of political as well as economic democracy in America." "This underlying cause [of strikes] is the denial of primary industrial liberties."[55] But Senator Wagner had to couch the NLRA's purpose in the language of economic recovery and interstate commerce. The preamble to the NLRA declares:

> The inequality of bargaining power between employees who do not possess full freedom of association or actual liberty of contract, and employers who are organized in the corporate or other forms of ownership association substantially burdens and affects the flow of commerce, and tends to aggravate recurrent business depressions, by depressing wage rates and the purchasing power of wage earners in industry by preventing the stabilization of competitive wage rates and working conditions within and between industries.[56]

This approach to economic recovery reflected the thinking of secular stagnationists such as economist Alvin Hansen, Senate aide Leon Keyserling, and Secretary of Labor Frances Perkins, who rejected the associationalist explanation of the economic crisis of the 1930s. The cause of the Great Depression, they argued, was not uncontrolled competition; competitive industries such as coal mining, clothing, and textiles no longer dominated the American industrial economy. By the 1930s, oligopolistic mass production industries—the industries most resistant to free collective bargaining—dominated the U.S. economy. According to secular stagnationists, in the absence of fiscal policy and collective bargaining, a mature industrial economy has a natural tendency toward underconsumption and economic stagnation, as private oligopolistic enterprises tend to overproduce goods and depress wages.[57] According to this view, individual wage earners had negotiated labor contracts with massive private corporations, whose unmatched bargaining power drove down wages in order to control costs; low wages contributed to economic stagnation because workers could not afford the goods they produced.[58] Widening economic inequalities during the 1920s, when unionization rates had dropped to about 10 percent of the workforce, further aggravated underconsumption by wage earners. Spending by the wealthy, furthermore, had limited impact on consumer demand; even conspicuous consumption by the leisure class could not offset mass overproduction and underconsumption. In addition, sound investment opportunities had dwindled, leading to increasingly speculative investments and contributing to the instability of the industrial economy. Secular stagnationists thus promoted the social Keynesian goals of greater economic equality combined with state interventions to stabilize production and investment.[59]

This provided the rationale for protecting wage earners' rights to engage in concerted activities. Wagner and his aide Leon Keyserling (who drafted the NLRA) argued that extending collective bargaining rights to industrial workers would counteract inequality in bargaining power, thus raising wages and increasing mass demand.[60] Collective bargaining, in other words, would promote the state's interest in economic recovery. By avoiding command-and-control policies, maintaining private property relations, and refraining from class-based politics, collective bargaining exemplified a modern liberal approach to economic and social policy.

The NLRA also contends that industrial unrest interferes with the free flow of interstate commerce, which points to another state interest in regulating industrial conflict—promoting industrial peace. Widespread employer resistance to the new labor policies and to organizing drives had contributed to the massive strike wave throughout 1933 and 1934, and the NRA labor boards had failed to alleviate this industrial unrest. According to William H. Leiserson, a student of John R. Commons and a prominent figure in the development of the New Deal labor relations policy, one of the principal purposes of the New Deal's expansion of workers' rights was to support the peaceful resolution of labor disputes. The Supreme Court, ruling that sit-down strikes were not protected by the NLRA, verified this purpose in *NLRB v. Fansteel Metallurgical Corp.* (1939):

> We repeat that the fundamental policy of the Act is to safeguard the rights of self-organization and collective bargaining, and thus by the promotion of industrial peace to remove obstructions to the free flow of commerce as defined in the Act. There is not a line in the statute to warrant the conclusion that it is any part of the policies of the Act to encourage employees to resort to force and violence in defiance of the law of the land. On the contrary, the purpose of the Act is to promote peaceful settlements of disputes by providing legal remedies for the invasion of the employees' rights.[61]

In either case, the legislative rationale for the new strike policy rested on commercial purposes. Guaranteeing wage earners' rights to organize, bargain collectively, and to strike, according to the NLRA, would increase their bargaining power and diminish industrial unrest associated with employers' resistance to independent labor organizations; both objectives served the state's interest in economic stabilization and recovery. The NLRA sanctions the right to strike only for these purposes, and not to promote industrial democracy, worker participation, economic justice, or workers' civil rights.[62] Although social Keynesianism supported the progressive goal of greater equality, it was the equality of bargaining power rather than the equality of citizens that it sought.

The social Keynesian justifications for a federally protected right to strike implicitly repudiated a central tenet of nineteenth-century worker republicanism, reaffirmed as recently as 1914 in the Clayton Act, that "the labor of a human being is not a commodity." According to this principle, free labor is not simply an article of commerce, but a prerequisite for self-rule and American citizenship. The Knights of Labor and early labor leaders such as William Sylvis had rejected the view that free labor contracts guaranteed labor liberty, not because wage earners lacked the bargaining power to negotiate a fair wage, but because the wage system itself denied this central tenet. By resting the right to strike on social Keynesian grounds, the NLRA constructed the right to strike as a commercial right rather than as a civil liberty.

The free collective bargaining model and the right to strike as a commercial right, however, proved to be more consonant with the values of modern American liberalism. Michael Sandel argues that modern American liberalism remains agnostic toward any substantive ideal of the good life, and consequently does not consider the collective nature of our purposes or set forth principles of substantive justice. Instead, modern American liberalism embraces a voluntarist conception of liberty, which permits individuals to pursue their private conceptions of the good life, and establishes a neutral state that pursues a procedural conception of justice.[63] The right to strike as a commercial right thus called for fewer revisions in modern American liberalism than did the compulsory arbitration model or the civil libertarian model of the right to strike.

The National Labor Relations Act and Modifying Authority Relations

Even though the right to strike as a commercial right proved to be more consonant with the values of modern American liberalism, it still called for considerable modifications in federal authority. The recent *Schechter* decision, and industry resistance to the early New Deal labor policies in general, had demonstrated to Senator Wagner and Leon Keyserling that employers would challenge the NLRA as an unconstitutional intrusion of federal authority. Wagner and Keyserling consequently needed to craft a statue that would withstand rigorous examination by a conservative Supreme Court. Compared to the civil libertarian and the compulsory arbitration model, constituting the right to strike as a commercial right required the fewest modifications in federal authority, in that the NLRA rests on the narrowest constitutional grounds and delegates the least authority to the labor board. The trade-off, however, was a very narrow right to strike.

Wagner and Keyserling confronted two potential constitutional objections, the first involving procedural due process, and the second, the scope of federal government jurisdiction. Throughout the late-nineteenth and early-twentieth centuries, the Supreme Court had overturned state and federal labor laws as infringements on the liberty of contract implied by the due process clause of the Fourteenth Amendment. *Lochner v. New York* (1905) invalidated a law limiting the maximum hours of bakery workers; *Adair v. United States* (1908) nullified the 1898 Erdman Act's ban against yellow dog contracts; *Coppage v. Kansas* (1915) countermanded a similar provision in state laws; *Adkins v. Children's Hospital* (1923) invalidated minimum wage laws for women and children in the nation's capital.[64] The NLRA anticipated a similar constitutional challenge by arguing that no true liberty of contract exists between individual employees and their employers. The second sentence in the act states that the corporate form of ownership created unequal bargaining power between the employer and the unorganized employees. This permitted employers to drive a hard bargain and to keep wages low, which contributed to underconsumption and economic stagnation. Federal support for collective bargaining, according to the NLRA's preamble, would establish "actual liberty of contract." The NLRA thus accepted the wage system and the voluntarist assumptions of pure-and-simple unionism.

The second constitutional hurdle concerned the federal government's limited jurisdiction over labor disputes. Prior to the NLRA, the Constitution permitted federal intervention in strikes only when they escalated into uncontrollable civil unrest, interfered with federal laws, or disrupted interstate commerce. Maintaining the flow of interstate commerce had warranted federal involvement in railway labor disputes, culminating in the 1926 Railway Labor Act. Traditionally, however, the Supreme Court had differentiated between manufacturing and commerce, and in the *Schechter* case the Court continued to uphold a narrow definition of interstate commerce, distinguishing between those goods that had crossed state boundaries at some point but had come to rest outside interstate commerce and those in the flow of interstate commerce. The authors of the NLRA consequently constructed employees' rights to organize, to bargain collectively, and to strike on the very narrow constitutional foundations of the commerce clause, without decisively responding to the argument that employment relations in manufacturing only *indirectly* affect interstate commerce. The first lines of the act proclaim:

> The denial by employers of the right of employees to organize and the refusal
> by employers to accept the procedure of collective bargaining lead to strikes

and other forms of industrial strife or unrest, which have the intent or the necessary effect of burdening or obstructing commerce by (a) impairing the efficiency, safety, or operation of the instrumentalities of commerce; (b) occurring
in the current of commerce; (c) materially affecting, restraining, or controlling
the flow of raw materials or manufactured or processed goods from or into the
channels of commerce, or the prices of such materials or goods in commerce;
or (d) causing the diminution of employment and wages in such volume as sub-
stantially to impair or disrupt the market for goods flowing from or into the
channels of commerce.[65]

Retreating from its previous position, the Supreme Court in *NLRB v.
Jones and Laughlin Steel Corp.* (1937) endorsed the more expansive view of
Congressional authority:

> When industries organize themselves on a national scale, making their relation
> to interstate commerce the dominant factor in their activities, how can it be
> maintained that their industrial labor relations constitute a forbidden field into
> which Congress may not enter when it is necessary to protect interstate com-
> merce from the paralyzing consequences of industrial war?[66]

This not only validated federal protections for wage earners' rights to organize, bargain collectively, and to strike, but also signified an important milestone in American political development. The expansion of the interstate
commerce clause represented the end of the laissez-faire era in state-market
relations and opened the way for limited federal regulation of the economy.
However, this affirmed the right to strike only as a commercial right, rather
than as a civil liberty or citizenship right, not subject to the same scrutiny
that constitutional rights receive from the Court. Moreover, as a statutory
right, the right to strike as affirmed by the NLRA is subject to legislative
abridgement and executive interference when it serves the interests of the
state. As a commercial right, the right to strike is more akin to an entitlement than a full-fledged right.

The *Jones and Laughlin* and *West Coast Hotel v. Parrish* (1937) decisions
also comprised the "switch in time that saved nine," and marked the shift in
the constitutional balance of power away from the judiciary and toward
presidential government.[67] Prior to the *Jones and Laughlin* decision, an activist Supreme Court had invalidated key New Deal legislation, including
Title I of the NIRA. Although Roosevelt's court-packing scheme had met
strong public and congressional opposition, it nonetheless succeeded in
checking the Supreme Court's opposition to the expansion of federal power
and presidential authority. The validation of the NLRA thus signified the
end of laissez-faire economic policies, the expansion of federal authority

under a broad interpretation of interstate commerce, and the rise of presidential power.

The NLRA fostered another modification in authority relations, namely, the expansion of federal administrative capacities to regulate labor conflicts. Prior to passage of the NLRA, these administrative capacities remained rudimentary except in times of emergency and war. The Department of Labor could only mediate labor disputes, and the NIRA labor boards had no enforcement authority and were subject to meddling by NRA administrators and the president himself. Senator Wagner, who had served on the NLB in 1934, realized that protection of wage earners' rights to organize and engage in concerted activities demanded the establishment of an independent agency with statutory powers to promote unionization and protect workers' rights. The NLRB thus had the power to supervise elections, and investigate charges of unfair labor practices and other violations of the act.

The NLRA, however, failed to delegate adequate powers to promote a robust right to strike, and political developments in the late 1930s and 1940s further curtailed the NLRB's administrative capacities. The NLRA only granted remedial powers to the labor board; the NLRB has no powers of prevention, nor may it bring criminal charges against employers who commit unfair labor practices, nor may wage earners sue employers for violating their rights under the NLRA. For example, the NLRA prohibits bargaining in bad faith and the wrongful discharge of workers for engaging in lawful collective action, but the NLRB may only demand that employers engage in good faith bargaining, and reinstate fired workers with net back pay. Strikebreaking employers pay no fines or punitive awards.

Furthermore, Senator Wagner and the existing labor board insisted upon the formation of an independent regulatory agency, outside the Department of Labor, which they regarded as the captive of rival AFL supporters. The existing labor board had close ties with CIO unions, and supported the new industrial union movement in the face of AFL resistance. Moreover, the existing labor board had been an adjunct to the NRA, which undercut the labor board on several occasions. Independence, however, isolated the new NLRB and left it vulnerable to employer attacks. Until the Supreme Court validated the NLRA, the National Association of Manufacturers and the Liberty League openly encouraged defiance of the NLRB. Over one hundred court injunctions prohibited the NLRB from enforcing the Act.[68] Even after the *Jones and Laughlin* decision, employers continued to defy the NLRB. Some of the bloodiest strikes erupted in the late 1930s because employers resisted their employees' rights to organize. Strikes against Ford, against the Little Steel companies, and against coal operators in Harlan County, Kentucky, revealed the limited enforcement powers of the early NLRB.[69]

Independence also left the new NLRB vulnerable to congressional attacks. As previously noted, the Dies Committee and Smith Committee investigations of the NLRB led to the resignation of the chairman, the reduction in the allocation for the NLRB's Economic Research Division, and the
redirection of the agency toward a more moderate agenda. Following the
war, the 1947 Taft-Hartley Act instituted many of the restrictions Representative Smith had proposed in 1940, including the elimination of the Economic Division, the subordination of the NLRB to the federal courts, the bifurcation of the agency leadership, and prohibitions on the NLRB engaging
in mediation and conciliation. Isolated and vulnerable, the NLRB became
less and less of a stalwart advocate for industrial unionism and collective
bargaining.

The legalization of the right to strike represented one of the most historic
achievements of the modern liberal American state. No longer would the
state treat most strikes as insurrections, conspiracies, or invasions of contract and property rights. The National Labor Relations Act ended the
state's default policy of strikebreaking and laid the foundations for the rule
of law in labor relations. However, by constructing the right to strike as a
statutory, commercial right, the New Deal established this right upon a
vulnerable legal base. Unlike civil liberties and civil rights, the rights of employees to engage in concerted activity have an insecure and ambivalent
constitutional foundation.

This achievement confirms Michael Sandel's observation about the loss of
the civic component in American political discourse concerning economic
relationships:

> Economic policy attended more to the size and distribution of the national
> product and less to the conditions of self-government. Americans increasingly
> viewed economic arrangements as instruments of consumption, not as schools
> for citizenship. The formative ambition gave way to the more mundane hope
> of increasing and dispersing the fruits of prosperity . . . From the standpoint of
> the republican tradition, the demise of the political economy of citizenship con-
> stituted a concession, a deflation of American ideals, a loss of liberty.[70]

The modern liberal American state vouchsafed a limited freedom to strike
in order to promote economic recovery, equal bargaining power, industrial
peace, and the system of free collective bargaining. These are worthy goals,
but they represent a final relinquishing of the nineteenth-century republican
goals of labor liberty, self-rule, civic virtue, and social justice.

6

"Get down to the type of job you're supposed to be doing"
World War II and the Labor Management Relations Act

Many labor law historians today regard the 1947 Labor Management Relations Act (LMRA), or Taft-Hartley Act, as one of the principal causes of the recent erosion of the right to strike and the current decline in the American labor movement.[1] Passed after fourteen years of unprecedented growth in the labor movement and after the public had become weary of massive postwar strikes, the LMRA prohibits a wide range of concerted activities, including sympathy strikes, secondary boycotts, wildcat strikes, jurisdictional strikes, political strikes, strikes to obtain the closed shop, and coercing other workers into supporting a strike. Thus, Katherine Stone argues:

> In order to retain the protection of the law, the union must surrender many of its economic weapons. The right to strike is restricted or impliedly waived; secondary boycotts and sympathy strikes are prohibited.
>
> The employers' economic weapons, however, are not similarly curtailed by the law. . . . He can lock out his employees. He can weaken the union by discharging shop leaders, reducing wages, laying off part of the workforce, or changing the production methods. The Act does not prohibit these "tactics" unless done with a specific and provable anti-union intent.[2]

Likewise, Christopher Tomlins asserts that the law's primary message to American workers was to "lie down like good dogs."[3] This echoed the views of labor leaders and their supporters in 1947 who denounced the new law as "a slave labor bill" and a "sharp turn to the right."[4]

The law turn in American labor studies, however, has put too much emphasis on the LMRA itself and the legal limits it placed on collective action. The LMRA was the product of the labor movement's ongoing struggle to define the right to strike in the context of war, the end of social reform, and the resurgence of American business. The erosion in this right thus has its roots in the interaction of broader American political developments and working-class formation during and after World War II. The most important consequence of this interaction was the disengagement of labor policy from social reform, a consequence that impeded the emergence of a social democratic welfare state in the United States.[5]

Although the 1935 National Labor Relations Act had constituted the right to strike narrowly as a commercial right, it nonetheless had done so within a social Keynesian framework that coupled economic and social reforms. That is, a protected right to strike promoted industrial recovery as well as workers' social citizenship rights. The NLRA, moreover, had a critical impact on American working-class formation, enabling the emergence of an industrial union movement and the quadrupling of union memberships by the end of World War II. After the war, union densities in basic industries, such as steel and automobile manufacturing, exceeded 90 percent levels, levels comparable to those in European social democratic countries that provided the political base for a comprehensive welfare state.[6] So impressive was the labor movement's growth that industrial relations scholar Sumner Slichter declared that a laboristic society had replaced a capitalistic society in the United States.[7]

During the war, however, the federal government discarded the NLRA's social Keynesian goals, as the national interest shifted from industrial recovery to national defense and economic stabilization. This occurred when the new union movement was still in its infancy and not fully incorporated into political and governmental institutions. Consequently, labor unions were inadequately represented in the war industries planning agencies, and wartime labor policies were divorced from social reforms. Instead, a wartime accommodation, in which labor leaders acceded to compulsory arbitration in exchange for union security, governed relations between the labor movement and the state. After the administration linked arbitration with wage controls, however, the federal government could not simultaneously stabilize labor relations and control wages in the absence of structural reforms. The collapse of wage controls and the no-strike pledge in 1945–46 precipitated one of the nation's most massive strike waves ever, which provided the proximate cause for restrictions on the right to strike.

The LMRA completed the disengagement of federal labor relations policy from social policy. The act rejected social Keynesian reforms in favor of a legalistic framework of industrial relations that protected individual rights and promoted a narrow contractualism in collective bargaining—features that necessarily limited collective action rights and established a more grudging right to strike. This constituted a significant retreat from the New Deal's more ambitious social Keynesian goals of structural reform and economic equality, and its affirmation of the right to strike.[8] In addition, liberal industrial relations professionals promoted the LMRA's narrow contractualism and legalistic framework, revealing that the diminution in the right to strike was not simply the result of "a sharp turn to the right," but also due to liberal ambivalence regarding this right.

World War II and the End of Social Reform

Wartime has often provided democracies with opportunities for social reform, as political leaders look for some higher purpose to justify the personal sacrifices and upheaval that citizens must endure. Thus, the Gettysburg Address recast the American experiment as "dedicated to the proposition that all men are created equal." Wilson's 1917 address to Congress sought a declaration of war against Germany in order to "make the world safe for democracy." Roosevelt's 1944 State of the Union address to Congress called for "a second Bill of Rights, under which a new basis of security and prosperity can be established for all." In Britain, World War II engendered the "Beveridge Report" and the modern welfare state. As Richard Titmuss observed in his 1950 essay "War and Social Policy":

> The reality of military disaster and the threat of invasion in the summer of 1940 urged on these tendencies in social policy. . . . The long, dispiriting years of hard work that followed these dramatic events on the home front served only to reinforce the war-warmed impulse of people for a more generous society.[9]

World War II, however, marked the end of the New Deal era of social reform in the United States and a retreat from the policies of social Keynesians. This failure of the United States to develop into a welfare state in part reflects the weak incorporation of the labor movement into the massive wartime economic planning process.

As noted in chapter 4, wartime typically presents favorable economic and political conditions for organized labor, as low unemployment and the need for national unity force the state to accommodate union demands. However, the outbreak of war in 1940 came at an inauspicious moment for the U.S. labor movement. The new federal strike policy was barely three years old, and no consensus, not even within the labor movement, had crystallized on the fundamentals of the industrial relations system. In the late

1930s, violent recognition strikes against farm owners in Delano, California; mine operators in Harlan County, Kentucky; the Little Steel companies; and Ford demonstrated the unsettled state of federal labor relations policy on the eve of World War II.[10] The Dies and Smith committees' investigations into the NLRB, and the subsequent resignation of NLRB chairman J. Warren Madden were further evidence that federal labor policy remained contested terrain just prior to the war.[11]

Moreover, on the eve of World War II the industrial union movement remained embryonic and divided.[12] Industrial unions had not yet organized large regions of the South and the West. Efforts to establish a beachhead among southern textile workers and farm workers had collapsed, and major employers in steel, auto manufacturing, coal mining, rubber, electrical goods, meatpacking, and lumber had either refused to recognize unions or to bargain with them. Most employers who did bargain with industrial unions only signed one-year contracts. In addition, splits within the labor movement undermined labor unity and led the CIO to disaffiliate from the AFL in 1938.[13] Internal struggles between Communists and moderates further divided CIO unions, including the United Automobile Workers (UAW).[14] UMW president John L. Lewis, perhaps the most influential labor leader of the era, refused to endorse Roosevelt in the 1940 election, subsequently resigned from the CIO presidency, and withdrew the UMW from the new labor federation.

Some progressive labor leaders, such as Philip Murray, Walter Reuther, and Sidney Hillman, initially regarded wartime mobilization and planning as an opportunity to promote a quasi-corporatist form of industrial democracy that transcended pure-and-simple unionism. Thus, to oversee wartime mobilization, CIO president Murray urged the president to create tripartite industry councils modeled after Pope Pius XI's social encyclical of 1931.[15] Reuther likewise recommended industrial councils, albeit for a more technocratic, social democratic plan to convert excess capacity in automobile plants to aircraft production.[16] However, in 1940 labor leaders were in a tenuous position to bargain with the state over wartime public policies, so these plans received little attention from the administration.

President Roosevelt instead placed winning the war above domestic concerns; referring to his new role, the president declared that "Dr. Win the War" had replaced "Dr. New Deal."[17] With the unemployment rate at its lowest level in more than ten years and wages rising during 1940 and 1941, domestic issues seemed less pressing. The administration instead needed Congress and industry to support its military plans and diplomacy.[18] President Roosevelt consequently placed the wartime planning agencies in the hands of business executives such as former General Motors president William Knudsen, who directed the Office of Production Management, and former Sears executive Donald Nelson, who chaired the OPM's successor, the War Production Board.[19]

The administration did appoint some labor representatives to wartime agencies, such as Sidney Hillman, whom Roosevelt appointed OPM codirector in 1940. But Hillman's role was largely advisory and consultative, and Roosevelt had appointed him without consulting other labor leaders, who regarded him as Roosevelt's retainer.[20] Many labor leaders, including Lewis, felt that Hillman had forsaken their rights under the NLRA when he intervened in 247 defense industry labor disputes without securing guarantees that federal contractors would obey the act.[21] Moreover, Hillman resigned after Roosevelt reorganized the OPM into the War Production Board and demoted him; no labor representative replaced him.

The administration subsequently appointed labor leaders and union staff to the Labor Production Division, the War Manpower Commission, and the individual industry branches of the War Production Board, but these positions were only advisory and concerned with narrow issues of transferring and training workers for defense production.[22] According to the U.S. Civilian Production Administration's report, the War Production Board largely ignored Labor Production Division recommendations and treated its members with suspicion. Labor advisory boards never met with their industrial counterparts, and their responsibilities were narrowly confined to wartime labor issues.[23] The labor movement consequently lacked the standing to promote industrial democracy or broader social reforms. Unlike in Britain, the labor movement could not turn the wartime experience to its advantage to support the social citizenship rights that President Roosevelt advocated in his 1944 economic bill of rights. Wartime planners instead made a conscious decision to keep wartime industrial planning temporary, confined largely to defense industries, and institutionally divorced from other administration agencies and other domestic policies.

Wartime Labor Policies

The ebbing of social reform during World War II was most apparent in the wartime labor disputes policies. With the outbreak of war in Europe, the national interest in labor disputes shifted from promoting collective bargaining and industrial recovery to ensuring uninterrupted defense production, labor peace, and economic stabilization. Most labor leaders submitted to wartime compulsory arbitration, automatic union membership for new hires at unionized workplaces, and wage controls, but this accommodation, unlike the NLRA, included no policy statement promoting the principles of industrial democracy or collective bargaining. The wartime accommoda-

tion eventually deteriorated after the policy goals of uninterrupted production, labor peace, and economic stabilization in the absence of social reform
proved to be irreconcilable.

Wartime Labor Arbitration and the No-Strike Pledge

Even before the United States entered the war, conflicts between the
wartime state and the labor movement were visible. During 1940–41, im-
pending war stimulated growth in defense industry employment and presented the best economic conditions for organizing in over a decade. This
sparked the largest strike wave since 1919, as workers pressed for union
recognition and labor contracts at Ford, Goodyear, General Electric, International Harvester, Remington-Rand, the Little Steel companies, as well as
in southern coal mines, meatpacking plants, and the defense industry.

Labor disputes in the defense industry proved to be particularly nettle-
some. Although defense industry planners flouted the NLRA in favor of
meeting production quotas and deadlines,[24] nothing angered the public
more than defense industry strikes. Thus, when work stoppages erupted in
1940–41 at the Vultee Aviation and the North American Aviation plants in
southern California and the Allis-Chalmers plant in Milwaukee, members
of Congress, the president, CIO officials, and the press denounced the strikers as unpatriotic, and State Department officials deployed National
Guardsmen to suppress the labor conflicts. The House of Representatives
passed a bill suspending the Norris–La Guardia Act and authorizing the use
of force to break strikes. Although the Senate tabled the bill out of defer-
ence to the president, Congress approved the Smith Act, which permitted
the imprisonment of strike leaders for anti-American activities.

In January 1942, President Roosevelt convened a national labor-
management conference and asked for a voluntary suspension of the right
to strike for the duration of the war in exchange for compulsory arbitration.[25] Labor leaders consented, recalling the repression following World
War I and hoping to secure more vigorous enforcement of the NLRA. Unlike the NLRA, however, Executive Order 9017, which established the National War Labor Board (NWLB), presented no declaration of principles. Its
sole objective was to settle "labor disputes which might interrupt work
which contributes to the effective prosecution of the war." The administration only authorized the NWLB to decide cases on their particular merits,
without attending to any general social policy objectives.[26] The NWLB
would not facilitate labor organization, promote collective bargaining, protect workers' rights, foster economic equality, establish industrial democracy, or address employment discrimination.[27] In practice, members of the
NWLB supported collective bargaining in order to stabilize labor relations

and ruled against employers who resisted union recognition and collective bargaining. But once a contract was negotiated, the NWLB regarded it as ironclad and prohibited all strikes to protest employer breaches of contract.

Maintenance of Membership

Among the most contentious and thorniest issues the NLRB arbitrated involved union demands for security clauses in their contracts. Security clauses authorize the closed shop, the union shop, dues checkoff, or the agency shop, and compel new employees to support the labor organization.[28] Unions demanded security clauses because most of the recently organized industries had championed the open shop after World War I. In addition, the new industrial union movement remained vulnerable, in that many industrial unions had won employer recognition only months before the start of the war.[29] Moreover, throughout the war, hundreds of thousands of new workers, many from the South and with nonunion backgrounds, inundated recently unionized workplaces, threatening to destabilize collective bargaining relationships. Given the no-strike pledge, what incentives did these new employees have to join and pay dues, if the union did not have the economic power to protect their rights and win further wage gains?

From a practical point of view, the NWLB recognized that supporting union security was essential to stabilizing labor relations.[30] Stable collective bargaining promoted responsible union leaders who were committed to the no-strike pledge. However, because Executive Order 9017 lacked a declaration of principle affirming the federal government's support for labor organization, the NWLB could not actively promote the closed shop. Instead, the board fashioned a compromise solution, "maintenance of membership" clauses, requiring automatic enrollment of new employees into the union, permitting employees to withdraw only during the first thirty days of the contract, and allowing payroll deduction of union dues. The NWLB noted:

> The maintenance of a stable union membership . . . makes for faithfully keeping the terms of the contract. . . . If the union leadership is responsible and cooperative, then irresponsible and uncooperative members cannot escape discipline by getting out of the union and thus disrupt relations and hamper production. If the union leadership should prove unworthy, demagogic and irresponsible, then worthy and responsible members of the union still remain inside the union to correct abuses, select better leaders, and improve production.[31]

The wartime labor disputes policy was a mixed blessing for the labor movement. On the one hand, it ensured the automatic enrollment of millions of new union members, as well as the stabilization of union finances. During the war, membership in CIO-affiliated unions doubled, and the size of the unionized workforce increased by 50 percent, from 9.5 million to 14.8 million.[32] By 1945, 48 percent of eligible workers were covered by collective bargaining agreements, and in primary industry, the figure approached 80 percent.[33] The policy thus relieved labor leaders of the burden of recruiting, building a union identity, securing recognition, collecting dues, leading strikes, and so on. On the other hand, the NWLB could not handle the flood of new cases it received daily, so illegal strikes often erupted as the only way to get action from employers or the NWLB.[34] National labor leaders had to police the no-strike pledge, often in the face of local resistance, or else the NWLB would eliminate maintenance of membership and dues checkoff. Labor organizations' primary activities changed from organizing and mobilizing the workforce and facilitating industrial democracy to negotiating and enforcing the contract. This encouraged a shift in power away from more militant shop-floor labor leaders toward more responsible national-level union leaders, and placed more emphasis on the collective bargaining agreement as a legally binding contract. The war labor disputes policy thus contributed to the growing bureaucratization of labor organizations and the split between the rank-and-file and the national leadership. As such, it anticipated key features of the LMRA.

Wage Controls and the Little Steel Formula

National War Labor Board officials confronted another dilemma: how to promote industrial peace without exacerbating wartime inflation. Initially, the maintenance-of-membership policy helped to stabilize industrial relations, but collective bargaining combined with full employment, cost-plus defense contracts, and administered pricing contributed to the destabilization of prices and wages. The Bureau of Labor Statistics recorded a 5 percent increase in the cost of living in 1940, and an 11 percent increase in 1941. Wage inflation rose at a faster rate, reaching 17 percent in 1941 and 24 percent in 1942.[35] These inflationary pressures eventually led to a modification of the administration's labor policies.

On April 27, 1942, President Roosevelt called for reorganizing the wartime planning agencies to stabilize wages and prices. The president's guidelines covered all NWLB arbitration awards, and placed the NWLB under the Office of Economic Stabilization and the Office of Production Management. In the fall, the president extended the NWLB's wage controls to all wage negotiations, not just those the NWLB arbitrated. This fundamentally altered the NWLB's functions and authority, giving the board the herculean task of reviewing *all* wage increases and submitting its decisions

to the director of Economic Stabilization. The NWLB now had two competing responsibilities: labor dispute arbitration and wage stabilization.

The NWLB had previously developed its own wage guidelines, because it
had frequently adjudicated wage disputes. Despite the administration's decision to keep social policy issues separate from the administration of
wartime economic policies, the NWLB could not arbitrate labor disputes on
their merits without remedying wage discrimination, providing a living
wage, equalizing intraindustry wage inequalities, and adjusting for regional
differences in the cost of living. The new wage guidelines, however, eliminated most of the NWLB's discretion and imposed a strict economic discipline. These guidelines, known as the "Little Steel formula," which arose
out of wage disputes between the United Steelworkers and Inland Steel, Republic Steel, Bethlehem Steel, and Youngstown Sheet and Tube, permitted
wage increases to compensate for the rise in the cost of living between January 1, 1941, and April 27, 1942, which was approximately 15 percent.
This became the limit for all collectively bargained wage increases for the
duration of the war: 15 percent above what they had been on January 1,
1941.

Labor leaders complained bitterly that Roosevelt had reneged on their
agreement to suspend the right to strike in exchange for arbitration. UMW
president John L. Lewis protested that Roosevelt had established the
NWLB in 1942 "to hand down in every wage controversy a decision based
upon a *judicial determination of the issue*" (emphasis in original). The
NWLB's Little Steel formula, however, subordinated compulsory arbitration to the administration's wartime economic policies. "Under its arbitrary
and miserably stupid formula, [the NWLB] chains labor to the wheels of industry without compensation for increased costs, while other agencies of
the government reward and fatten industry by charging its increased costs
to the public purse."[36] Labor unions now had no bargaining power whatsoever, but were still expected to enforce the no-strike pledge. Wartime stabilization policies, furthermore, imposed greater restraints on wages than on
other sources of inflation. Great scrutiny accompanied wage negotiations,
due to the public nature of collective bargaining, but no similar controls applied to profits, which increased from $9 billion in 1940 to $24 billion in
1944.[37]

Moreover, the wartime accommodation had little to offer the United
Mine Workers. The UMW had already organized nearly 99 percent of the
bituminous coal industry, and their contracts had union shop security
clauses—far better than maintenance-of-membership clauses. In addition,
the UMW had previously won all the wage increases that the NWLB would
grant under the Little Steel formula. Lewis consequently rejected the role of
"the responsible union leader" and openly attacked the board for "fouling
its own nest."[38] Lewis and the UMW instead decided to violate the no-strike

pledge and challenge the Little Steel wage formula in the spring of 1943, when more than five hundred thousand coal miners went on strike.[39] This was not just a wage strike but a political strike, in open defiance of the White House and the NWLB. In response, the federal government seized the coal mines and for five months managed the industry. Lewis subsequently rejected the NWLB's wage settlement, and, when the contract expired on November 1, led 530,000 miners out on strike again. Stabilizing labor relations and controlling wage inflation ultimately proved to be irreconcilable policy objectives. By 1943, the no-strike pledge showed signs of strain, and by the end of the war, the accommodation that supported the labor disputes policy had collapsed.

The Smith-Connally War Labor Disputes Act

These massive wartime strikes fueled antiunion sentiment throughout the country. Wayne Morse, public member of the NWLB and a prolabor liberal, accused the strikers of treason and asserted that "in time of war, when a union seeks to defy the government of the United States, I am in favor of breaking that union." Gen. George Marshall claimed that the coal strike and a railway strike prolonged the war by six months and increased U.S. casualties by one hundred thousand—an unsupportable claim, but one that demonstrated the military leadership's impatience with wartime work stoppages.[40] Defense administration officials, including the NWLB, sought enhanced powers to seize plants, enjoin strikes, conscript strikers, and imprison strike leaders. The Selective Service threatened to cancel the draft deferments of strikers. Military leaders demanded national service legislation to draft civilians for defense industry work, a measure that would have subjected strikers to criminal penalties.

Consequently, in the summer of 1943 Congress passed the Smith-Connally War Labor Disputes Act, which broadened the president's emergency powers to seize struck plants and prosecute strikers.[41] The Smith-Connally Act, however, did little to stem the collapse of the wartime accommodation. Thus, President Roosevelt seized the coal mines, but the miners remained on the picket lines. The president finally directed Secretary of the Interior Harold Ickes to negotiate with Lewis, and on November 3 they agreed on a 25 percent raise, repudiating the Little Steel formula.[42] Other labor leaders petitioned the NWLB for wage increases to match the UMW's settlement and discovered that the Smith-Connally Act's provision for a secret strike vote provided them with additional leverage, without actually committing them to a work stoppage.

Meanwhile, wildcat strikes and semiauthorized work stoppages continued to spread. Local United Rubber Workers (URW) leaders in Akron called a citywide strike to protest the NWLB's inaction on its wage adjustments. The military seized the rubber plants, and the URW international president resigned. Wildcat stoppages in Detroit automobile plants led to a UAW crackdown on local leaders and nearly caused a UAW vote of no confidence against the no-strike pledge. A Christmas Eve strike by 150,000 steelworkers also challenged the no-strike pledge; the strikers returned to work only after Roosevelt intervened and forced the NWLB to grant retroactive wage increases. More than one million railway workers struck in December, and threatened a nationwide strike on December 31, to protest the Office of Economic Stabilization's rejection of the NWLB's wage increase of twenty cents per hour. Although the strike rate had plummeted to only four million workdays in 1942, strike rates escalated throughout the rest of the war, rising to 13.5 million work days lost in 1943, and nine million in 1944.[43] These aggregate figures, moreover, present only part of the picture, because most strikes were brief wildcat strikes that typically went unrecorded.[44] Thus, in 1944 and 1945, one-half of all workers in production industries engaged in work stoppages.[45]

The Postwar Strike Wave

The strike rate continued to mount in 1945–46, precipitating the largest strike wave in U.S. history and setting the stage for new limitations on the right to strike. In September 1945, 43,000 petroleum workers and 200,000 coal miners struck. In October, the strike rate doubled when 44,000 northwestern lumber workers, 70,000 midwestern teamsters, and 40,000 San Francisco Bay Area machinists walked out. The strike rate redoubled in November, when 225,000 automobile workers initiated the historic General Motors strike. In January 1946, 174,000 electrical workers, 300,000 meatpackers, and 750,000 steelworkers stopped work. In April, 340,000 bituminous coal miners walked out, and in May railway workers nationwide went on strike. General strikes erupted in Stamford, Connecticut; Lancaster, Pennsylvania; Rochester, New York; Pittsburgh, Pennsylvania; and Oakland, California.[46] During the first six months of 1946, three million working Americans struck, making it, according to the Bureau of Labor Statistics, the most concentrated period of industrial strife in the country's history. Throughout 1946, strikes idled an unprecedented 4.9 million workers.

Most of these strikes erupted as a result of workers' anxieties about reconversion to a peacetime economy. The war had generated low unemployment, a rising standard of living, and, for many, the best economic conditions in nearly a generation. Average weekly wages had risen about 70 percent between January 1941 and July 1945, in large part because of increased overtime. Behind wartime prosperity, however, were temporary, artificial conditions and unresolved issues, and many wage earners feared a return to economic stagnation. Reconversion would remove a major prop for the economy, while adding twelve million service men and women to the labor force. In 1944, cancellations of naval contracts had already eliminated overtime for many hourly workers, and average weekly wages began to drop after V-E Day, declining 25 percent in the defense industry that year.[47] After the federal government abruptly canceled all defense orders, weekly wages plummeted by 20 percent, and unemployment in war-related industries increased by 25 percent.[48]

In addition, wartime planning administrators decided on a rapid reconversion to a peacetime, free enterprise economy.[49] According to the Civilian Production Administration report, Julius Krug, the War Production Board's last director, assumed that "the free enterprise system would remain the basis for our economic activity; should Government intervene to maintain high levels of employment, it would do so mainly by means of fiscal policy; controls would not be used to restore prewar economic relationships or to accomplish social or economic reforms; and wartime controls would be abandoned as soon as possible."[50] Krug then acted swiftly to remove wartime regulations and controls, despite widespread fears of postwar inflation, depression, and unemployment.[51]

Underlying wage earners' fears was a broader struggle over the role of organized labor in the postwar economy. Progressive labor leaders, on the one hand, looked on reconversion as an opportunity to expand collective bargaining beyond the scope of pure-and-simple unionism and to extend organized labor's influence into areas of management control. Walter Reuther, for example, called for the continuation of wartime economic controls and the conversion of defense production to raise consumption levels to 40–50 percent above their prewar levels. In this manner, Reuther proposed converting wartime industry to housing construction to meet the needs of returning GIs and working Americans.[52] For proposals such as these, automobile executive George Romney dubbed Reuther "the most dangerous man in Detroit."[53]

Employers, on the other hand, were intent on reasserting managerial prerogatives. New Deal reforms, wartime economic controls, weakened shop floor discipline, and the expanding scope of collective bargaining had seriously eroded management authority. Thus, when labor economist E. Wight Bakke interviewed sixty business executives in 1945–46 he discovered that the growth of collective bargaining had left them with "anxiety . . . about the future, uncertainty as to where the process will end."[54] General Motors president Charles E. Wilson argued in a Senate subcommittee hearing that "what we have come to know as the American system" must be saved from a social revolution "imported from east of the Rhine. Unless this is done, the border area of collective bargaining will be a constant battleground . . . as the unions continuously attempt to press the boundary farther and farther into the area of managerial functions."[55] Business leaders sensed a loss of power particularly on the shop floor, with the spread of wildcat strikes, the rise of assertive shop stewards, and increasing agitation for the unionization of foremen.[56]

In response to the postwar strike wave, in November 1945 President Truman convened the National Labor-Management Conference, and asked the representatives to extend compulsory arbitration through the reconversion period. He also announced his intent to maintain wartime wage and price controls throughout the reconversion period and eventually to restore free collective bargaining with a minimum of government interference. The employers' representatives, after declaring their support for collective bargaining, denounced the administration's wartime price controls, signaling to labor leaders that they would have to fight for wage increases. The meeting ended in stalemate when labor leaders refused to identify any management rights that lay beyond the scope of collective bargaining. President Truman's failure to secure a voluntary accord during the reconversion period set the stage for the passage of new legislation to regulate labor disputes.[57]

The Postwar Settlement

Ultimately, three massive strikes established the boundaries of the postwar labor-management settlement: the United Automobile Workers' strike against General Motors; the United Steelworkers' strike; and the United Mine Workers' strike. The 113–day UAW strike, initiated days after the National Labor-Management Conference ended, was the most significant. UAW president Walter Reuther regarded the work stoppage as an opportunity for the industrial union movement to move beyond pure-and-simple unionism, "to wage an economic struggle planned to advance the welfare of the community as a whole."[58] Arguing that GM had enjoyed strong profits during the war and could afford better wages, Reuther called for a 30 percent wage increase with no increase in automobile prices. Moreover, to prove that wage increases were not passed along in the form of inflated prices, Reuther demanded that GM open its books to the UAW and the Office of Price Administration, the federal agency that administered price controls during the war—a demand that struck at the foundation of managerial prerogatives.

"We are not operating like a narrow interest group," Reuther insisted.[59] Instead, he wanted to reconnect collective bargaining and social policy, using wage negotiations to redistribute income and to promote structural reforms.[60] "Unless we get a more realistic distribution of America's wealth," he argued, "we don't get enough to keep America going."[61] These demands were well within Truman's postwar wage-price guidelines, which permitted wage increases as long as they produced no price increases.[62] Moreover, they promoted the social Keynesian objectives of the NLRA, which sought greater economic equality and linked the rights of concerted activity to broader social reform. Reuther subscribed to Senator Wagner's more expansive view of collective bargaining that regarded it as a way to encourage industrial democracy and cooperative management.[63] GM negotiators, however, rebuffed this attempt to extend collective bargaining into company pricing policies. One GM negotiator complained to Reuther:

> Why don't you get down to your size and get down to the type of job you are supposed to be doing as a trade union leader, and talk about money you would like to have for your people and let that labor statesmanship go to hell for a while? It's none of your damn business what the OPM does about prices![64]

Initially the Truman administration supported Reuther's proposal. In December Truman appointed a fact-finding board to investigate the strike, which recommended examining GM financial records and taking the company's ability to pay into account. GM rejected the board's findings, walked out of the meetings, and instead endured a 113–day strike. President Truman backed down, refusing to force GM to submit to his wage-price guidelines.

The UAW-GM contract eventually followed the pattern set by the steelworkers. United Steelworkers' president Philip Murray, observing the impasse in the GM strike and the Truman administration's vacillation, refused to turn the steel strike into a similar confrontation over wage-and-price controls and the scope of collective bargaining. Instead, the steelworkers agreed to average wage increases of 18.5 cents per hour, with corresponding price increases, and conceded the employer's right to manage. This contract set the pattern for most major industries and secured for CIO members the largest wage increase so far. But these contracts also doomed what remained of the administration's wage-and-price stabilization policies and Murray's industrial councils plan. Henceforth, most collective agreements included a management rights clause declaring the employer's unilateral authority to set prices, determine production goals, discipline workers, layoff employees, and determine overall business strategy. Collective bargaining became a matter of private interest and the right to strike an instrument for narrow, pure-and-simple union goals, divorced from broader social reforms.[65]

Unions that challenged the postwar settlement discovered that the modern liberal American state was still willing to suppress strikes, especially in the atmosphere of the early cold war. Thus, during a national railroad labor dispute in May 1946, the president ordered the seizure of the railways and urged Congress to grant him the power to conscript the strikers and to extend the Smith-Connally War Labor Disputes Act beyond its 1947 expiration. These threats convinced the strikers to return to work.[66]

The United Mine Workers also defied the postwar settlement, deciding to test the administration's resolve. Like the UAW strike, the UMW strike encompassed more than pure-and-simple union issues. The UMW sought to extend collective bargaining into broader social welfare concerns, such as mine safety and health care, and after the administration seized the mines, Lewis challenged the authority of the state. Truman, facing criticisms that he was soft on labor, and wanting to preempt the strike issue before the congressional elections, gladly accepted the challenge. Lewis provided a convenient target, because he had broken with the CIO and the Democrats in 1940 and had violated the wartime no-strike pledge. "The Administration must find out sometime whether the power of Mr. Lewis is superior to that of the federal government," averred the White House.[67]

After the miners defied Truman's order to return to work, the administration obtained injunctions against the UMW, and federal courts held Lewis in contempt. The Supreme Court, in a 5–4 decision, sustained the injunction, in spite of the Norris–La Guardia Act, declaring that the president could still obtain an injunction under his power as commander in chief when a strike threatened national security and public welfare.[68] Lewis capitulated and ordered an end to the strike. Victory over the UMW leader imparted to President Truman the national prestige he needed and established the precedent for later presidents seeking injunctions during emergency strikes. It also demonstrated that those who defied the boundaries of the postwar settlement would face the forceful intervention of the federal government.

This postwar settlement manifested significant changes in American liberalism and state-market relations. During the late 1930s and 1940s American liberals retreated from reformist, New Deal policies that redistributed economic power and moved toward compensatory policies that promoted growth and stability.[69] Unionized workers could participate in this system and enjoy job security, productivity-based wage increases, and fringe benefits, as long as they did not challenge these premises. Working Americans could exercise their right to strike over the terms of their employment contracts, but they could not seek codetermination or industrial democracy. The passage of the 1946 Employment Act, which promoted a modest commercial Keynesian agenda of economic growth and stability rather than a

social Keynesian agenda of economic equality and structural reform, epitomized this retreat from New Deal reformism.

Senator Wagner had regarded strikes to be the result of dysfunctional employment relations and believed that the state could harness collective action to promote greater social equality, a higher standard of living, and economic recovery. But by the postwar era, many American liberals considered
strikes to be the result of overreaching labor leaders and unbridled labor organizations and a direct threat to economic stability, national security, and
community welfare. Sumner Slichter, a leading liberal postwar industrial relations scholar, articulated the growing liberal ambivalence toward labor
union power and the right to strike; labor leaders exercised *more* power, he
asserted, than captains of industry.[70] Unions, he feared, could become
tightly controlled oligarchies with little concern for democratic control.
Short of that, unions promoted their own particularistic goals at the expense of the broader interests of the community.[71] Slichter wrote:

> During the last year [1947] . . . unions in key places have shown a reckless will-
> ingness to inflict calamitous losses upon the community in order to get pre-
> ferred treatment for their members, in order to win trivial gains, or in order to
> compel government to make changes in public policy. . . . The reckless and ir-
> responsible use of the strike which has occurred so frequently in essential in-
> dustries during the last year calls for well-planned and vigorous action to de-
> fend the public interest.[72]

Although he never fully designated his criteria (other than proclaiming
that "the man in the street knows perfectly well"), Slichter declared that
strikes in hospitals, gas and electric utilities, the railroads, the coal and steel
industries, telephone service, and even elevator service could not be tolerated: "Why, therefore, *pretend* that men in these industries have the right to
strike?"[73] Furthermore, strikes that attempt to press for changes in public
policy, he claimed, violate the underlying conditions of a free society.
Slichter consequently proposed that federal officials have emergency powers
to order strikers back to work and to charge violators with unfair labor
practices.

Thus, calls to limit collective action came not just from the business community and the conservative coalition in Congress. Postwar liberals like
Slichter no longer regarded industrial unrest as symptomatic of underlying
social problems, nor as expressions of legitimate grievances. Instead, they
argued that strikes pitted the self-interest of labor unions against the
broader interests of the community. But given the opposition that labor

leaders such as Walter Reuther and Phillip Murray had encountered, how could labor unions strike to defend a broader public interest?

The Labor Management Relations Act of 1947

Many labor leaders and sympathizers regard the 1947 Labor Management Relations (Taft-Hartley) Act as a repudiation of the 1935 National Labor Relations Act and as a product of "the sharp turn to the right" in the 1946 congressional elections, in which the Republicans gained control of the House and the Senate. Passed over President Truman's veto in the aftermath of the postwar strike wave, these wide-ranging amendments to the NLRA established new limits on labor unions and collective action. The LMRA bans a variety of strikes (listed below), allows employers to petition for a decertification election during a strike (Section 9[c]), and gives the president additional powers during emergency strikes (Section 206). Nonetheless, the LMRA was hardly a repudiation of collective bargaining or the right to strike. Section 13 specifically states: "Nothing in this Act . . . shall be construed so as to interfere with or impede or diminish the right to strike." Those who regard the LMRA as a "slave labor act" that demanded that organized labor "lie down like good dogs" should compare it to the post–World War I backlash, when state and federal forces violently suppressed the steelworkers' strike, the West Virginia coal miners' strike, and the railroad shopmen's strike, canceling all of the labor movement's wartime gains.

Many liberal politicians, moreover, did not share the labor movement's unmitigated scorn for most of the provisions of the LMRA. President Truman, although he vetoed the act, had already called for many of its provisions in his 1947 State of the Union address, including mandatory cooling-off periods, powers to intervene in emergency strikes, and bans on secondary boycotts and jurisdictional strikes; he subsequently exercised his executive authority under the act's emergency strike procedures six times—more than any other president since then. In 1948, organized labor helped to defeat many of the LMRA's congressional supporters and to elect Democratic majorities to both chambers. Congress nonetheless retained the LMRA with only minor modifications, even though labor law reform remained organized labor's top legislative priority for the next forty-six years.

The LMRA's restrictions on the right to strike instead took place within the context of broader political developments, manifesting modern American liberalism's turn toward a less intrusive state after World War II. First, it institutionalized the wartime disengagement of social policy from labor relations policy. Second, it crystallized key features of the postwar settlement between management and organized labor, containing collective bargaining within a narrowed, contractual framework. Finally, it established a restrained labor relations policy for the United States during the cold war. The LMRA thus confirmed the wartime departure from the more progressive, reformist liberalism of the New Deal era.

The LMRA and the Disengagement of Labor Relations Policy from Social Policy

The 1935 NLRA, to repeat, was not merely a labor relations policy; it was also one of the most extensive social policies passed during the New Deal. Although he couched the act in the language of commercial rights, Senator Wagner hoped to promote an expansive conception of collective bargaining as a form of industrial democracy, to foster the organization of labor in basic industry, and to improve working Americans' standard of living. By contrast, the purpose of the LMRA was not to promote these social goals but to stabilize industrial relations within the existing social structure: "It is the purpose and policy of this Act . . . to protect the rights of individual employees in their relations with labor organizations." Thus, Section 7 guarantees the rights of employees to refrain from work stoppages and other concerted activities, and Section 8(b) prohibits strikes to obtain a closed shop agreement and strikes to prevent nonunion employees from entering the workplace or to demand their discharge. The act also protects the rights of employers by prohibiting certain unfair labor practices by labor organizations, just as the NLRA had prohibited specified unfair labor practices by employers. These unfair labor practices cover a wide range of collective actions, including secondary boycotts, sympathy strikes, jurisdictional strikes, strikes by uncertified unions (Section 303), and strikes that violate the labor contract (Section 301).[74] By prohibiting unfair labor practices by labor organizations, the LMRA sought to equalize the rights of unions and employers.[75] Although the LMRA acknowledges collective bargaining and labor organization, it doesn't promote them but, rather, subordinates them to individual rights.

The LMRA also disengaged labor relations policy from social policy by limiting the authority and administrative capacities of the NLRB. During the 1930s, the NLRB had actively promoted unionism, and particularly the new industrial union movement—an orientation entirely consistent with the facilitative purposes of the NLRA. This active advocacy of collective bargaining and industrial unionism had provoked investigations by the Smith Committee, which recommended most of these modifications in the Smith Act of 1940.

The House version of the 1947 LMRA had initially proposed eliminating the NLRB altogether, but the final version refashioned it into a neutral agency by creating an independent general counsel (Section 3[d]), eliminating the Economic Research Division (4[a]), and prohibiting the NLRB from engaging in mediation—a function reserved for the new Federal Mediation Service (3[e]). Creation of an independent general counsel, who has almost as much authority as the chairman, divided the agency and removed the agency's prosecutorial functions from the control of the chairman.[76] The NLRB thus became the *only* agency in the federal government with this bifurcated administrative structure, contravening the administrative reforms recommended under the 1946 Administrative Procedures Act.[77] Without the Economic Research Division, the NLRB could not undertake empirical studies to determine the actual impact of secondary boycotts, jurisdictional strikes, national emergency strikes, and the like. Prohibiting mediation and conciliation prevented the labor board from becoming involved in the substantive details of industrial disputes and collective labor contracts, which might have given it the power to ascertain more accurately whether an employer was engaging in bad-faith bargaining, and otherwise to take a more active and informed role in policy making and dispute resolution. Denying the NLRB these administrative capacities left it with only a case-by-case method for administering federal strike policy.

Finally, the LMRA denied to the NLRB independent enforcement power, requiring the agency to apply to the federal courts to issue temporary restraining orders when complaints are filed (Section 10[b]) and to enforce its orders (Section 10[e]). Sections 3 and 10 have transferred much of the NLRB's policy-making authority to the courts and reinforced the legalistic character of federal strike policy. Instead of facilitating labor organizing and collective bargaining, the NLRB in subsequent years became a tenuous and circumspect agency that focused on due process, formal procedures, and technical questions of legal interpretation. Stripped of important administrative functions, institutionally isolated, and concerned for its political survival, the NLRB turned away from an active social agenda, such as promoting unionization among the working poor, as they had in the late 1930s.[78]

During the New Deal era, Senator Wagner had proclaimed a more active and pragmatic conception of the state: "We think of the ideal state, not as a fixed goal, but as a process of becoming. . . . And it is in the shifting scales of action and progress, and not by reference to a fixed star, however luminous, that the ideals of the modern state must be realistically judged."[79] But the LMRA, like the 1946 Employment Act, envisioned a less energetic state. The state henceforth would avoid directly intervening in economic decisions and in the market and instead would foster economic stability and balance. The LMRA assumed a formally impartial role for the state in the regulation of labor disputes, as a disinterested enforcer of formally equal rights between unions and employers, and as a neutral defender of individual employees' free choice. Henceforth, the regulation of industrial conflict was disengaged from a broader social policy agenda. Bold reforms in social policy and labor law during the postwar era, such as equal employment opportunity and the War on Poverty, have originated with other federal agencies, and social movements have turned to other forms of social protest, apart from the workplace.

The LMRA and the Narrowing of Collective Bargaining

In advocating for his bill, Senator Wagner proclaimed, "The struggle for a voice in industry through the process of collective bargaining is at the heart of the struggle for the preservation of political as well as economic democracy in America."[80] Collective bargaining, according to Wagner, was not an adversarial process but a form of industrial democracy and "a cooperative venture guided by intelligence, rather than a mere test of relative strength."[81] Murray's plans for industrial councils and Reuther's demand for union involvement in the pricing decisions of General Motors similarly embraced this progressive conception. By contrast, the LMRA rejected this broad view of collective bargaining and reinforced a legalistic, contractual form of collective bargaining. This constrained conception of collective bargaining now defines the right to strike.

The LMRA limited collective bargaining in two ways. First, Section 2(5) affirmed that the employer's right to manage is not a mandatory subject of collective bargaining. Collective bargaining takes place only over the terms of employment narrowly defined and, by implication, does not compel employers to bargain over "permissive" subjects that involve "the core of entrepreneurial control," such as layoffs, plant closings, production processes, investment decisions, product prices, and the like.[82] Furthermore, Section 14(a) excluded low-level managerial and supervisory employees from collective bargaining. This provision quashed the nascent movement to unionize foremen and supervisors, who had attempted to organize during World War II. Although low-level supervisors frequently perform the same tasks as nonsupervisory workers, and often have no significant decision-making authority, they represent management's first line of authority over the shop floor.[83] Excluding them from collective bargaining not only eliminated their right to strike but made them available as striker replacements. These provisions erected a high wall of separation that shields the employer's right to manage from the sort of cooperative management that Wagner had contemplated. Collective bargaining—and therefore the right to strike—are now confined to a narrow range of employment issues.[84]

Second, the LMRA restricted collective bargaining to single employers. Section 8(b) bans strikes to force an employer into larger bargaining units.

Thus, it inhibits industrywide trade agreements, such as those the National Civic Federation advocated in the early 1900s, as well as the UMW's Central Bituminous Coal Fields Agreement of the 1920s and 1930s. Collective bargaining may not promote industrial councils or others forms of planning at the industry level. Employees, moreover, may only exercise their right to strike at the level of the firm. Strikes such as those to unionize the West Virginia coal operators in the 1920s are now unprotected under federal law.

The LMRA thus impeded the more cooperative, expansive forms of collective bargaining that progressives had supported before 1947 and instead promoted what David Brody calls "workplace contractualism"—a set of private, legal-bureaucratic procedures for resolving disputes at the workplace.[85] Workplace contractualism transformed the collective agreement into a definite and legally binding agreement between a union and an employer. Section 8(d) states:

> To bargain collectively is the performance of the mutual obligation of the employer and the representative of the employees to meet at reasonable times and confer in good faith with respect to wages, hours, and other terms and conditions of employment, or the negotiation of an agreement, or any question arising thereunder, and the execution of a written contract.

Workplace contractualism not only established a complex web of contractual rights for the unionized employee but it also fashioned new limits on collective action. Section 301 declared that employers may sue labor organizations in federal court for any violation of the contract—a limitation that did not exist in British law until 1982. Consequently, if a labor contract includes a no-strike clause, then the employer may sue the union for damages if workers engage in an unauthorized strike, or if the strike was a reaction to the employer's repeated violations of the contract. Moreover, existence of grievance procedures implies a no-strike obligation.[86] In practice, this feature of the act prohibits unregulated "quickie" strikes to resolve shop floor disputes and defend employee rights. The no-strike pledge and grievance procedures were both features of the wartime labor disputes policy, illustrating the roots of workplace contractualism in the wartime accommodation.

The LMRA and the Cold War

Finally, the LMRA strike policy not only reflected the wartime accommodation and the postwar settlement but also changes in U.S. national security interests. In 1947, administration officials were preoccupied with the cold war and with national preparedness. For example, Congress approved the 1947 National Security Act, which completely reorganized the national defense agencies and created the National Security Council. Fearing a possible outbreak of hostilities with the Soviet Union, administration officials worried that a major strike by defense industry workers, coal miners, steelworkers, and others, could hamper the capacity of the United States to respond to rapidly developing international threats. War and the war powers have shaped federal interventions in strikes since the late nineteenth century, and they continued to do so during the cold war. The LMRA consequently extended the president's emergency powers to intervene in strikes that threatened the national interest. Sections 206–210 established procedures for investigating, enjoining, and delaying such strikes by means of an eighty-day "cooling off" period for labor and left open the possibility of "appropriate action."

In addition, Section 9(h) of the LMRA denied federal protections for any labor organization whose leaders failed to sign affidavits that they were not Communists. During the New Deal and World War II, Communists had rejected dual unionism (establishing alternative Communist-dominated unions) in favor of "burrowing from within," often providing the most stalwart support for the CIO organizing drives of the 1930s, but also rendering loyal support for the no-strike pledge during the war, when survival of the Soviet Union became an overriding goal. CIO leaders like Walter Reuther tolerated Communist support during these years, but they increasingly attacked Communist influence after the war.[87] The LMRA's "non-Communist" affidavit provision helped to purge Communist labor leaders and their supporters as threats to national security and ensured that unions would exercise the right to strike for pure-and-simple union goals.

The emerging cold war system, however, also sustained the right to strike. In its new international role as the leader of the free world after World War II, the United States could hardly suppress all forms of industrial conflict. So it fostered the system of free collective bargaining and the right to strike for pure-and-simple union purposes as an alternative to class conflict and class rule. Section 7 proclaims: "Employees shall have the right to self-organization, to form, join, or assist labor organizations, to bargain collectively through representatives of their own choosing, and to engage in other concerted activities for the purpose of collective bargaining or other mutual aid or protection." This was a far cry from the federal government's reversal after World War I, when the Red scare incited the Palmer raids and the armed suppression of the steel strike.

Liberal industrial relations scholars of the era, such as Sumner Slichter, Arthur Kornhauser, Robert Dubin, and Arthur M. Ross went so far as to extol free collective bargaining as the system of industrial jurisprudence best suited to a free society.[88] Free collective bargaining, they asserted, promotes harmonious relations among competing interests, a fair distribution of rights and opportunities, a balance between special interests, and cooperation among various groups in pursuit of common interests.[89] To operate effectively, free collective bargaining requires basic background conditions of mutual trust, good will, open communications, a willingness to listen to reason and to compromise, and strong, responsible, and democratic unions.[90] Under free collective bargaining, negotiations focus on concrete and finite issues, rather than broad, abstract principles, and unions recognize employers' managerial prerogatives.[91] Although unions and employers represent particular and sometimes conflicting interests, labor and management also share overlapping interests, which free collective bargaining will support. As such, it promotes competing and diverse interests through the peaceful adjustment of their differences.[92]

Free collective bargaining thus epitomized the norms of postwar interest group liberalism. Its proponents acclaimed the diversity of interests and the existence of limited conflict among these interests. They expressed optimism that these conflicting interests could establish a private system of rules and procedures that would manage these conflicts fairly, free from the compulsion of the state, and balance their interests with the broader public interest. Through the institution of free collective bargaining, the American state could manage the countervailing powers of unions and employers, and thus promote the values of a free society. Free collective bargaining could absorb industrial conflict within certain limits; indeed, some industrial conflict was functional and healthy, providing a means of relieving social pressures before they exploded.[93] At the dawn of the cold war era, free collective bargaining thus represented an acceptable liberal alternative to the model of irreconcilable class conflict espoused by the United States's international rivals. The Soviet Union, which compelled workers to join Communist-directed labor organizations that had no right to strike, compared unfavorably to this system.

By 1947, the federal government had finally established the legal framework and administrative structures of the modern liberal right to strike, marking the end of seventy years of labor upheaval. The rule of law now prevailed over the rule of force, and collective bargaining replaced the law of the jungle. After being tested during the war and the postwar strike wave, the U.S. policy now fully supported the right to strike for the purposes of free collective bargaining.

Labor law critics today decry the numerous legal bans that the LMRA imposed on the right to strike. These bans, however, were not simply the product of a conservative backlash but were rooted in the social struggles and political developments of the war and postwar era. Most importantly, they grew out of changes in American liberalism marked by the end of social reform. These changes disengaged labor relations policy from social policy and separated the labor movement from broader social struggles.

More significant than the LMRA's bans on specific forms of collective action, moreover, was the disengagement of the right to strike from citizenship rights. Early labor leaders had defended the right to strike as a component of free labor citizenship. Senator Wagner supported this right as an aspect of industrial citizenship through an expansive form of collective bargaining. The NLRA had also affirmed this right for social Keynesian purposes, and the social citizenship rights they promoted. Modern American liberalism, however, grudgingly acknowledges this right in order to negotiate private agreements between employers and unions.

7

"Let us stand with a greater determination"

The National Labor Relations Act and the Bifurcation of Collective Action in the 1960s

During the decade of the 1960s, a wide variety of social activists and re-formers engaged in collective action to press for the expansion of citizen-ship rights in the United States. African Americans demanded civil rights re-forms to end invidious discrimination and segregation, and to secure equal voting rights and equal opportunity. Antipoverty warriors sought the ex-pansion of social citizenship rights, as well as the maximum feasible partic-ipation of the urban poor. Welfare rights organizations agitated to eliminate second-class treatment of welfare recipients, and to gain the right to a min-imum annual income. However, during the 1960s political reformers, social activists, and labor leaders did not push for the enlargement of the right to strike or for its extension to new groups of the working poor, nor did social activists turn to collective action at the workplace to promote social justice for the working poor and the racially oppressed.

Instead, with a few noteworthy exceptions, political reformers and social activists ignored the politics of the workplace, and embraced the politics of community.[1] Community organizing, community protests, community ac-tion programs, and community redevelopment projects represented the most progressive responses to the problems of social inequality and urban poverty. "Community" became a shibboleth in progressive political dis-course, and the politics of the community became the preferred form of pro-gressive political activity. Concerted activity at the workplace, meanwhile, remained largely disconnected from movements to secure the citizenship rights of the working poor, industrial conflict was institutionally isolated from the rest of society, and the labor question was no longer a defining issue in American society.[2] The bifurcation of collective action into the politics of the workplace and the politics of community constituted one of the most distinctive and puzzling characteristics of American social movements throughout the 1960s.

The bifurcation of collective action during the 1960s is puzzling because the most common forms of community-based protest during the rights-conscious 1960s originated as forms of work-based collective action. Community activists did not invent picketing, protest marches, rallies, boycotts, civil disobedience, and sit-ins; these forms of protest originated with the labor movement. Wage earners in the late nineteenth and early twentieth centuries had protested at work to demand their freedoms of speech and association, their due process rights, and their right to organize and to have a voice in the workplace, just as social activists in the 1960s demanded their rights and liberties. The celebrated 1963 March on Washington, for example, drew its inspiration from the proposed 1941 March on Washington, which A. Philip Randolph (president of the Brotherhood of Sleeping Car Porters) organized to protest employment discrimination in the defense industry.[3]

The bifurcation of collective action is also perplexing because many of the social conditions that spurred community-based collective action in the 1960s were rooted in the labor market. Despite the affluence and full employment policies of the era, the working conditions of the invisible poor during the 1960s resembled those of the forgotten men a generation earlier. The poverty rate still ranged between 22 percent in 1960 and 12 percent in 1969.[4] In 1967, the *Manpower Report of the President* reported subemployment (unemployed and underemployed) rates in ten predominately urban areas varying from 24 percent to 47 percent.[5] High unemployment and low wages affected the black community in particular; according to the Department of Labor, unemployment for nonwhites during the early 1960s exceeded 10 percent—more than double the rate for whites.[6] As one commentator of the era observed, "For Negroes in poverty areas, unemployment rates were higher than the worst national rates for the entire labor force recorded since the depression of the 1930s."[7] The *Report of the National Advisory Commission on Civil Disorders* noted that the black community not only endured high unemployment rates, but that "Negro workers are concentrated in the lowest skilled and lowest paying occupations. . . . Negro men in particular are more than three times as likely as whites to be in unskilled or service jobs which pay far less than most."[8] The NLRA had helped to lift millions of industrial workers out of low-wage jobs into the middle class, but during the rights-conscious 1960s few social activists or policy makers strove to extend to unskilled and service workers the rights to organize, to bargain collectively, and to strike.

Early labor leaders and social reformers appreciated the connections between the politics of community and the politics of work, and realized that social justice demanded reforms in the living *and* working conditions of the laboring classes.[9] Early labor leaders united the politics of community and the politics of work with their ideal of the cooperative commonwealth. According to David Montgomery, strikes and labor boycotts constituted the primary form of urban protest for the working poor during the nineteenth century.[10] During the Gilded Age, strikers and community members often perceived strike issues as community issues—as who would control the community—and not just as a private dispute over the labor agreement.[11] Thus, when the Homestead strikers attacked the boatload of Pinkertons in 1892, they were not only defending their union but their community as well.

Policy makers and social reformers during the Progressive Era also recognized this linkage and realized that the "labor question" encompassed not just conditions at the workplace but conditions within the community as well.[12] Jane Addams, whose Hull House represented the model of a community-based social service institution, understood this connection and struggled to organize sweated labor in her Chicago neighborhood.[13] Addams remarked:

> That a Settlement is drawn into the labor issues of its city can seem remote to
> its purpose only to those who fail to realize that so far as the present industrial
> system thwarts our ethical demands, not only for social righteousness but for
> social order, a Settlement is committed to an effort to understand and, as far as
> possible, to alleviate it. . . . This is especially true in periods of industrial disturbance.[14]

Why, then, did social activists not follow a similar path in the 1960s?

In this chapter I argue that this bifurcation of collective action has its roots in the National Labor Relations Act. The NLRA helped to liberate the working poor by affirming their rights to organize and to engage in collective action at the workplace, but it also constrained the politics of work, by channeling it into a narrow collective bargaining framework and by excluding significant segments of the working poor. Assumptions in the act mediated the forms of collective action available to the working poor in the 1960s. I also argue that the social reforms of the 1960s achieved only limited success because they failed to strengthen the working poor's rights to engage in collective action at the workplace. First I look at the specific exclusions and implicit boundaries that the NLRA instituted. Then I consider the impact of these exclusions on the War on Poverty and the welfare rights movement. Finally, I examine two social movements that transcended this split between the politics of work and the politics of community: the 1968

Memphis sanitation workers' strike and the 1965–1970 strike by what later became the United Farm Workers (UFW) union.

National Labor Relations Policy and the Regulation of the Politics of the Workplace

One of the sources of the bifurcation of collective action was the 1947 Labor Management Relations Act, which, as I argued in the previous chapter, institutionalized the disengagement of labor relations policy from social policy. To review, the LMRA banned a variety of concerted activities such as secondary boycotts, sympathy strikes, and strikes to force employers into larger bargaining units, thus preventing labor conflict from spilling out of the narrow boundaries of an employer-employee dispute into a community-wide protest. Strikes such as the UMW engaged in to unionize West Virginia coal towns in the 1920s are now illegal under federal law. Hence, by the 1950s, industrial relations moderates noted with approval that the industrial relations system channeled worker discontent into orderly collective bargaining and limited the "core of conflict" between labor and management to the rules governing the employment relationship.[15]

The LMRA also diminished the authority and administrative capacities of the National Labor Relations Board, transforming the agency from a bold advocate of structural reform into a cautious, neutral adjudicator of labor disputes, concerned with due process, formal procedures, and narrow, technical questions of legal interpretation.[16] Thus, Herbert Hill, former counsel for the NAACP, complains that during the 1960s the NLRB initially abdicated its responsibility to uphold Title 7 of the 1964 Civil Rights Act, which the board claimed fell outside its jurisdiction.[17] Reforms in social policy and labor law during 1960s consequently originated with other federal agencies, such as the Office of Economic Opportunity, the Department of Labor, and the Equal Employment Opportunity Commission, and social movements turned to other forms of social protest, apart from the workplace, to pursue these reforms.

Finally, the LMRA rejected the progressive view of collective bargaining and instead reinforced a more limited workplace contractualism that treats the labor agreement as a private, legal-bureaucratic procedure for resolving disputes at the workplace.[18] Thus, Section 2(5) specifies that collective bargaining take place over the terms of employment—wages, hours, and working conditions—and, by implication, does not sanction bargaining over permissive subjects that involve the "core of entrepreneurial control," such as layoffs, product prices, production processes, plant closings, and investment decisions.[19] These permissive subjects may influence not only the workforce but the broader community as well.[20] William Julius Wilson notes that the loss of manufacturing employment and the suburbanization of industry account for much of the economic dislocation, social disorganization, and community deterioration of poor, inner-city neighborhoods.[21] Strikes to protest their impact, however, are not protected under the NLRA; employees who strike against an employers' decision to move jobs out of their community face the threat of immediate discharge.

Less apparent than the LMRA as a source of the bifurcation of collective action are restrictions in the 1935 National Labor Relations Act. Throughout the 1930s, Senator Wagner advocated employees' rights to organize, bargain collectively, and engage in concerted activity as essential for establishing social justice and industrial citizenship.[22] By helping to bring millions of low-wage industrial workers into the middle class, the NLRA has proven to be one of the most successful social policies of the twentieth century. Initially, Senator Wagner and his supporters had intended to extend federal protections to all workers, industrial and nonindustrial alike. Thus, during the debates over the Wagner Act, New York Representative Vito Marcantonio argued: "If the industrial workers are entitled to protection, then by the same token the agricultural workers are entitled to the same protection."[23] In 1936–37, Senator Robert La Follette hoped that exposure of grower strikebreaking against the Southern Tenant Farmers Union and against farm workers in California's Central Valley would lead to the extension of the NLRA to agricultural workers.[24] Congressional leaders, however, concerned about maintaining the New Deal Democratic Party coalition, rejected this. The success of the New Deal in Congress depended on the support of the party's southern wing, a powerful constituency within the Democratic Party coalition that opposed federal policies that would alter the balance of power between whites and blacks in the south.

The NLRA, consequently, excludes large segments of the working poor. Section 2 of the act specifies that "the term 'employee' . . . shall not include any individual employed as an agricultural laborer, or in the domestic service of any family or person at home." Like the Economic Security Act and the Fair Labor Standards Act, the NLRA thus omitted most of the southern black labor force, 70 percent of whom labored as farm workers and household servants at the time.[25] This exclusion has reinforced the segmentation of the labor market into unionized, well-paid and secure jobs for white males, and unprotected, nonunionized and lower-paid jobs for other segments of the working poor. Moreover, because collective bargaining agreements typically include privatized welfare benefits such as health insurance, pensions, and supplemental unemployment payments, this exclusion has also contributed to the bifurcation of U.S. social policy and the exclusion of millions of the working poor from other social citizenship rights.[26] The working poor may not exercise their right to strike to promote their social citizenship rights, including their rights to employment and to economic security, nor may they exercise their right to strike to promote broader community concerns.

The NLRA excludes other segments of the nonindustrial workforce. Section 2 further states that "the term 'employer' . . . shall not include the United States, nor any State or political subdivision thereof." In other words, the act does not protect the rights of public employees to engage in collective action. During the postwar era, public employment provided one of the principal routes for advancement of blacks into the middle class, offering hundreds of thousands of jobs to black school teachers, public health workers, social workers, bus drivers, police officers, community action administrators, postal workers, and the like.[27] Following President Kennedy's Executive Order 10988 in 1962 and the initiatives of progressive mayors such as Robert Wagner Jr., large numbers of public employees acquired some protections to unionize and to bargain collectively. Statutes, ordinances, and judicial decisions, however, constrain these rights and generally prohibit public employees from exercising their right to strike.[28]

Besides explicitly excluding farm workers, household workers, and government employees, the NLRA also lacks an antidiscrimination clause.[29] Since the 1890s, the constitutions of AFL construction unions and the railroad brotherhoods had contained color bars denying membership to all blacks, while other unions had segregated black workers into Jim Crow locals or permitted de facto discrimination in wages, job assignments, training, and so on. Because the act establishes procedures to elect an exclusive bargaining representative based on a majority vote but makes no provisions for the rights of minorities, it initially sanctioned all-white closed shops. Senator Wagner had proposed an antidiscrimination clause, but, according to Keyserling, "the American Federation of Labor fought bitterly to eliminate the clause and much against his will Senator Wagner had to consent to the elimination in order to prevent scuttling the entire bill."[30] The NAACP consequently denounced the act because it denied blacks access to some of the most desirable jobs. The 1964 Civil Rights Act finally outlawed these discriminatory practices, but black wage earners had to seek relief through the courts and the Equal Employment Opportunity Commission—not the NLRB.

The NLRA also fails to assist nonindustrial workers in more subtle ways. The NLRA presupposed an industrial workforce and provided the tools for organizing the industrial union movement of the 1930s. By banning specific unfair labor practices by employers, such as discriminatory discharge, blacklisting, labor espionage, company unions, and refusal to bargain, the act denied to employers those weapons that had maintained open shop employment relations for fifty years. By promoting wholesale administrative procedures like card signing and elections to select a collective bargaining representative and the checkoff to automatically deduct union dues from paychecks, the act relied on economies of scale to lower the costs of organizing and collective bargaining at massive industrial employers. Nonindustrial workers face a different environment for labor organizing. Nonindustrial employers seeking a union-free environment may contract out to nonunion firms, employ more casual, part-time, or temporary workers, or create a work environment that encourages frequent turnover. In addition, nonindustrial employers tend to have smaller workforces, which do not benefit from the economies of scale that the NLRA's administrative procedures create.

Finally, as I argued in chapter 5, the NLRA affirmed the right to strike as a commercial right, that is, a liberty constructed upon the narrow and vulnerable constitutional foundation of the interstate commerce clause, rather than upon the Bill of Rights or the Thirteenth or Fourteenth Amendments. As a commercial right, the right to strike lacks the moral and political urgency of civil rights and civil liberties—citizenship rights with unequivocal constitutional foundations. Civil rights violations receive the strict scrutiny of the court, and civil rights laws permit victims to sue, but strikers may not seek criminal charges or sue for damages against strikebreaking employers. The right to strike as affirmed by the NLRA is not a citizenship right per se but an entitlement subject to legislative abridgement, as the 1947 amendments demonstrated.

Urban Poverty and the Politics of Community in the 1960s

The separation of the politics of the workplace from the politics of the community was one of the unstated assumptions that policy analysts accepted in the early 1960s when they addressed the problem of urban poverty. According to the prevailing structuralist theory that dominated progressive thinking during that period, persistent poverty in America's inner cities had little to do with the working poor's low levels of unionization or unequal bargaining power over the terms of their employment. Instead, structuralists viewed poverty as a *community* problem, rooted in the unequal opportunities and social pathologies of the ghetto system, apart from the inequalities that persisted in employment relations. As a community-based problem, urban poverty called for community-based responses—targeted programs that brought manpower training, social services, health services, educational reforms, and urban redevelopment programs into poor neighborhoods, as well as efforts to organize the poor on a community basis. Few advocated organizing the poor at their workplaces or extending to the working poor NLRA rights to engage in concerted activity.

Progressive policy analysts during the Great Society era presented two variants of the structuralist theory of poverty. Keynesians within the Council of Economic Advisors and the Bureau of the Budget observed that persistent residual poverty remained immune to fiscal policies that had stimulated robust economic growth. Unlike the forgotten men of the 1930s, who had endured general economic stagnation, the invisible poor of the 1960s remained impoverished in the midst of affluence. Walter Heller, chairman of the Council of Economic Advisors, concluded that structural barriers to individual economic opportunities—educational disadvantage, institutional racism, and technogical change—prevented the inner-city poor from taking advantage of an expanding economy. The 1964 *Report of the Council of Economic Advisors,* which provided the foundation for the War on Poverty, concluded: "In the future economic growth alone will provide relatively few escapes from poverty. Policy will have to be more sharply focused on the handicaps that deny the poor fair access to the expanding incomes of a growing economy."[31] This economic variant of structuralist theory justified specialized poverty programs to remove these barriers to individual opportunities.

A political variant of structuralist theory emerged from one of the most intense academic debates of the 1950s and 1960s, one that concerned the nature of power in American communities. Interest group theorists such as Robert Dahl and Nelson Polsby argued that a wide variety of competing, countervailing interests disperse power throughout the community, whereas elite theorists such as Floyd Hunter responded that, behind the appearance of interest group competition, elites with shared interests dominate community decision making.[32] Structuralists Richard Cloward and Lloyd Ohlin and others developed a more refined version of elite theory by defining power as the systematic organization of bias within community politics, which creates institutional barriers to social mobility and political influence.[33] Despite their disagreements, all sides shared the tacit assumption that the principal sources of power, whether dispersed, concentrated, or structural, were rooted in the community, apart from the workplace.

According to this more radical version of structuralist theory, urban poverty is the product of powerlessness, rather than personal inadequacy, a culture of poverty, economic stagnation, or the working poor's low level of organization at the workplace. The organization of bias within community institutions permits vested interests to dominate agenda setting and the allocation of resources to their advantage.[34] Structuralists argued that since the New Deal era federal urban policies had largely benefited urban progrowth coalitions—loose alliances of local public officials, real estate developers, construction contractors, building trades unions, local businesses, chambers of commerce, and local newspaper publishers.[35] Local elites modified the federal interstate highway program into metropolitan commuter systems, which carved up older urban working-class neighborhoods, while permitting the middle class to flee to the suburban fringe. Local growth machines used federal urban renewal funds to clear decaying urban neighborhoods but not to build low-income housing. The Federal Housing Authority built large housing projects in inner cities, apart from middle- and working-class neighborhoods, further concentrating and isolating the urban poor from the rest of the community.[36] Redlining by mortgage lenders and discriminatory practices of real estate businesses and white homeowners concentrated the black urban poor into ghetto neighborhoods. This political variant of structuralist theory contended that the ghetto system duplicates the inequalities in community power structures.

The structuralist theory of urban poverty helped to explain how poverty can persist in a prosperous society that officially promotes equal opportunities and marked an advance over theories that blamed widespread poverty on individual moral and psychological defects or on a self-perpetuating culture of poverty. But it ignored Senator Robert Wagner's argument that unequal bargaining power between individual employees and their employers leads to low wages and that the failure to protect wage earners' rights to organize, to bargain collectively, and to strike contributes to poverty. In particular, structuralist theory neglected the origins of urban poverty in the unequal power relations that had persisted for generations between the southern agricultural workforce and growers. New Deal agricultural policies had largely benefited growers, providing incentives to take land out of agricultural production, to shift from tenancy to wage labor, and to modernize agricultural production with labor-reducing farming practices.[37] These structural changes displaced upward of ten million southern agricultural workers, most of whom entered urban labor markets, participating in the largest internal migration in U.S. history.[38]

New Deal policies, however, had offered few protections for the agricultural workforce. Farm workers had engaged in strikes during the 1930s, but growers in southeastern Arkansas and in Delano, California, had destroyed the fledgling Southern Tenant Farmers' Union (STFU) and the California farm workers' movement.[39] Farm workers subsequently presented no organized resistance to structural changes in southern agriculture during the New Deal and after World War II. Displaced farm workers instead pursued individual responses to structural economic changes by migrating to urban labor markets that offered better individual economic opportunities, thus entering urban labor markets with virtually no labor organizations, and little experience with the organized labor movement.

For generations, semiskilled industrial work had provided decent job opportunities for new entrants into urban labor markets, but at the height of the Great Migration, the industrial sector was contracting.[40] By 1950 the number of workers employed in services equaled the number employed in industry.[41] During the 1950s, Daniel Bell and other social critics noted the relative decline in the number of semiskilled factory workers, and by the

1960s he announced that the United States had become a "post-industrial society," in which services are the dominant economic sector. A disproportionate number of black migrants subsequently found low-wage, unskilled, service sector jobs as hotel maids, janitors, sanitation workers, nurse's aides, and food-service workers—segments of the labor market ill-suited for the type of mass labor organizing sustained by the NLRA. The NLRA's exclusion of agricultural and domestic service workers, and its lack of an antidiscrimination clause, inhibited the organization of the black working poor in the 1960s and limited their capacity to engage in workplace-based collective action to promote civil rights and economic equality. Lacking power resources at the workplace, the African American working poor turned instead to community leaders—ministers, student leaders, teachers, and community organizers—to champion their demands for social justice.

Neither version of the structuralist theory of urban poverty fully appreciated these broader changes affecting the working poor since the 1930s. Structuralists instead focused on the current barriers to individual economic opportunities and the current community power structures rather than the origins of these structural inequalities. As a result, few suggested that urban poverty might be related to unequal employment relations or that extending the right to engage in concerted activities to the working poor might alleviate urban poverty.

The War on Poverty and Community Action

President Johnson's 1964 State of the Union message heralding the War on Poverty reflected this focus on community. "The central problem," he declared, "is to restore man's satisfaction and sense of belonging to a *community* where he can find security and significance."[42] Thus was born the Great Society's main initiative to improve the lives of the urban poor. Although in many ways a renewed commitment to the objectives of the New Deal, the War on Poverty differed from the New Deal in one crucial way: it attempted to organize and empower the poor as a residential community rather than as wage earners. Policy makers and social reformers sought to reduce structural poverty by providing community-based services, by organizing the poor for community-based collective action, and by removing artificial barriers to individual employment opportunities.[43] As such, it accepted the existing boundaries between work-based politics and community-based politics.

The most innovative section of the 1964 Economic Opportunity Act created community action programs (CAPs) to provide inner-city neighborhoods with federally supported social services such as job training, family planning, and community development projects. The most radical aspect of

CAPs was their attempt to organize and empower the poor on a residential basis. Section 202(b) of the act mandated CAPs, "developed and conducted with the maximum feasible participation of residents of the areas and members of the groups referred to." Robert Kennedy succinctly summed up this objective: "Part of the sense of helplessness and futility comes from the feeling of powerlessness to affect these [big city] organizations by providing real responsibility for the poor. This . . . calls for maximum feasible participation of *residents.*"[44] By linking residents of poor urban neighborhoods with federal government granting agencies and supporting their participation in the planning, coordination, and delivery of federal social services, CAPs sought to bypass the local power structures that had excluded the interests of the poor community and had distorted New Deal urban programs.

Community unions, which attempted to link the urban poor with the labor movement, were among the most innovative CAPs. UAW president Waiter Reuther said such community unions would "provid[e] the poor with their own self-sufficient economic organizations in the community."[45] Jack Conway, a former UAW official and the director of the Presidential Urban Areas Task Force that drew up guidelines for CAPs, asserted:

> We believe that just as the auto worker and the steel worker and other industrial employees gained self-respect and dignity through organization, so, too, can the poor gain self respect and dignity by the same method. . . . The community union is a new concept, a new form of institution, but it is well within the best traditions of the trade-union movement. A community union could mesh traditional trade union functions with modern community-center functions. It could, for example, bring tenants together to bargain collectively with slum lords. It could have its own grievance procedure and steward system so that the complaints of a neighborhood could be voiced effectively.[46]

Community unions, however, did not engage in the most traditional union functions: work stoppages and other workplace-based forms of collective action.

Efforts to establish militant grassroots community unions fell short of Reuther's and Conway's aspirations. Jealousy often arose between labor organizers and community leaders, who feared that the former would dominate these community unions. Given the existing social disorganization and lack of resources in poor communities, organizing the urban poor on a residential basis proved to be extremely difficult. Like CAPs generally, most community unions eventually gave up and became community agencies that applied for, and administered, federal grants.[47]

Moreover, by 1966, community action programs had lost the support of the Johnson administration. Conflicts between CAPs and local elites threatened the Democratic Party's decades-old coalition between the White House and Democratic mayors, who accused the Office of Economic Opportunity of fomenting class conflict and racial strife. When Congress amended the Economic Opportunity Act, they eliminated the goal of "maximum feasible participation," removed popular programs like Head Start from the OEO, and gave city agencies greater control over federal urban grants. Congress began dismantling the objectionable agency in 1969, and finally eliminated the OEO in 1974. Community action programs eventually operated like traditional social service agencies, offering legal, family planning, and training services, providing patronage jobs for social service professionals, and only giving lip service to the goal of maximum feasible participation.[48]

Daniel Moynihan argued that the goal of maximum feasible participation, while laudable, was poorly conceived, and that CAPs were more the creation of activist social scientists than the working poor. "The war on poverty was not declared at the behest of the poor: it was declared in the interest of persons confident of their own judgment in such matters."[49] The underlying problem, however, was not who had instigated the War on Poverty; rather, it was their failure to address one of the principal sources of inequality. Those who shaped the War on Poverty failed to recognize that employers constitute one of the most powerful components of the community power structure. In contrast, the architects of the NLRA realized that, in order to improve living standards, the state needs to increase the bargaining power of the working poor by affirming and protecting their right to engage in collective action at the workplace.

The National Welfare Rights Organization and the Politics of Community

Social activism during the 1960s also reflected the era's focus on community. During the 1960s, a welfare rights movement emerged out of the War on Poverty and agitated for the transformation of social provisions from a benefit into a citizenship right. Like the community action programs, the welfare rights movement turned to community-based politics to challenge the community power structure and to demand the rights of the poor. And like the CAPs, the welfare rights movement accepted the existing boundaries between the politics of the community and the politics of the workplace, neglected to link demands for welfare rights with demands for workplace rights, and ultimately failed to transform the American welfare state.

A distinguishing characteristic of the American welfare state is its failure to treat welfare as a social citizenship right. British sociologist T. H. Marshall argued that economic security ought to be a universal right in order to guarantee to everyone full and equal membership in the community.[50] Despite Roosevelt's 1944 proclamation of an economic bill of rights, social provision in the United States, however, remains, according to Michael B. Katz, "in the shadow of the poorhouse," with low levels of benefits, means-tested programs, no national health care, and a bifurcated system that separates more generous Social Security programs from relief for the poor.[51] William Julius Wilson states: "In contrast to many European nations, the United States has not created comprehensive programs to promote the *social* rights of American citizens. Antipoverty programs have been narrowly targeted and fragmented."[52] This system of poor relief, with its means testing and low levels of benefits, creates invidious distinctions that have treated welfare recipients as second-class citizens.

Welfare recipients, civil rights activists, social workers, VISTA (Volunteers in Service to America) volunteers, and legal services lawyers joined forces in the mid-1960s and organized more than five hundred community-based welfare rights organizations to challenge this system of poor relief and to encourage the militancy of the poor.[53] JOIN (Jobs or Income Now), a community union based in the inner-city neighborhoods of Chicago, was typical. In a lengthy "Welfare Bill of Rights," JOIN demanded a guaranteed minimum income, adequate welfare benefits, the elimination of welfare as a tool for controlling and stigmatizing the poor, control of welfare services by the recipients, elimination of arbitrary removals from welfare rolls, privacy rights for welfare recipients, and so on. It demanded that "recipients have the right to unionize":

> Like other groups, welfare recipients should organize to protect their rights and to insure the dignity of their families. Welfare officials should negotiate with recipients so that legitimate complaints can be heard. No one should be cut off [from] welfare or threatened by a caseworker if he of she organizes for his or her rights.[54]

This Welfare Bill of Rights, however, made no mention of extending to the working poor the right to strike, or other NLRA rights.

Welfare rights organizers instead mobilized community protests as an instrument of social activism, employing forms of collective action, ironically, that the labor movement had developed in the late nineteenth and early twentieth centuries.[55] Protestors picketed welfare offices, participated in sit-ins, formed grievance committees, and presented demands, just as industrial workers had during the Great Depression. However, unlike earlier work-based collective action, welfare rights groups never protested against employers, and never demanded more jobs, better wages, improved working conditions, employee representation, collective bargaining, or related things. Instead, they protested against community welfare agencies, demanding more assistance and services, the elimination of arbitrary and invidious administrative rules, and greater access for the poor. Protests remained community-based forms of collective action.

More radical welfare rights activists, such as Frances Fox Piven and Richard A. Cloward, supported mass protests of the urban poor, not just as a tactic to obtain expanded benefits for the protestors, but as a strategy to disrupt the welfare system and to bring about broad structural reform.[56] Mass protests, they believed, would create a huge increase in the relief roles, overwhelming the welfare system. A breakdown of the welfare system would spark a political crisis, followed by the federalization of the welfare system. Piven and Cloward believed that would lead to a guaranteed national income policy, similar to those in social democratic systems. They did not, however, seek an extension of the right to strike to excluded segments of the working poor.

The welfare rights movement secured some modest changes in social provision in the United States. Legal aid lawyers counseled poor individuals on a range of common legal problems, including problems in securing and retaining welfare benefits. This altered the attitudes of welfare recipients, who came to regard social provision as a legal entitlement rather than as an unearned benefit. Consequently, between 1967 and 1972 the number of Aid to Families with Dependent Children (AFDC) recipients rose from 5 million to 10.7 million.[57] Funding for AFDC quadrupled, and participation rates of those eligible for AFDC jumped from 33 percent in 1960 to about 90 percent in 1971. Legal advocates also broke new ground in the development of class-action suits to protect the legal rights of the poor. This helped to eliminate some of the more invidious administrative rules and to secure important procedural rights for people on relief. Test cases ruled that suitable-home regulations, man-in-house restrictions, employable mother rules, and residency requirements violated the constitutional rights of recipients.[58] Welfare recipients also won protection against unannounced household visits by welfare officials, the right to a hearing, the right to notification of termination, and the right to appeal.[59]

The welfare rights movement, however, failed to realize their principal objective of a federally guaranteed minimum income. Greater legal rights did not secure for the urban poor a greater portion of the national wealth, nor did the Supreme Court accept the argument that the poor had an entitlement to adequate AFDC benefit levels based on need.[60] Local welfare agencies instead adopted legal-bureaucratic norms of equity that upheld formal, procedural rights while limiting benefits and discouraging applicants with burdensome—but equitable—procedures. Once urban unrest subsided in the early 1970s, the welfare explosion led to a backlash.[61] Opponents attacked the premise of an entitlement to welfare, arguing that welfare promoted dependency, permissiveness, and a vicious cycle of poverty.[62]

Turning the concept of social citizenship rights on its head, some social critics began to argue for compulsory work requirements as a condition for receiving welfare benefits.[63] This presaged a retreat from many of the social policies of the modern liberal American state, including its affirmation of workers' rights to collective activity.

Two related reasons—the first conceptual, the second tactical—explain the failure of the welfare rights movement to restructure social policy. Conceptually, the movement treated welfare rights not as *social citizenship* rights but as *individual legal* rights. Individual welfare recipients have due process rights, such as the right to a hearing and the right to appeal termination of benefits. Recipients also have privacy rights, such as the protection against unannounced visits, as well as rights against arbitrary treatment, such as the employable mothers rule. But social provision per se remained an entitlement only, that is, a legal right created by statute rather than by the Constitution, and subject to legislative restrictions. As such, welfare rights are still consistent with means testing, low benefit levels, and stigmatization of the poor.[64] One has no basis to criticize inadequate welfare benefit levels within the modern liberal rights framework, as long as everyone's benefits are equally inadequate.

Tactically, the welfare rights movement failed to restructure social policy because it ignored workplace-based collective action and neglected reforms in employment and labor relations policies. Piven and Cloward admit this failure to link welfare rights with workplace rights:

> It was not clear how activists could, as a practical matter of organizing, mount an attack on poverty by attacking its main cause—underemployment and unemployment. What our plan proposed instead was a way of attacking the lack of income resulting from unemployment. . . . It was appealing to some organizers for that reason.[65]

Indeed, it was not clear how to mount an attack on poverty, given the way in which the NLRA restricted workplace protest and channeled it into a narrow, collective bargaining framework. This framework isolates workplace issues from broader community issues; workers may not strike against employers who abandon an inner-city neighborhood, or who refuse to expand employment. Nor may workers strike to protest inadequate social provisions by the state or federal government. Although workers may strike for better wages and more job security, they may only do so on a fragmentary, firm-by-firm basis. Moreover, inner-city service sector employers remained unorganized, and the industrial relations system proved inadequate for organizing a fragmented workforce and relatively small employers. Welfare rights activists would have to challenge the NLRA itself to permit community-based collective action to spill over its banks into the realm of employment relations and to extend NLRA collective action rights to excluded sectors of the working poor.

As a practical matter, as Piven and Cloward discovered, organizing welfare recipients on a community basis also had its limitations. Welfare recipients often lacked the social organization and daily contact with other members of welfare rights groups to sustain a movement. Once they had obtained or restored their benefits, welfare recipients no longer had an incentive to remain active. In addition, the national welfare rights movement faced growing conflicts between its middle-class white male leadership and its impoverished black female constituency. The movement's rhetoric promoted participatory democracy and cooperation, but cleavages based on class, race, and gender created conflict and disagreement. Mounting friction led organizers and members to leave the organization, eroding its limited resources. The movement increasingly focused on lobbying in Washington, which drew more of its resources away from community-based organizing.[66]

The failure to organize and activate the working poor at their workplaces contributed to these difficulties. Labor organizations, unlike these welfare rights organizations, provide ongoing services and benefits and daily contact with other members. Wage earners consequently have more of a vested interest in their organizations at work. The automatic payment of membership dues through payroll deductions, moreover, provides labor organizations with a more stable resource base. In addition, enhancing NLRA collective action rights for the working poor would provide them with the means to improve their terms of employment, which directly affects the welfare of their communities. Strengthening these rights also would potentially broaden the labor movement and provide more of a political base for the transformation of social provision into a social citizenship right. The existing system of industrial relations, however, provides inadequate protections for the working poor to organize and engage in workplace-based collective action to support a guaranteed annual income, full employment, universal health care, and other social citizenship rights associated with the modern welfare state. Because the Great Society did not challenge the system of labor relations and workplace authority that had existed since 1947, it had only limited success in achieving its goals.[67]

Linking the Politics of Workplace and Community

An alternative explanation for the separation of the politics of the workplace from the politics of the community during the 1960s places the blame squarely on the labor movement for failing to organize the working poor. One researcher has documented a significant decline in union organizing expenditures, from $1.03 per nonunion member in 1953 to $.87 in 1964.[68]

Others accuse the labor movement of actively discriminating against black workers. Herbert Hill, former labor secretary for the NAACP, has documented discrimination by white-dominated unions and their resistance to Title 7 of the 1964 Civil Rights Act.[69] The labor movement, with its focus on organized white male workers, squandered an opportunity to ally with the emerging black civil rights movement in the early 1960s. Hill writes:

> The combination of a dynamic black protest movement and a body of innovative law emerging within a context of rapid industrialization and urbanization created a new situation and new possibilities for unionization in many southern communities. But the tired old barons of the AFL-CIO were incapable of understanding this development, incapable of understanding the nexus of race and class in a rapidly changing south.[70]

The 1960s, however, were not unique in this failure—the "tired old barons" of the organized labor movement had been failing to organize the working poor since the 1890s.[71] The mainstream AFL leadership dismissed the industrial workforce as incapable of organization, and even resisted the emerging CIO and its constituent unions during the 1930s. CIO unions eventually had to disaffiliate and form their own federation. During this period the most dynamic union organizers, such as the Reuther brothers, David Dubinsky, and Sidney Hillman, came up from the shop floor. Organizing requires workers themselves to take the initiative; often only those outside the mainstream labor movement can envision the potential for social activism and progressive social reform.

Such was the case on two significant occasions during the 1960s, when the working poor turned to strikes and boycotts to demand social justice at work and in their communities. In Memphis, a sanitation workers' strike in 1968 provided the prelude to Dr. Martin Luther King Jr.'s Poor People's Campaign for economic justice.[72] In California, a series of farm workers' strikes and consumer boycotts against grape and lettuce growers eventually coalesced into the United Farm Workers (UFW) union or La Causa (Spanish, "the cause")—one of the most important social movements of the era.[73] In Memphis and California, activists bridged the politics of the workplace and the politics of the community in order to improve the lives of some of America's lowest-paid wage earners.

In both instances, strikers initially strove for conventional pure-and-simple union objectives. Strikers in Memphis sought union recognition, a collective bargaining agreement, improvements in wages, safety improvements, and the elimination of racial discrimination in pay and work rules. Strikers in California likewise demanded union recognition, collective bargaining agreements, and improved pay, as well as the elimination of the labor contractor system, improved living conditions in the labor camps, and sanitary facilities in the fields. Such demands comprised the most basic concerns of workplace-based politics. As these movements evolved, however, each eventually transcended pure-and-simple unionism, adopted a civic discourse that emphasized social justice, human rights, and racial equality, and built communitywide movements.

The Memphis Sanitation Workers' Strike

In Memphis, sanitation workers demanded their civil rights with signs declaring "I AM A MÁN." Local black clergy, recognizing the strike's significance for the civil rights movement, provided broad community support for the sanitation workers and invited Dr. Martin Luther King Jr. to address the community and lead a march with the strikers. By the time he arrived in Memphis, Martin Luther King Jr. had grasped the necessity of mobilizing the black community for a nationwide protest to obtain economic justice for poor black workers. The Memphis strike provided inspiration for his Poor People's Campaign, scheduled for Washington, D.C., later that spring.[74] During his visit to Memphis, King denounced the strike injunction, the denial of union recognition and collective bargaining, and attacks on picketers and speakers as violations of their civil liberties and fundamental rights:

> We have an injunction and we're going into court tomorrow morning to fight this illegal, unconstitutional injunction. All we say to America is, "Be true to what you said on paper." If I lived in China or even Russia, or any totalitarian country, maybe I could understand the denial of certain basic First Amendment privileges, because they hadn't committed themselves to that over there. But somewhere I read of the freedom of assembly. Somewhere I read of the freedom of speech. Somewhere I read of the freedom of the press. Somewhere I read that the greatness of America is the right to protest for right.[75]

The United Farm Workers' Strike

Similarly, the California farm workers and their supporters came to regard La Causa not just as a unionization drive but as a struggle for social justice and freedom, and as a movement for Mexican American pride. Cesar Chavez explained: "We hate the agribusiness system that seeks to keep us enslaved, and we shall overcome and change it not by retaliation or bloodshed, but by determined nonviolent struggle by those masses of farm workers who intend to be free and human." On another occasion Chavez said, "A farm contractor does not contract work in the full sense of the word . . .

he buys and sells humans."[76] During Chavez's 1966 Lenten march from Delano to Sacramento, marchers proudly displayed symbols of the Mexican American community, such as flags with Aztec eagles and icons of Our Lady of Guadalupe. The Catholic bishops of California issued a statement declaring farm labor a moral problem and asserting that papal and Vatican Council doctrines supported the farm workers' right to unionize and to strike.[77]

Among the most distinctive features of these strikes were the links they forged between the politics of the workplace and the politics of community. King, Chavez, and their followers recognized that one of the main sources of power in the community is control over the workplace. This realization encouraged the formation of coalitions between community organizations and labor organizations. In Memphis, black church leaders united into COME—Community on the Move for Equality. COME, a community-based civil rights organization, provided strategic planning, organized marches and boycotts, distributed leaflets, collected donations, supplied meals for the strikers, and brought the strike to national attention. In his last speech before his assassination, King urged the black community to continue supporting the strike through boycotts and demonstrations: "The question is not, 'If I stop to help this man in need, what will happen to me?' 'If I do not stop to help the sanitation workers, what will happen to them?' That's the question. Let us rise up tonight with a greater readiness. Let us stand with a greater determination."[78]

In California, the organization founded by Cesar Chavez, the National Farm Workers Association (NFWA), similarly had close ties with organizations in the Mexican American community. Cesar Chavez was a farm worker who began his organizing career with the Community Service Organization (CSO), a militant civil rights and civic-action organization sponsored by Saul Alinsky's Industrial Areas Foundation and rooted in the barrios and *colonias* or neighborhoods.[79] During his years with the CSO, Chavez helped members of the Mexican American community register to vote and obtain their citizenship papers and defended them against police brutality and urban renewal projects in the barrios. He also learned the basics of labor organizing, such as focusing on the grass roots and establishing community service centers to address the needs of the working poor. During his ten years organizing for the CSO, Chavez came to realize the need to organize farm laborers, and eventually he resigned as general director to lead the NFWA organizing drive.

During the campaign, Chavez recognized the importance of the Catholic Church as a source of moral and economic power. The Church is an extremely important institution in the Mexican American community, a source of ethnic pride and cultural identity; its papal encyclicals on labor and social justice helped to legitimize Chavez's organizing efforts. In "The

Mexican American and the Church," a 1968 address to farm workers during the Delano grape strike, Chavez urged his listeners to call on the church to help them organize at the grassroots level: "What do we ask the Church to do? . . . We ask for its presence with us, beside us, as Christ among us. . . . We ask the Church to sacrifice with the people for social change, for justice, for love of brother."[80] The Catholic Church consequently offered essential community-based support, with the participation of reform-minded priests and Mexican American congregations. As a source of ethnic pride and cultural identity, La Causa promoted the broader concerns of the Mexican American community, and like the Memphis strike, instilled in its members the realization that they were also full members of the United States community, equal in standing with every other citizen.

Although neither of these strikes spawned a national movement or brought about fundamental changes in federal social policies, wage earners in both cases realized significant organizational gains and improvements in their working and living conditions. The sanitation workers won union recognition, nondiscrimination and grievance arbitration clauses in their labor agreement, dues checkoff, the city's package of employee benefits, and a fifteen-cent raise.[81] The farm workers attained union recognition from the Delano area growers, an increase in hourly wages from $1.10 to $1.80, grower contributions to health and welfare and social service funds, a union-managed hiring hall, and safety rules limiting pesticide use.[82]

Moreover, strikers achieved these improvements without the benefit of the NLRA, which specifically excludes public employees and farm workers. Indeed, in most jurisdictions, public employee strikes are illegal. Although farm worker strikes are legal, the NLRA does not protect farm workers from blacklisting, discriminatory discharge, or strikebreaking. On the other hand, coverage by the NLRA would have channeled these workers' social activism into the normal forms of workplace politics, separated from community politics, and would have inhibited their evolution into broader social movements demanding social justice. In fact, had the NLRA not excluded farm workers, the nationwide grape boycott would have violated federal labor relations law. It was King's and Chavez's genius to see beyond the current structures of social policy and social activism and to realize that economic justice for second-class citizens demands collective action both at the workplace and in the community.

The issue of work once again commands attention in debates concerning urban poverty and social policy. William Julius Wilson, for example, argues that the disappearance of work from impoverished urban neighborhoods since the early 1970s has contributed to the disintegration of vulnerable neighborhoods, the breakdown of social organization, and the rise of violence in the inner cities.[83] Wilson proposes an aggressive, social democratic agenda of employment and training programs aimed at broad segments of the American population to improve the lives of the urban poor and to integrate them into the mainstream of American life.

This renewed interest in the relationship between employment and urban poverty has refocused the social policy debate in a fertile direction. But the current debate continues to neglect the working poor's low levels of organization and representation at the workplace. Social democratic programs such as those Wilson proposes will not succeed as long as they do not confront the need for social democratic politics to support them. If the goals of social policy include the empowerment of the poor and their inclusion in American society, then policy makers need to address the sources of vulnerability and exclusion in labor relations. The reduction of urban poverty also calls for programs to encourage the mobilization of the working poor at the workplace, and to extend to those excluded from the NRLA the right to strike.

8

"Playing hardball"

Permanent Striker Replacements and the Limits of Industrial Justice

No other topic today better illustrates modern American liberalism's incoherence and ambivalence toward the right to strike than the permanent striker replacement issue. Although the National Labor Relations Act affirms that "nothing in this Act shall be construed so as to interfere with or impede or diminish in any way the right to strike,"[1] and clearly bans employers from firing strikers, it also permits employers to hire strikebreakers ("permanent replacement workers," in liberal legal jargon) and prohibits the employer from summarily discharging strikebreakers to make room for the strikers after the labor dispute has ended. Federal labor law also prohibits strikers from interfering with strikebreakers, and, if necessary, the state may provide police escorts to subdue striker resistance. Moreover, after one year the employer may petition the National Labor Relations Board for a union decertification election in which only the strikebreakers may vote. This procedure permits permanent striker replacements to terminate the union as their collective bargaining representative. Some scholars argue that the increasing use of permanent replacement workers has seriously shifted the balance of power between organized labor and employers and that it accounts for the dramatic decline in the U.S. strike rate, which has plummeted to its lowest level since before the New Deal.[2]

Labor law scholars sympathetic to the labor movement contend that this paradoxical provision arises from a loophole in federal labor law that undermines the fundamental principles of the NLRA; they support labor law reform to eliminate this inconsistency in the law and to restore balance to federal strike policy. I disagree with this analysis and instead argue that the permanent striker replacement issue arises not just from an aberration in U.S. labor law but from the fact that the NLRA does not treat the right to strike as a citizenship right. If work is central to one's standing as an American citizen, then the state should protect workers' rights to suspend work during a labor dispute, and either protect their right to return to work after the dispute is resolved or provide compulsory arbitration of the dispute. Instead, the NLRA treats the right to strike merely as a commercial right, as a form of pressure in the collective bargaining process. As such, it does not bear the same urgency for modern liberalism as do civil rights and civil liberties. Instead, the right to strike has degenerated into the right to quit.

The permanent striker replacement issue is a symptom of modern American liberalism's grudging endorsement of the right to strike. First I will look at the emergence of the permanent striker replacement strategy in the 1980s and its impact on U.S. industrial relations. Then I will review the legal history of the permanent striker replacement issue and the recommendations of labor law reformers for a ban. I conclude that these reforms would be ineffective, because the permanent striker replacement strategy emanates from more fundamental problems in federal labor relations policy. Finally, I argue that the toleration of legalized strikebreaking is symptomatic of the limitations of the modern liberal conception of industrial justice. The state consequently sets minimal standards for good-faith bargaining, and suspends judgment about the fairness of bargaining proposals and the use of strikebreakers in a labor dispute. Banning the use of strikebreakers would involve the state in questions of substantive justice, and it would place restrictions on what Michael Sandel calls the "unencumbered self."

The Emergence of the Permanent Striker Replacement Issue

Strikebreaking has a long and ignoble past, but the permanent striker replacement strategy as a means of promoting a union-free workplace is a relatively recent development.[3] From the early 1950s until the mid-1970s, employers generally sought stable collective bargaining relations and relied on paternalism, positive personnel practices, and passive containment of labor organizations to the existing unionized sectors and regions of the United States. Employers during this golden age of industrial relations rarely hired permanent striker replacements.[4] However, wage differentials between the nonunionized and unionized segments of the workforce began to increase during the 1960s and 1970s, partly due to the labor movement's failure to expand during the postwar era, which heightened employers' incentives to substitute nonunionized for unionized labor. Organized labor's inability to obtain passage of the 1977 common situs picketing bill and the 1978 labor law reforms, despite the Democratic Party's control of the executive and legislative branches, signaled to the business community the labor movement's vulnerability.[5] Finally, increasing international competition within U.S. product markets led employers to cut costs by supporting tax cuts and deregulation, and demanding concessions at the bargaining table.[6] Consequently, beginning in the early 1980s, employers began to pursue a more assertive bargaining position toward unions.[7] The increasing use of permanent striker replacements was part of some employers' more aggressive union avoidance strategy.[8]

The first widely publicized case involving the permanent striker replacement strategy was the Professional Air Traffic Controllers Organization's strike in 1981.[9] The members of PATCO, which had endorsed Ronald Reagan for president in 1980, worked under high-stress conditions for the Federal Aviation Administration, an agency known for its militaristic employment relations. In the summer of 1981, thirteen thousand air traffic controllers walked out after contract talks had broken down. The strikers expected the Reagan administration to negotiate, but, with breathtaking speed, the administration fired all of the strikers, and, without closing any airports, transferred the air traffic controllers' tasks to FAA managers, military air traffic controllers, and trainees. Within weeks, the federal government had decertified PATCO. Of course, because they were public employees, the NLRA did not apply to the air traffic controllers, who had no legal right to strike. So the Reagan administration did not simply replace the strikers—it fired them and brought criminal charges against the strike leaders. Never before had the federal government fired and brought criminal charges against striking federal employees.[10] The Reagan administration's response sent a shock through the labor movement, as well as a signal to the business community that the administration supported a more aggressive approach to labor relations.[11]

More typical of the permanent striker replacement strategy in the private sector was the Phelps Dodge strike in Morenci, Arizona, which demonstrated to other employers the feasibility of the permanent striker replacement strategy.[12] In the spring of 1983 the Phelps Dodge Corporation, which mines and smelts copper, adopted an aggressive bargaining position toward Local 616 of the International Union of Mine, Mill and Smelter Workers, demanding the elimination of the productivity-based wage increase formula that had become a pattern in the copper industry. Union negotiators refused, since bargaining away this hard-won wage formula would destabilize wages within the industry and precipitate a spiral of wage cuts among other copper producers. Local 616 decided to strike.

The limited cost savings that would be realized by this concession, and the union's peaceful negotiations with other firms in the copper industry, indicate that Phelps Dodge's unyielding stance was not caused by business necessity. Phelps Dodge president Richard Moolick revealed that the company had bargained in bad faith and had chosen the bottom of the economic cycle, when the union's bargaining power was weak, to break the union.[13] "My position was there's no time like the present to go after the unions on a united basis," Moolick told Jonathan Rosenblum in 1990, concerning a conference he attended with the presidents of other mining companies in February 1983.[14] A federal appeals court in 1989 concluded that Phelps Dodge management had conspired among themselves to violate the strikers' civil rights.[15]

Had Local 616 been able to prove to the National Labor Relations Board that Phelps Dodge had bargained in bad faith, the employer could not have permanently replaced the strikers, and the NLRB would have ordered it back to the bargaining table. However, in most cases, determining that an employer has not fulfilled the duty to bargain is a subjective judgment. Section 8(d) of the NLRA "does not compel either party to agree to a proposal or require the making of a concession." Moreover, hiring permanent striker replacements is not prima facie evidence of bad-faith bargaining. Because Phelps Dodge had met regularly with the employees' representatives, had made no overt threats or promises, and had never publicly stated their intent to bargain to an impasse, the regional NLRB ruled in the employers' favor: the work stoppage constituted an ordinary economic strike, which permitted the employer to hire permanent replacements.

This determination provided additional state protections for Phelps Dodge. After picketers forced one of the mines to close, Phelps Dodge obtained a court injunction and police escorts for the striker replacements. On the employer's request, Arizona governor Bruce Babbitt furnished National Guard troops, armed personnel carriers, and a fleet of helicopters to guard the strikebreakers. One year later, Phelps Dodge petitioned the NLRB for a union decertification election. The permanent striker replacements formally dismissed Local 616 as the employee's representative and terminated Phelps Dodge's duty to bargain with the strikers.

Other employers followed suit. In the domestic airline industry, Continental Airlines (1983), Trans World Airlines (1989), and Eastern Airlines (1989) employed permanent replacements against striking flight attendants and mechanics. Greyhound Bus Lines employed permanent replacements unsuccessfully in 1983 and successfully in 1990. The International Paper Company hired permanent replacements in 1987 in Jay, Maine, despite previous awards recognizing the cooperative collective bargaining relations at that mill. In one of the largest strikes of the decade, Caterpillar replaced thousands of automobile workers in 1991. In 1994 Bridgestone Firestone Tire replaced thousands of striking rubber workers in Illinois, Indiana, Iowa, and Oklahoma, and the *New York Daily News* replaced hundreds of its own employees. Even the National Football League operated with re-placement players during a contract dispute in 1985. Between 1985 and 1989, employers resorted to permanent replacements in about one-fifth of all strikes.[16]

Meanwhile, U.S. strike rates plummeted to their lowest levels since 1933, leading many labor scholars to argue that the permanent striker replace-ment strategy has altered the balance of power between unions and man-agement and has seriously eroded the right to strike.[17] Michael LeRoy re-ports that 31 percent of employers in major strikes in 1985 and 35 percent in 1989 announced their intention to hire permanent replacements; he ar-gues that aggregate strike activity dropped during this period as a direct re-sult of these increasing threats.[18] Paul Weiler notes that "the bleak prospect of permanently losing his job is obviously likely to chill an employee's will-ingness to exercise his statutory rights to engage in 'concerted activities.' " William Gould, NLRB chairman under President Clinton, states:

> The lawfulness of the permanent replacement tactic is a factor in the erosion of
> the right to strike and the labor movement itself. The industrial relations cli-
> mate of the past decade ought to make us reassess the compatibility of job loss
> as a price for the strike's exercise and the ideal of a civilized and democratic so-
> ciety.[19]

Permanent Striker Replacement and the Courts

Many scholars in the field of labor relations law argue that the legality of the permanent striker replacement strategy emanates from an obsolete, aberrant, and poorly argued precedent, *NLRB v. Mackay Radio and Tele-graph Company* (1938).[20] The case originated as an unfair labor practice complaint over the discriminatory discharge of five strike leaders in 1936, at a time when the constitutionality of the NLRA remained in question. The NLRB ruled that the employer had unfairly discriminated against the strike leaders, and the appeals court and the Supreme Court reaffirmed the deci-sion. Then, in an obiter dictum, the Supreme Court added that an employer who has committed no unfair labor practices has "the right to protect and continue his business by supplying places left vacant by strikers. And he is not bound to discharge those hired to fill the places of the strikers, upon the election of the latter to resume their employment in order to create places for them."[21]

The fairness of employing permanent striker replacements was not an issue in the case; indeed, the defendant had not employed permanent replacements. Hence, Weiler criticizes the *Mackay* doctrine as based on a poorly considered "casual *dictum*."[22]

The *Mackay* decision has generated a line of precedents that elaborate on the doctrine and attempt to eliminate inconsistencies with the NLRA. The NLRA specifically prohibits employers from interfering with their employees' statutory rights, including discharging employees for exercising their right to strike. To those uninitiated in the finer points of labor law, this appears to prohibit permanently replacing strikers. The Supreme Court has resolved this apparent contradiction by distinguishing permanent replacement from termination. Permanently replaced workers are in a state of legal limbo, in which they do not work and receive no wage but remain employed in a statutory sense. They therefore have the right to reinstatement if positions become available and the right to vote in NLRB-authorized representation elections for one year after the strike began.[23] For wage earners this distinction may seem absurd, and the retention of these rights meager consolation for losing their livelihood, but because it is illegal to fire strikers, it is entirely consistent with the NLRA.

The Court has also addressed possible inconsistencies between the *Mackay* doctrine and the 1947 Labor Management Relations Act. Typically, unions demand the reinstatement of all strikers as one condition for settling a strike. However, the LMRA specifically protects individual employees' rights *not* to engage in concerted activities—what is called "the right to refrain." In *Belknap v. Hale* (1983) the Court ruled that replacement workers terminated to make room for returning strikers may sue the employer for discriminatory discharge and breach of contract.[24] This limits the capacity of employers and strikers to reach a negotiated settlement, and has reinforced the use of permanent replacements as a hard-bargaining tactic.

Since the 1960s the Supreme Court and the NLRB have also placed some limitations on the use of permanent striker replacements. The Court has determined that employers may not offer permanent replacements better wages and working conditions than the striking workers had, such as superseniority and additional vacation pay. Offering replacements a better deal than those they replace constitutes discrimination against employees for union activity—an unfair labor practice. The Court has also ruled that employers may not presume that permanent replacement eliminates the employer's duty to bargain with the strikers; only a decertification election may end this obligation. The NLRB has ruled that an employer has the authority to lock out employees and hire temporary replacements during a contract dispute in order to force concessions in the collective agreement, but it must reinstate the strikers after the dispute is resolved.[25] Each of these rulings has placed significant limitations on the permanent striker replacement strategy in order to make it consistent with the NLRA, but these limits have not deterred many employers.

The Court has also extended the *Mackay* doctrine to union members who cross the picket line. Under the LMRA, strikers may not coerce coworkers into participating in a job action. However, may a union fine strike defectors? May it insist that the employer discharge crossovers if the union wins the strike? May employers reward crossovers? In *NLRB v. Allis-Chalmers* (1967) the Supreme Court recognized unions' authority to fine strike defectors. This provided them with an important disciplinary sanction, but in 1969 the Court decided that unions could not compel an employer to fire crossovers, and in 1972 the Court ruled that a defector could avoid disciplinary action by resigning from the union. Labor organizations attempted to close this loophole by imposing constitutional restrictions prohibiting resignations during a strike. In *Pattern Makers League of North America v. NLRB* (1985), however, the Court ruled that union constitutions may not prohibit crossovers from resigning.[26] Critics charge that these decisions further weaken union discipline and erode the right to strike.

Another Supreme Court decision has strengthened an employer's capacity to lure strike defectors. In *Trans World Airlines vs. Independent Federation of Flight Attendants* (1989), the Court ruled that an employer may entice more recently hired employees to remain at, or come back to, work during a strike by promising them better positions. Even if the union wins the strike, it may not insist that the employer demote crossovers to make room for union members with more seniority. In other words, crossovers not only avoid discipline but they reap a reward. In her majority opinion, Justice Sandra Day O'Connor reaffirmed the *Mackay* decision, arguing that it would be unfair to treat more recently hired permanent striker replacements better than the crossovers, thus extending permanent replacement worker status to strike defectors. By rewarding junior employees who break ranks, and prohibiting the union from disciplining them, the Supreme Court has further weakened the right to strike.[27]

Critics argue that these decisions not only stack the deck in favor of employers but that they also destroy collective bargaining, and ultimately undermine the objectives of the NLRA. The theory of collective bargaining regards economic pressure as essential for bringing the employer to the bargaining table; weakening the right to strike diminishes this pressure. Moreover, when an employer hires permanent replacements, strikers lose interest in resolving the labor dispute that precipitated the strike, and instead must concern themselves with winning their jobs back. This inflames the conflict, as replaced strikers turn to violence and corporate campaigns. Furthermore, the permanent striker replacement strategy encourages employers to bargain in bad faith to provoke a strike, with the aim of breaking the union. Finally, even when the union survives, this strategy leads to distrust, hostility, and bitterness; it undermines cooperation, and generally destroys the conditions necessary for collective bargaining. As Peter Capelli notes, "Hiring permanent replacements means a labor strike is now a fight to the death, rather than a periodic test of wills."[28]

During the late 1980s and early 1990s labor leaders and advocates of labor law reform petitioned Congress to pass legislation banning the use of permanent striker replacements. In 1988, the House of Representatives passed the Workplace Fairness Act (H.R. 4552), which would have prohibited the employment of permanent replacements during the initial ten weeks of a strike. In 1990 the House passed H.R. 3936, and H.R. 5 in 1991 and 1993, which would have placed a complete ban on the use of permanent striker replacements. Despite repeated attempts to pass labor law reform legislation, supporters in Congress could not overcome vetoes and filibusters. In 1995 President Clinton issued Executive Order 12954, which prohibited federal contractors from hiring permanent striker replacements. The Third Circuit Court of Appeals overturned the executive order in *Chamber of Commerce of the United States v. Reich* (1996).[29] The Bush administration has not asked the Supreme Court to review the case, and Congress shows no signs of reviving the issue.

The Erosion of the Right to Strike, the NLRA, and the Reagan NLRB

The permanent striker replacement strategy appears to be the principal encroachment on the right to strike today; it seems to emanate primarily from an aberrant and ill-conceived Supreme Court precedent, and apparently a ban on permanent striker replacements would restore the NLRA and strengthen the right to strike. As I have argued in previous chapters, however, deficiencies in the modern liberal right to strike extend much deeper than judicial decisions. The permanent striker replacement strategy reflects problems with the NLRA itself, its commitment to balance in industrial relations, and the weak administrative capacities it supports. Even if labor law reformers could close this one loophole—which appears increasingly unlikely—the overall policy would still remain ambivalent, and it would still permit employers to break strikes.

First, proponents of the ban give far too much credit to the *Mackay* decision and ignore the statutory basis of the striker replacement strategy. During their hearings on the NLRA in 1935, members of the Senate Committee on Education and Labor explicitly acknowledged an employer's right to hire permanent replacements during a strike: "[The Act] provides that a labor dispute shall be 'current,' and that an employer is free to hasten its end by hiring a new permanent crew of workers and running the plant on a normal basis."[30] Whereas the act specifically banned a number of antiunion activities, it did not forbid hiring replacement workers. If employing permanent striker replacements subverts collective bargaining, why did the act not explicitly prohibit it? And why did the La Follette Civil Liberties Committee, which exposed numerous oppressive labor practices from 1936 to 1939, not investigate the employment of permanent striker replacements?

The statutory basis of the permanent striker replacement strategy is even more evident in the 1947 amendments to the NLRA, which constrain unions' capacity to defend themselves against this tactic. Until the Labor Management Relations Act outlawed them, the closed shop and secondary boycott provided unions with effective economic weapons to resist permanent replacement. Unions could expel strike defectors and, if the union won the strike, force the employer to discharge them. Union members at other workplaces could refuse to handle the products and supplies of a struck employer who had replaced strikers, and they could decline to perform subcontracted work. These forms of self-help and mutual aid existed at the time that the Court enunciated the *Mackay* doctrine, but the 1947 amendments banned the closed shop, strikes to prevent nonunion employees from entering the workplace or to demand their discharge, sympathy strikes, and secondary boycotts. The LMRA also established the union decertification procedure, and denied NLRA protections to supervisory employees, who frequently replace strikers. Moreover, the LMRA acknowledged permanent striker replacement by explicitly prohibiting replaced economic strikers from voting in representation elections.[31] Labor leaders immediately recognized this threat. During the 1948 congressional campaigns, unions attacked the LMRA specifically because it permitted employers to replace strikers and then petition for a decertification election.[32] The permanent striker replacement strategy thus does not arise simply from an offhand remark made in a moldy Supreme Court decision but from the NLRA itself, and especially from the 1947 amendments.

The use of permanent striker replacements is also consistent with the NLRA's commitment to balance and neutrality in labor-management relations. Opponents of the ban argued that the Workplace Fairness Act would tilt the playing field unfairly to the advantage of organized labor. Both sides in the dispute, opponents assert, must risk something—employers risk the loss of production and business, strikers risk the loss of wages and their jobs—but banning permanent striker replacements would greatly diminish strikers' risks and would encourage more strikes. Lynn Martin, then secretary of labor, presented this argument in her testimony to the House Subcommittee on Labor-Management Relations in 1990:

> The balance in collective bargaining is promoted by the threat to use economic weapons, because actual usage often bears too great a cost to workers, employers, and, yes, to the public. . . . A meaningful strike threat may force an

employer to make concessions. On the other hand, the threat of replacement serves as a deterrent to striking and may result in other concessions. . . . If the right to permanently replace economic strikers were prohibited expressly, there would be little incentive for unions to moderate the use of the strike weapon.[33]

Paradoxically, as Paul Weiler's proreform article "Striking a New Balance" illustrates, both advocates and critics argue that the need to balance employees' and employers' bargaining power justifies their respective positions on the ban.

This conception of balance ignores what Claus Offe refers to as the structural asymmetry of power between labor and capital, and mistakenly equates the unequal. Organizing, mobilizing, and exercising power, as well as the comprehension and aggregation of interests, are much more challenging tasks for labor organizations than for employers:

> For the sake of their power, unions are forced to maintain a precarious balance between mobilization of resources and mobilization of activity, between size and collective identity, between bureaucracy (which allows them to *accumulate* power) and internal democracy (which allows them to *exercise* power). None of these dilemmas applies with comparable seriousness to business and employers organizations for the reason that they do not depend on internal democracy, collective identity, or the willingness to engage in solidary action, because of the very fact that they are *already* in a structural power position which renders complications such as these avoidable.[34]

Business interests are objectively given, and businesses pursue them instrumentally. Labor unions, however, have to discover their interests through more dialogical patterns of collective action, which depend on discussions between leaders and the rank and file, strike rallies, strike votes, and other aspects of internal democracy.[35] Businesses are not concerned with internal democracy, and employers do not face the equivalent of "crossover employers" or "permanent employer replacements." Even with a ban on permanent striker replacements, the balance of power would still favor employers.

Proponents of the ban also ignore the weaknesses of the NLRB, and the role that the Reagan NLRB played in the erosion of the right to strike. Although nominally an independent regulatory agency, the NLRB has always been the center of political conflict, as past administrations have used the presidential appointment process to politicize the NLRB.[36] The weakness of stare decisis in administrative law combined with the willingness of new appointees to overturn precedent has contributed to policy oscillation, instability, and confusion about the precise boundaries of the right to strike. Congressional investigations of the Eisenhower and the Kennedy-Johnson boards fueled this tendency. Moreover, the statutory affirmation of the federal appeals courts' authority over the NLRB encourages losing parties to regard NLRB decisions as tentative. The fact that losing parties appeal nearly half of all labor board decisions exhibits the controversy and lack of finality surrounding NLRB decisions.[37]

During the Reagan administration, NLRB policy reversals and administrative delays became particularly problematic, and contributed to the erosion of the right to strike. As with his appointments to other regulatory agencies, Reagan appointed officials to the NLRB who shared his agenda supporting deregulation and opposing constituencies affiliated with the Democratic Party.[38] Observers regarded Reagan's appointment of Donald Dotson as chairman of the NLRB as especially hostile to organized labor and collective bargaining, which, Dotson charged, led to "labor monopoly, the destruction of individual freedom, and the destruction of the marketplace as a mechanism for determining the value of labor."[39] In two years, the Dotson board overturned twenty-nine major precedents. James Gross writes, "The Dotson Board's speedy and extensive review of precedents that conservatives considered pro-union brought about a shift in national labor policy that freed employers in many important ways from constraints of workers and unions." Former NLRB member Peter Walther stated that these reversals tacitly encouraged antiunion employers to follow the various legal strategies outlined above.[40]

The Dotson board's scrutiny of numerous test cases and the Reagan administration's deep cuts in the agency's budgetary allocation led to a growing case backlog, reaching seventeen hundred cases by June 1984, the largest ever, and four times what it had been in 1978. As a result, the average processing period increased from 273 days in 1984 to 395 days in 1989. Between 1984 and 1989, the median case-processing times were the highest in NLRB history, averaging two to three times as long as they were in the 1970s. In some cases, it took seven years before the board finally dispensed with an unfair labor practice complaint.[41] Delays generally impose asymmetrical costs on employees, who must bear the costs of unfair dismissals or other disciplinary actions, and weaken the incentives for employers to bargain in good faith. More timely NLRB decisions in these cases would have contributed to the resolution of the labor disputes and the determination that many were unfair-labor-practice strikes, in which employers may not hire permanent replacements.

The striker replacement strategy, consequently, is indicative of more profound problems in federal labor relations policy. Over the decades, organized labor has experienced growing limitations on employees' rights to engage in collective action: bans on secondary boycotts and sympathy strikes, limits on union security arrangements, limits on union discipline, and the like. Employers have discovered how to oppose unions while remaining within the letter of the law by exercising the NLRA's free speech provisions to make veiled threats, by challenging NLRB determinations of appropriate bargaining units, by exploiting sources of delay in processing cases and administering representation elections, by surface bargaining (meeting the minimum requirements of their duty to bargain but with no intention of reaching an agreement), and so on. Employers have also discovered that the remedial nature of national labor relations policy imposes negligible sanctions on those who flout the law during organizing campaigns and collective bargaining. A ban on permanent striker replacements, moreover, would still permit employers to hire temporary replacements, and it would do nothing to address these other weaknesses in federal labor relations policy.

Industrial Justice and the Permanent Striker Replacement Issue

The permanent striker replacement issue reveals not only the limitations of U. S. labor relations policy but also modern American liberalism's grudging acceptance of the right to strike, and it taps into fundamental weaknesses with modern notions of industrial justice. Originally, Senator Wagner promoted independent labor organizations and an expansive version of collective bargaining in order to secure for workers a voice in industry and to establish a new equity for working Americans. But as the NLRA has evolved, the Supreme Court has construed fairness in neutral, procedural, and voluntaristic terms, and it has avoided reading any substantive standards of justice into the NLRA. The state's role now is to act as a neutral referee, rather than to promote an ideal of citizenship or fair outcomes in the collective bargaining process. The permanent striker replacement strategy does not violate these neutral, procedural, and voluntaristic standards of industrial justice. This strategy, however, deprives workers of their livelihoods, destroys workers' organizations, undermines collective bargaining, devastates marriages, and disrupts community harmony. As such, modern strikebreaking demonstrates how impoverished is the modern liberal concept of industrial justice.

Harvard political theorist Michael Sandel faults modern American liberalism for promoting the ideal of a neutral state that attempts to maximize the individual's liberty to choose his or her own end, without imposing any civic ideal of the good society.[42] In modern American liberalism, fairness demands that the state remain indifferent toward competing conceptions of the good life, so long as the conditions for voluntarism are preserved. This, he argues, has diminished citizenship to the concept of the "unencumbered self," "a person without character, without moral depth," and without the allegiances that one owes other human beings as such: "Not egoists, but strangers, sometimes benevolent, make for citizens in the deontological republic; justice finds its occasion because we cannot know each other, or our ends, well enough to be governed by the common good alone."[43]

Likewise, the modern liberal American state attempts to promote industrial justice without entering into substantive moral discourse that would provide a conception of the common good in collective bargaining law. It is not the purpose of current collective bargaining law to help prepare working Americans to function as full citizens in a self-governing republic, or to support industrial democracy, or to ensure a just wage. Instead, the state treats collective bargaining law as a framework of rights neutral with respect to the varying purposes of competing individuals. That is, the current conception of industrial justice provides no independent standard to judge the morality of the employer who wants to break a union, the striker who remains loyal in the face of hardship, the strikebreaker who takes a striker's job in the midst of conflict, or the crossover who betrays his or her allegiances to workmates. Without a substantive conception of industrial justice, there is no way of specifying the validity of the outcome in advance. Instead, federal labor relations policy tries to design a procedure that is fair per se, so that the outcome is just per se, independent of any substantive standard of industrial justice. This demands that the state remain indifferent toward the union buster, the striker, the strikebreaker, and the crossover, in order to construct a neutral liberal space within which contending parties with differing aims can come to a consensus. Under such a conception of industrial justice, neutralism and voluntarism comprise the pillars of free collective bargaining.

Neutralism in free collective bargaining manifests itself in the state's refusal to rule on the fairness of the terms of collective bargaining proposals. Before 1960 the NLRB and the courts considered imposing good bargaining standards to promote mature negotiations and balanced bargaining relations, and to limit the abuse of bargaining power.[44] Such standards would have permitted the NLRB to declare that an employer's unreasonable demands, or his or her use of certain economic weapons, such as the lockout or permanent replacements, constituted prima facie bad-faith bargaining.

In *NLRB v. Insurance Agents* (1960), however, the Warren Court declared that the NLRA prohibits the state from influencing the terms of a collective bargaining agreement, and determined that regulating either party's choice of economic weapons would permit the state to interfere with the substantive outcome of the bargaining process. Justice Brennan summarized the modern American liberal theory of collective bargaining and its relation to the right to strike:

> Collective bargaining, under a system where the Government does not attempt to control the results of negotiations, cannot be equated with an academic collective search for truth—or even with what might be thought to be the ideal of

one. The parties—even granting the modification of views that may come from a realization of economic interdependence—still proceed from contrary and to an extent antagonistic viewpoints and concepts of self-interest. The presence of economic weapons in reserve, and their actual exercise on occasion by the parties, is [therefore] part and parcel of the system that the Wagner and Taft-Hartley Acts have recognized. . . . Surely it cannot be said that the only economic weapons consistent with good-faith bargaining are those which minimize the pressure on the other party and maximize the disadvantage to the party using them.[45]

This guarantees that collective bargaining is an adversarial process between two contenders, rather than the cooperative process of comanagement that Senator Wagner envisioned. The Court reaffirmed this view in *American Shipbuilding v. NLRB* (1965), when it held that an employer that locks out its employees during a contract dispute does not commit an unfair labor practice, again asserting that the NLRA does not give the state authority to assess the relative power of adversaries nor to deny the use of an economic weapon to one party on this basis.[46] By implication, the use of permanent striker replacements is consistent with the theory of free collective bargaining and the modern liberal conception of industrial justice.

This neutralism, however, limits the modern liberal American state's authority to intervene when an employer decides to bargain to an impasse, provoke a strike, permanently replace the strikers, and decertify the union. Technically, these actions constitute an unfair labor practice under the NLRA, but without substantive standards for judging the reasonableness and fairness of an employer's proposals and actions, a shrewd employer can evade the statutory duty to bargain in good faith. Under the law, an employer must have "an open mind and a sincere desire to reach agreement," and "a sincere effort must be made to reach common ground." An employer engages in bad-faith bargaining when it fails "to participate in the deliberations so as to indicate a present intention to find a basis for agreement."[47] The determination that an employer has engaged in bad-faith bargaining, consequently, depends on a subjective assessment of the firm's "state of mind."

The NLRB and the courts have developed some minimal guidelines for inferring whether an employer has engaged in bad-faith bargaining. Refusal to meet with union representatives on a timely basis, refusal to compromise on any issue, refusal to make counterproposals, refusal to recognize statutory obligations in writing, refusal to put the agreement in writing, refusal to provide corroborating financial data of business necessity, and negotiating directly with employees rather than their authorized representatives indicate to the NLRB a refusal to bargain in good faith. The NLRB must consider the totality of circumstances—the board must establish a pattern of behavior in order to interpret the employer's state of mind in the collective bargaining process.[48] But as long as an employer fulfills these minimal procedures, and the state suspends judgment on the substantive fairness of proposals, a canny and dissembling negotiator can bluff his or her way past these guidelines, and make unreasonable demands in order to provoke a strike.

The modern liberal conception of industrial justice also presupposes voluntarism—the principle that freedom consists of "pursuing our own good in our own way, so long as we do not attempt to deprive others of theirs, or impede their efforts to obtain it."[49] The only obligations that modern liberalism recognizes are those that individuals voluntarily consent to. Thus, the 1935 NLRA protects worker self-organization and collective bargaining in order to promote "full freedom of association" and "actual liberty of contract." The 1947 LMRA protects the right to refrain from union activities and prohibits the closed shop, in order to defend individual rights against coercion by labor unions. The theory of free collective bargaining disavows compulsory arbitration and promotes voluntary collective agreements between employers and employees. Voluntarism in labor law permits "employees to freely exercise their right to join unions, be good, bad or indifferent members, or abstain from joining any union without imperiling their livelihood."[50] Voluntarism also ensures that, after the collective agreement lapses, the employer has virtually no further legal obligations toward its striking employees.[51]

During public debates over the proposed Workplace Fairness Act and President Clinton's 1995 executive order, representatives of the National Association of Manufacturers, the United States Chamber of Commerce, and the National Association of Independent Businesses argued that the proposed ban on permanent replacement workers would violate the NLRA's commitment to voluntarism by infringing on individual workers' right *not* to strike. Section 7 of the 1947 amendments protects an employee's right to refrain from concerted activities, and declares that forcing an employee to engage in such activities, and compelling an employer to discriminate against him or her, constitute unfair labor practices. As Reed Larson, president of the National Right to Work Committee, testified to the House Committee on Economic and Educational Opportunities:

> The prime goal of union officials is to control workers. Indeed, no less an authority than Secretary Reich has acknowledged this fact. . . . "In order to maintain themselves, unions have got to have some ability to strap their members to the mast. The only way unions can exercise countervailing power is to hold their members' feet to the fire."[52]

Broadening the right to strike, Larson indicated, would conflict with modern American liberalism's commitment to voluntarism. Permanent replacements and defectors who cross the picket line are merely pursuing their own good in their own way; enforcing the strike impedes their liberty. Replacing one's employees, taking the job of someone entangled in a labor dispute, and betraying one's allegiance to fellow employees, do not offend the concept of voluntarism, but hindering these actions does. These are matters of personal conscience, not relevant from the standpoint of industrial justice.

The reduction of industrial justice to neutralism and voluntarism, and the refusal to consider standards of substantive justice have contributed to the poverty of modern liberal discourse in the field of labor relations. Thus, throughout the legislative hearings concerning the Workplace Fairness Act, none of the expert witnesses ever morally condemned the use of permanent striker replacements.[53] Proponents argued that the use of permanent striker replacements led to an imbalance in bargaining power, subverted the NLRA, reduced productivity, and was unfair, but none ever argued that it violated norms of civic obligation and civic virtue. Even the euphemism "permanent replacement workers" exhibits an awkward attempt to circumvent moral judgment.

The frequent use of gaming metaphors in discussions of labor relations policy further illustrates the poverty of modern liberal discourse in industrial relations. Proponents of the ban argued that it would help to create "a fair contest" or "a level playing field."[54] As UAW president Owen Bieber observed: "What we have now is a riverboat gambler policy, with more and more employers forcing strikes and gambling that after years of costly litigation, no unfair labor practice will be found."[55] Likewise, opponents of reform contended that fairness demands that both players have something at risk in the contest.[56] Note, for example, Justice Sandra Day O'Connor's opinion in *Trans World Airlines v. International Federation of Flight Attendants* (1989):

> We see no reason why those employees who chose not to gamble on the success of the strike should suffer the consequences when the gamble proves unsuccessful. Requiring junior crossovers, who themselves cannot displace the newly hired permanent replacements, and "who rank lowest in seniority" to be displaced by more senior full-term strikers is precisely to visit the consequences of the lost gamble on those who refused to take the risk.[57]

Justice O'Connor accepts the premise that the state ought to act as a referee, neutral toward "winners" and "losers" and toward competing aims, and suggests that fairness in gambling is an appropriate paradigm for just labor relations. This reinforces the outlook that equates social justice with the rules of fair play, focusing on procedure while bracketing the morality of the game and the individual players' ultimate purposes.

In his personal account, *Confessions of a Union Buster,* former labor relations consultant Martin Jay Levitt frequently refers to his previous occupation as a game. "School, jobs, credit, taxes, lawsuits, sex: life was a series of games, not in the sense of entertainment, but games in that every circumstance was a contest that would produce a winner and a loser." Levitt describes how he helped employers "play hardball" with their employees by developing "a game plan" in which he "stretched every rule in the book."[58] The permanent striker replacement strategy was one of the gambits he engaged in. He chose his ends freely, but not out of an ideological or moral commitment to union-free work environments; he describes himself not as a crusader but as a conquistador. Union busting was a thrilling blood sport, rather than a quest for justice and fairness. Labor-management consultants like Levitt provide an object lesson in what Sandel's unencumbered self may lead to.

Permanent striker replacements and strike defectors provide a contrasting example. Opponents of the ban regard striker replacements as independent-minded free agents who resist unionism, and who only want to work free of union coercion and striker violence.[59] Union leaders and proponents of the ban, not surprisingly, consider them amoral opportunists who betray their fellow wage earners by selfishly depriving others of their livelihoods. Anecdotal accounts, such as Getman's study of the paper workers' strike in Jay, Maine, indicate that they are neither heroes nor villains, but wage earners so desperate for work that they become pawns in this game. These unencumbered selves suffer the loss of their union affiliations, ostracism by their neighbors, alienation from family members, and the contempt of the community, for insecure jobs that frequently are not permanent.

The paradoxical law that permits the employment of strikebreakers arises from defects in the liberal conception of industrial justice. Neutralism and voluntarism fail to secure equality and liberty in labor relations. Modern American liberalism fails to provide its proponents with adequate language to criticize employers who betray their employees and strike defectors who abandon their loyalties. Instead, proponents are left with the paltry complaint that those who employ strikebreakers do not play fairly. The right to strike is the right to engage in *concerted* activity, but the modern liberal conception of justice brackets all discussion of common purpose. Banning the employment of permanent striker replacements may remove an inconsistency in the National Labor Relations Act, but it will not resolve the modern liberal ambivalence toward the right to strike. A more robust defense of the right to strike in the United States will require the revival of a civic discourse that recognizes the intimate connection between employment rights and American citizenship.[60]

9

"We deplore strikes because of the inconvenience"

Modern American Liberalism and the Right to Strike

As the three preceding chapters have demonstrated, during the postwar era American workers witnessed a slow deterioration in the right to strike. Since World War II, workers may only exercise this right within a narrow range of workplace issues, disconnected from broader social policy concerns and disengaged from progressive social struggles. Even within the domain of industrial relations, the right to strike remains precarious, because employers may hire strikebreakers and eventually seek decertification of the union. The restricted and precarious status of this right in the United States today does not arise simply from quirks in social policy or in labor law but stems from a deeper, underlying ambivalence in modern American liberalism toward this right. On the one hand, modern American liberalism supports the right to strike as a legitimate and fundamental principle of collective bargaining, and affirms this right as a necessary component of a free society. On the other hand, modern American liberalism does not provide a vigorous defense of this right. In *theory*, modern American liberalism acknowledges the right to strike, but in *practice* it reveals a grudging acceptance of this right, a "yes, but . . ." that merely concedes the right to strike, but denies its status as a citizenship right.

In this chapter I analyze this ambivalence toward workers' rights to engage in collective action, with the focus on four branches of modern American liberalism: industrial pluralism; Keynesian liberalism; economic liberalism; and rights-based liberalism. None provides a robust defense of the right to strike as a fundamental citizenship right. Modern American liberalism cannot furnish a coherent justification, because the right to strike is essentially a collective right, and because it necessarily conflicts with other rights. In the final chapter I argue that it makes more sense to regard the right to strike as a citizenship right (rather than as a commercial right) and that the revival of civic republican discourse would provide a more coherent and less equivocal justification for it.

Industrial Pluralism, Free Collective Bargaining, and the Right to Strike

Of all branches of modern American liberalism, industrial pluralism arguably had the greatest impact on the development of industrial relations during the postwar era, dominating the field from the late 1940s to the present. Industrial pluralism influenced a diverse group of academics, including labor economists, sociologists, legal scholars, and political scientists, as well as a large number of industrial relations practitioners and government officials. The most prominent adherents were among the era's most respected university professors and men of public affairs; they included John Dunlop, George Shultz, Clark Kerr, Archibald Cox, Arthur Kornhauser, Richard Lester, William F. Whyte, and Jack Barbash.[1] Because industrial pluralists promoted organized labor and collective bargaining, one might expect that they would have unequivocally supported the right to strike. In fact, industrial pluralists expressed deep reservations about this right and supported it only under limited conditions.

Although industrial pluralism was rooted in the New Deal labor relations framework and the policies of the National War Labor Board, this outlook was very much a product of the broader liberal intellectual thought of the postwar period.[2] At its foundation was an ideological rejection of class conflict as the driving force in labor-management relations. This was combined with a recognition that industrialization had rendered obsolete the individualistic assumptions of nineteenth-century liberalism. The pluralistic social theory of the 1950s provided a middle path for the study of industrial conflict.[3]

According to industrial pluralists, industrial conflict is neither the product of the capitalist relations of production nor a manifestation of dysfunctional employment relations, but rather a natural product of the social complexity that accompanies industrialization. Industrial disputes arise out of the employees' discontent over low wages, dissatisfying working conditions, or low status, that is, from the employees' subjective state, rather than from subordination, unjust treatment, or the wage system.[4] Industrial conflict, therefore, is not pathological but natural, and, within certain limits, functional, providing a safety valve for worker discontent and permitting the industrial system to make necessary adjustments.[5] Despite their adversarial relationship, labor and management have a mutual interest in the free enterprise system and in maintaining uninterrupted production, raising productivity, and resolving their day-to-day disputes.[6] Over the long run, therefore, the industrial relations system tends toward equilibrium.[7] With their rejection of class struggle and acceptance of limited intergroup conflict, industrial pluralists thus fell squarely within the mainstream of consensus liberalism.

Industrial pluralists believed that because industrial conflicts are not symptomatic of a dysfunctional or unjust society, they are manageable problems that lend themselves to technical adjustments by industrial relations experts. Minor interventions by the state (or by private mediators acting on the state's behalf) can help smooth out the bumps in labor relations without compelling a settlement, seizing a business, or nationalizing an industry. Thus, industrial pluralists did not challenge the existing system of authority, property relations, production, or distribution.

Instead, industrial pluralists expressed an abiding faith in collective bargaining as the proper procedure for fine-tuning the employment relationship. Free collective bargaining presupposed mutual respect, open communication, a problem-solving orientation to disputes, and willingness to compromise.[8] It also provided a practical means of containing industrial conflicts. Frederick Harbison noted:

> First, [collective bargaining] provides a drainage channel for specific dissatisfactions and frustrations which workers experience on the job; second; it helps to "humanize" the operation of the essentially impersonal price system by making it generally palatable to workers as a group; and, third, it absorbs the energies and interests of the leaders of labor who might be inclined to work for the overthrow of capitalism if this avenue of activity were lacking.[9]

Arthur Ross was even blunter: "One of the virtues of collective bargaining in its various forms (including the strike) is that it permits the formulation of limited issues which are amenable to resolution and blurs over the large differences of principle which can never really be settled."[10]

From this, one might suppose that industrial pluralists were stalwart supporters of the right to strike, which is an essential component of collective bargaining. In their writings, however, one detects profound reservations, and at best an equivocal acceptance of the right to strike as an instrument of collective bargaining.

> We value collective bargaining because it yields agreements that reflect the needs and desires of labor as well as management. We deplore strikes and lock-

outs because of the inconvenience they cause especially to bystanders. Yet the strike and the lockout are means of stimulating bargaining and inducing the parties to reach agreement.[11]

Industrial pluralists generally acknowledged the utility of the collective bargaining strike in which workers collectively stop working during an impasse in order to demonstrate their economic power and to test their employers' resolve. Sumner Slichter observed, "The willingness of each side to stand a shutdown is the real force behind the position taken by each side in the negotiations."[12] Such garden-variety economic strikes accorded with wage bargaining theory and with collective bargaining narrowly conceived, but they represent only one category of strike. Industrial pluralists, while voicing support for this sort of strike, showed little support for union recognition strikes, strikes to protest employer breaches of contract, wildcat strikes, and emergency strikes that do not fit into the framework of collective bargaining. Instead, they promoted administrative procedures as substitutes for these other forms of work-based protest. These alternative procedures have proven to be less satisfactory than direct economic action.

For example, industrial pluralists rejected the recognition strike and supported the NLRB-sponsored certification of representation election. Such an election follows strict administrative procedures, from the filing of a petition to a secret ballot conducted under NLRB supervision. Although this appears to substitute a democratic process for a bitter economic struggle, employers have learned how to exploit various features of federal labor law, such as permissive "employer free speech" provisions and "appropriate bargaining unit determination" procedures. The employer free speech provision permits an employer to mount a vigorous public relations campaign against unionization prior to a representation election, as long as the campaign involves warnings rather than direct threats. An employer has a right to hold captive-audience meetings where supervisors warn employees that unionizing might lead to plant closure, but union supporters do not have a corresponding right to campaign at the workplace. The appropriate bargaining unit determination procedure permits employers to delay the election by contesting the NLRB's decision regarding which workers may vote in the representation election; such delays are invariably disadvantageous to the union, even when the employer commits no unfair labor practices. After a successful election, moreover, the employer is under no obligation to sign a contract, although the National Labor Relations Act requires management to participate in the collective bargaining process. Since the 1960s, management consultants well versed in the subtleties and limitations of the NLRA have provided a burgeoning service to employers who want to stave off unionization without violating the letter of the law.[13]

Industrial pluralists also condemned the jurisdictional strike, which involves interunion rivalries rather than labor disputes with the employer.[14]

These strikes erupt when an outside union attempts to force workers to change their union affiliation. As such, they interfere with the collective bargaining system by forcing a work stoppage on an already organized workplace. Jurisdictional strikes, however, also occur when the employer improperly reassigns work from an employee in one union to another who is not in that union. In any case, jurisdictional strikes were much more common during the 1930s and 1940s, when emergent industrial unions challenged the jurisdictional lines of craft-based AFL unions, but they became rare after the 1955 AFL-CIO merger. Concern over this sort of internecine conflict prompted Congress to include provisions in the 1947 amendments that permit employers to petition the NLRB for a decertification election when they suspect that their employees do not support their union. This provides the employees with a democratic alternative to economic struggle, but, as noted in chapter 8, it also permits employers to seek decertification as part of a permanent striker replacement strategy.

Industrial pluralists also rejected wildcat strikes and "quickie" strikes during the term of the contract. In the past, workers turned to such strikes when employers violated work rules or otherwise violated the collective bargaining agreement; as such, they imposed an immediate sanction on the employer for any breach. Industrial pluralists, however, spurned direct action to enforce labor agreements, and have generally supported the Supreme Court's "Steelworkers' Trilogy" decisions, which encourage private arbitration of grievances as a peaceful alternative and infer no-strike clauses in labor agreements with grievance arbitration provisions.[15] Employees who believe the employer has violated their rights under the agreement or under law may file grievances through their union representative. If they are not resolved informally, the grievance goes to an independent arbitrator, who is hired by the local union and employer to make a final determination on the merits of the case. If the grievance still remains unresolved, the union may file an unfair labor practice complaint with the regional NLRB, and so forth. Unlike a wildcat strike, this process redefines the employers' breach of contract as a worker *grievance,* places the burden of proof on the employee, and permits the employer to continue the disputed action until there is a final determination.[16] Grievance arbitration, moreover, treats grievances on a case-by-case basis, even when several arise from the same disputed action. This is time consuming and places a financial burden on the union, which shares the costs of private arbitration. It also permits employers to "jam" the grievance process, which frustrates attempts to enforce labor agreements.[17]

Industrial pluralists also expressed apprehensions about major collective bargaining strikes, as well as "national emergency strikes"—work stoppages that interfere with national defense, public health, safety, and the general welfare. These include industrywide strikes by railway workers, coal miners, and steel workers, as well as local strikes by public utility and hospital employees. Such strikes presumably have an adverse effect on innocent by-standers, interfering with other businesses that depend on the struck em-ployers' services and products and sometimes harming the health and safety of the public at large.[18] By declaring that a work stoppage is a national emer-gency strike, the president may order the attorney general to seek an injunc-tion against an otherwise legal strike. The "national emergency strike" des-ignation, however, remains ill-defined, and industrial pluralists offered no convincing evidence that any major strikes have threatened public health and safety or national security since passage of the LMRA. Although anecdotal evidence suggests that certain strikes had the potential for harming the pub-lic interest (such as the 1977–78 coal strike, the last time a president declared a national emergency strike), officials still must weigh the potential harm of such strikes against the potential harm of suppressing them. LeRoy and Johnson, for example, argue that this provision tends to cast striking unions in a negative public light, that presidents have declared national emergency strikes more out of political expediency than national necessity, and that this has seriously eroded the right to strike in general.[19]

In conclusion, industrial pluralists did not regard strikes as justifiable ac-tions calling for support but as problems demanding solution. Thus, Clinton Golden, Virginia Parker, and others, under the auspices of the National Plan-ning Association, investigated the "causes of industrial peace." William F. Whyte similarly studied the "pattern for industrial peace," and Richard Lester examined the maturation of labor organizations, the narrowing scope of con-flict and the institutionalization of conflict into orderly procedures. By 1960, Arthur Ross and Paul Hartman proclaimed the "withering away of the strike," that free collective bargaining had made worker militancy obsolete and unnec-essary. In all cases, the researchers suggested that the goal of industrial rela-tions is stability, and that the system of free collective bargaining would ensure that stability, without any alterations in basic social arrangements, or the ex-pansion of workers' citizenship rights, or even any augmentation and exten-sion of collective bargaining.[20] A. H. Raskin, a *New York Times* editor who frequently contributed to the industrial relations literature, summed up this outlook: "I see no reason why in this institution alone, of all facets of our so-ciety, we should exalt the right to make war as the hallmark of industrial civi-lization when we seek to exorcize it everywhere else, even in global relations of sovereign powers."[21] From such a perspective, the current decline in the U.S. strike rate, and the deterioration of the right to strike, present no difficulties.

Keynesian Liberalism, Wage Stabilization, and the Right to Strike

Robert Lekachman has described the thirty-year period from the passage of the 1946 Employment Act until the economic crises of the mid-1970s as "the age of Keynes," during which Keynesian liberals dominated national economic policy making. Keynesian economics provided a supportive policy environment for unions, collective bargaining, and a limited right to strike, and the start of the downward spiral in U.S. strike rates coincided with the breakdown of the Keynesian consensus in the mid-1970s. Keynesian liberalism, however, also manifested an ambivalent and conflicted position toward the right to strike, and it could provide no steadfast defense of that right when the right to strike contributed to wage-push inflation in the 1970s.

The term "Keynesians" refers to an influential group of policy intellectuals and policy makers who advocated the use of fiscal policy instruments to manage the business cycle. Their policy objectives included increasing the U.S. gross national product while maintaining stable prices and low unemployment, with a minimal amount of state intervention in production, property relations, private investment decisions, and the distribution of income. The hallmark of Keynesianism was its acceptance of deficit public spending as a countercyclical measure during economic contractions.

Keynesians were among the best-known economists and economic advisors of the postwar era; they included Leon Keyserling (Senator Wagner's former aide and chairman of the Council of Economic Advisors during the Truman administration), John Kenneth Galbraith, Walter Heller, Gardner Ackley, James Tobin, Kermit Gordon, and Paul Samuelson. Although this includes a rather diverse group of economists, all were the direct intellectual heirs to the revolution in economic theory that John Maynard Keynes had initiated with the publication of his *General Theory of Employment and Money*. Social democratic governments in postwar Europe embraced Keynesianism as a plan for active state intervention in the economy. In the United States, Keynesian thinking directly influenced the 1946 Employment Act, and Keynesian economists enjoyed their greatest influence in public affairs through the Council of Economic Advisors. Keynesian theory provided a coherent framework of economic analysis that dominated modern American liberalism from the late 1940s until about 1980.[22]

Even though Keynes did not publish his *General Theory* until 1936, Keynesian thinking shaped the 1935 NLRA. Secular stagnationists like Keyserling, the author of the NLRA, adhered to a proto-Keynesian view that underconsumption was the underlying cause of the Great Depression. The NLRA thus affirmed employees' rights to engage in concerted activities as a means of raising wages, increasing mass consumption, and stimulating economic recovery. Indeed, John Maynard Keynes had lived through the British government's attempts to drive down wages during Britain's inflationary crisis of the mid-1920s and the subsequent general strike of 1926, and considered the efforts of the trade unions to defend their wages as economically sound. By the late 1930s, Keynesian thinking had advanced to the United States, and American Keynesians like Alvin Hansen wrote approvingly of collective action as being consistent with Keynesian goals.

Keynesian policies, moreover, fostered economic conditions conducive to exercising these collective action rights. Ever since the devastating defeats of the late nineteenth century, labor leaders had learned to exercise the right to strike strategically, during periods of economic growth and low unemployment. Keynesian policies supported these conditions, which reduce employers' willingness to resist lengthy work stoppages and limit the supply of replacement workers. Hence, Keynesian theory and practice originally buttressed workers' rights to engage in collective action.

Early American Keynesians, such as Alvin Hansen, had generally supported an interventionist state, democratic planning, greater economic equality, and stronger workers' organizations. These more social democratic goals were apparent in the National Resources Planning Board's proposals and in the rejected Full Employment Act of 1945.[23] However, American Keynesian liberalism underwent a transformation during the postwar era that lessened its support for structural reform and eventually led these later Keynesians to regard labor union power as a source of wage and price instability.[24] According to Margaret Weir, resurgent business groups associated social Keynesianism with the most liberal economic policies of the New Deal, and feared that the proposed Full Employment Act would strengthen organized labor after the war. Southern agricultural interests rejected the more intrusive social Keynesian policies as a threat to private control over the southern black agricultural workforce.[25] Consequently, postwar Keynesian liberalism developed a tentative and more moderate approach to economic management and social policy. The 1946 Employment Act retreated from the aim of economic planning for full employment, and instead established the Council of Economic Advisors, which has the more limited responsibilities of monitoring the economy and advising the president.

In addition, the intellectual culture of Keynesian economics underwent a transformation. Paul Samuelson's synthesis of Keynesian economics with more traditional neoclassical economics produced a more technocratic approach to economic policy, which narrowed the economic agenda to managing the business cycle through the manipulation of federal spending and taxing. Keynesian economists came to view the problems of growth, full employment, inflation, and investment as technical rather than structural, and accepted the existing social and political arrangements as given. In their view, the market system did not call for an intrusive state, but only required fine-tuning for the purposes of stabilization and growth.[26] The Keynesian liberals of the postwar era sought to raise the standard of living without interfering with market liberty, private property rights, or the distribution of power in society. As such, they remained indifferent to the struggle between labor organizations and employers. Keynesian liberalism was more concerned with the citizen as consumer than the citizen as worker.

Persistent inflation during the postwar years further weakened Keynesian liberals' support for workers' rights to engage in collective action. As early as 1945, Lord Beveridge and others realized that full employment, fiscal stimulus, and collective bargaining offered a recipe for inflation: "Under conditions of full employment, can a rising spiral of wages and prices be prevented if collective bargaining, with the right to strike, remains absolutely free? Can the right to strike be limited generally in a free society?"[27] This was the conventional "demand-pull" inflation such as depicted by the Phillips curve, for which Keynesians recommended modest fiscal and monetary adjustments to balance unemployment and inflation. Throughout the 1950s and 1960s, however, a slow increase in both inflation and unemployment revealed a shift in the Phillips curve, and suggested that inflation did not respond to simple Keynesian controls.

Economists began to refer to this new inflation as "wage-push" inflation when monetary authorities failed to eliminate inflation after raising interest rates and causing several mild business contractions. Strong unions offered a convenient explanation, and highly publicized strikes in the steel industry particularly provoked blame. Steelworkers walked out on four occasions during the 1950s to press for higher wages. During the 1952 strike, President Truman had attempted to seize the steel mills, and in 1959, after a 116-day work stoppage, President Eisenhower had implemented national emergency strike procedures to end the strike. On all four occasions, steelworkers won raises, and steel manufacturers boosted their prices.

According to the conventional explanation of wage-push inflation, corporations and unions in an oligopolistic economy have sufficient market power to set wages and prices independently of supply and demand. John Hicks, one of the foremost Keynesian economists of the period, described it as a "fix price system," in which businesses determine prices based on the normal costs of production plus a profit. If wages go up, corporations pass higher costs along to consumers through higher prices. As wages in one industry rise, wage earners in other industries also press for raises. If too many businesses engage in administered pricing, economic expansion stops short of full employment.[28] Deficit spending then only leads to more union demands for higher wages.

An alternative explanation argues that wage-push inflation is a consequence of the postwar settlement, and a by-product of the Keynesian solution for controlling social conflict.[29] An expanding economy supported higher wages without any redistribution of income and provided the conditions for the postwar labor-management accord. Employers submitted to narrow collective bargaining and to productivity-based annual wage increases in exchange for management authority over subjects that involve the core of entrepreneurial control—pricing, investment, product development, production technologies, and the like. Wage-push inflation was the price of preserving industrial peace and management authority. During the 1945–46 GM strike, Walter Reuther had challenged this arrangement when he demanded a 30 percent wage increase with no increase in prices. The strike settlement, however, provided wage increases with no price controls. The 1950 "Treaty of Detroit" between GM and the UAW further secured industrial peace in exchange for cost-of-living allowances and generous fringe benefits.[30] This became the model throughout the 1950s and 1960s, not only for the UAW but for industrial unions generally. Entirely eliminating inflation required altering the compromise that established management's au-thority to set prices and provided the unionized workforce with a middle-class standard of living.

Rather than challenging the postwar settlement, Keynesian liberals proposed incomes policies to supplement their fiscal and monetary policies. John Kenneth Galbraith observed that "at full employment there is no mechanism for holding prices and wages stable. This stabilization . . . is a function of the state . . . and [therefore] a system of wage and price restraint is inevitable in the industrial system."[31] Incomes policies, however, clashed with the right to strike under free collective bargaining.

The history of federal wage stabilization programs exhibits this conflict with the right to strike and illustrates how wage controls generate industrial conflicts that eventually undermine the controls. During World War II, federal wage guidelines depended on a voluntary no-strike pledge and federal arbitration of labor disputes. The no-strike pledge began to break down in 1944, and by 1946 the U.S. strike rate skyrocketed, due to workers' desire to catch up with inflation and unions' efforts to consolidate wartime gains. The postwar strike wave destroyed President Truman's efforts to stabilize wages and prices during the reconversion period.[32] Truman again imposed a wage stabilization policy during the Korean War. When the steelworkers struck for wage increases beyond these guidelines, Truman attempted to seize the steel mills. A coal miners' strike later that year dealt the final blow to the Korean War incomes policy. Presidents Kennedy and Johnson promoted voluntary wage and price guideposts pegged to the annual increase in labor productivity. A 1966 machinists' strike against the airline industry overturned these guideposts as well.[33]

Thus, some labor organization will eventually challenge an incomes policy. Unions may strike directly against the wage guidelines, as the coal miners did in a series of nationwide strikes between 1943 and 1946. In other cases, wage earners may strike to force the wage board to make concessions on a particular wage issue, as the steelworkers did in 1952. Any strike, however, threatens the existence and legitimacy of the wage stabilization policy. According to Melvin W. Reder, under Keynesian policies, the federal government has "its own objectives of economic performance whose achievement may be imperiled by the content of wage settlements."[34] Successful wage stabilization depends on government intervention to prevent wage disputes from erupting into strikes, or to force an end to a work stoppage. Such policies thus lead to the politicization of strikes and the weakening of the right to strike.[35]

Keynesians argued that authorities need to find some way to protect wage restraint programs from union challenges.[36] Some recommended removing NLRA protections for strikers, enjoining strikes, fining or jailing strike leaders, and seizing struck facilities. Others, during the 1970s, proposed neocorporatist arrangements to develop and administer incomes policies, believing that they would produce more acceptable guidelines. As Daniel Quinn Mills suggested, "The most favorable condition for government intervention in disputes is one in which national leadership of employers and unions have agreed in advance to assist the government in the settlement of disputes within the stabilization criteria."[37]

Institutional arrangements in the United States, however, do not support the adoption of neocorporatist incomes policies. Collective bargaining in the United States is highly decentralized and fragmented. No peak employers' organizations exist in the United States. The peak labor organization, the AFL-CIO, lacks the authority to intervene in its constituent unions' wage bargaining. Some unions, like the National Education Association, are not members of the AFL-CIO. The LMRA has eliminated industry-level bargaining structures, and NLRB "appropriate bargaining unit" determinations have reinforced bargaining at the local level. Statutory restrictions on broad-based concerted activity (such as the bans on secondary picketing and secondary boycotts) reinforce the decentralized character of U.S. industrial relations. Even if U.S. industrial relations could support societal-level bargaining, Keynesian liberals expressed unwarranted optimism that unions would support the state's objectives, rather than pursue their own agenda.[38]

Keynesian liberals were unable to manage the economic stagnation, rising inflation, and high unemployment of the 1970s within the existing political-economic arrangements. By 1980, the Keynesian consensus had disintegrated, as had the economic conditions supporting a limited right to strike. Keynesian liberal equivocation over workers' rights to engage in collective action paved the way for the Reagan-era wage policy that deliberately weakened labor unions and collective bargaining. The Keynesian liberal analysis of wage-push inflation warranted diminishing the power of those institutions that contributed to inflation as one alternative method of attaining the state's economic objectives. Consumers today enjoy low inflation partly because of the deterioration of the right to strike.

Economic Liberalism and the Right to Strike

Since the breakdown of the Keynesian consensus in the 1970s, economic liberalism has enjoyed a revival as a public philosophy and as one of the dominant policy discourses of the New Right.[39] In its simplest terms, economic liberalism promotes free markets as a means of unleashing greater efficiency and economic energies, and as a method of guaranteeing greater individual liberty. Economic liberals consider all forms of collective action as suspect, and present some of the strongest arguments against the right to strike.[40]

Most recently, economic liberalism has been associated with economists of the Chicago school, including such luminaries as Milton Friedman and Joseph Stigler. This branch of modern liberalism, however, has extensive international and historical roots. It extends to the Austrian school of economists— Friedrich Hayek, Ludwig von Mises, and Fritz Machlup, among others—and includes British economists such as Lionel Robbins and Frank H. Knight. Although popularly seen as conservative, they openly embrace the term "liberal," and identify themselves with classic liberal theorists such as Adam Smith, David Hume, and John Locke.[41] Their advocacy of unfettered markets places them at odds with certain other modern liberals, but their passionate defense of individual liberties, formal equality, and the rule of law, as well as their rejection of socialism, situate them squarely within the liberal tradition.[42]

Although economic liberals have sometimes asserted that they do not oppose the collective right to quit if employers do not meet workers' demands, they vehemently reject the right to strike if it means barring employment to other workers.[43] Arthur Shenfield argues that "the strikers' demand for an inalienable right to, and property in, a particular job cannot be made conformable to the principle of liberty under law for all."[44] Hayek asserted, "The whole basis of our free society is gravely threatened by the powers arrogated by the unions."[45] Henry Simons concurred:

[Unions] are essentially occupational armies, born and reared amidst violence, led by fighters, and capable of becoming peaceful only as their power becomes irresistible. . . . Peaceful strikes, even in the absence of overt violence, are a meaningless conception when they involve disruption of an elaborate production process with intricate division of labor.[46]

Although economic liberals accept the legitimacy of voluntary labor organizations, they reject the right to strike as a violation of individual liberty and the free market.

Their objections to the right to strike fall into two categories: economic objections, which criticize strikes as an unnatural interference with free markets; and political objections, which disapprove of strikes as unjust. Of these, the political arguments are more compelling.

Economic criticisms stress the efficiency of free markets and the natural order that markets create. Successful strikes artificially drive up labor costs by denying to other workers access to part of the labor market and increase wage inequality by forcing other workers to take lower-paying jobs. This worsens unemployment, because employers will have no incentive to hire more workers and will instead invest in labor-saving technologies. Consumers pay higher prices, and investors avoid strike-prone industries. Strikes permit the organized to win higher wages, but the subsequent misallocation of resources diminishes the welfare of the community. As William Hutt put it: "The disruption of the market system by the simple, concerted withdrawal of labor is in itself damaging to the community."[47]

Economic liberals also contend that strikes disrupt the spontaneous social order created by free markets. Hayek referred to this spontaneous order as "catallaxy" and argued that no other human agency has the capacity to create the degree of social organization that arises naturally through market processes.[48] The labor market is a complex system of information and communication, and it permits individuals to pursue their chosen occupations with a minimum of interference. Strikes disrupt this order by generating hostility on the job, undermining morale, reducing cooperation, and disrupting strikers' and employers' home lives. Disharmony spills out into the community, divides neighbors, and upsets daily life.

Although these economic criticisms raise valid objections to collective action, they do not provide irrefutable arguments for abolishing the right to strike. If the right to strike is, indeed, a *right,* then utilitarian objections alone cannot invalidate it. Arthur Okun countered:

> The domain of rights is full of infringements on the calculus of economic efficiency. Our rights can be viewed as inefficient, because they preclude prices that would promote economizing, choices that would invoke comparative advantage, incentives that would augment socially productive effort, and trades that potentially would benefit buyer and seller.[49]

If the right to strike is a right, the costs it imposes on society are no more relevant than the costs of the right to vote, the right to due process, or the prohibition against involuntary servitude. In practice, society restricts the harmful exercise of rights all the time. But the burden of proof rests on those who would abridge a right to demonstrate that it imposes an unacceptable harm. According to Kornhauser, Dubin, and Ross, between 1933 and 1954 "the number of workers participating in strikes is roughly the same order of magnitude as the number suffering industrial accidents," and strikes diminished the total available working time by less than .5 percent.[50] Although this does not measure all the related costs, it indicates that the economic inefficiencies alone do not justify revoking this right.

One may also raise doubts about the second objection. Whether ideal markets generate spontaneous order is a matter of speculation, but the history of the existing market system demonstrates that it generates social disorder—depressions, crashes, structural dislocations, externalities, and so on. Numerous strikes have occurred in response to the social discord generated by the market, rather than the other way around; the strike waves of the 1870s, 1890s, and 1930s are cases in point. The contention that abolishing the right to strike will eliminate social disharmony at the workplace ignores the lessons of the era of industrialization, when suppression of the right to strike only inflamed labor disputes. Indeed, the NLRA, by legalizing the right to strike, has reduced the overall violence and discord associated with labor disputes.[51]

The economic liberals' political objections are more difficult to dismiss. If the right to strike is a *right,* then its validity stands or falls on the principle of justice. Economic liberalism is not just an economic theory—it is a political theory, which proposes a particular theory of justice. Friedrich Hayek, the most philosophical of economic liberals, based his theory of justice on the political thought of David Hume, who asserted "three fundamental laws of nature, *that of the stability of possessions, of transference by consent, and of performance of promises.*"[52] These principles of justice undergird economic liberals' support for the liberty of contract, property rights, as well as the free market. The right to strike interferes with each of these.

Hayek described this theory of justice as "commutative" to underscore his rejection of distributive, or social, justice. For Hayek, who regarded "social justice" as a meaningless, even pernicious, concept, justice had nothing to do with substantive outcomes.[53] All values originate with the individual, and individual liberty—not social justice—is the condition for all other values. Commutative justice guarantees the greatest amount of individual liberty, defined as "the possibility of a person's acting according to his own decisions and plans, in contrast to the position of one who is irrevocably subject to the will of another."[54]

The rule of law follows from Hayek's principle of commutative justice. According to Hayek, the rule of law is a meta-legal doctrine that requires all laws to be general, abstract, applied equally, well-known, and predictable.[55] The law should simply create a framework in which individuals may define and pursue their own private purposes with the minimum amount of coercion. The law, therefore, should not have particularistic and intended substantive purposes. Finally, the rule of law requires constitutional protections to safeguard individual liberty from legislation that is merely expedient or that expresses popular desires.

The right to strike conflicts with the principles of commutative justice and the rule of law. A successful strike relies on coercion—"the threat of inflicting harm and the intention thereby to bring about certain conduct"[56]—in order to subordinate the wills of individuals to the collective purposes of the organization. In other words, the right to strike interferes with the liberty of contract in employment—"of transference by consent, and . . . the performance of promises." The right to strike violates the rule of law because it creates legal privileges and immunities for a particular class of individuals. By protecting strikers against job loss and immunizing them against injunctions, liability, and criminal prosecution, laws that support the right to strike violate the principle that just laws be abstract and general.[57] Laws affirming the right to strike (the Norris–La Guardia Act and the NLRA) also violate the requirement that just laws may not promote particularistic and intended substantive purposes, because these statutes ostensibly support unionization and collective bargaining.

The right to strike also infringes on property rights. A successful strike restricts the output of productive property in order to extract higher wages—in other words, it is a form of extortion. Economic liberalism establishes the right to property as a primary condition of a just society. John Locke argued, " 'Where there is no property, there is no justice,' is a proposition as certain as any demonstration in Euclid. . . . I can certainly know this proposition to be true as that a triangle has three angles equal to two right ones."[58] Although David Hume dismissed Locke's argument that the right to property preceded government in the state of nature, he established the right to property on convention, and asserted that justice requires "the stability of possession." Hayek drew on Hume and argued that private property establishes a private sphere wherein individuals may exercise their liberty: "The recognition of private or several property is thus an essential condition for the prevention of coercion."[59]

Economic liberals draw several pointed objections to the right to strike. Not only does the right to strike compromise the efficiency and natural order of the market but it also limits the individual's liberty of contract and the employer's right to property. Strikes attempt to prevent others from working for the struck employer, and to force the employer to agree to a collective agreement. Strikes also hold the employer's property hostage, denying to the employer its unmolested use. As such, the right to strike violates major precepts of commutative justice and the rule of law.

A closer inspection of the economic liberals' commitment to the liberty of contract in employment and the right to property, however, raises doubts that these rights ought to overtrump others. Economic liberals, like most modern American liberals, equate labor liberty with voluntary wage contracts, rather than with self-directed activity or with self-government.[60] Economic liberals, furthermore, apply a strict construction to the concept of liberty, denying that economic power is a form of coercion.

> Even if the threat of starvation to me and perhaps my family impels me to ac-
> cept a distasteful job at a very low wage, even if I am "at the mercy" of the only
> man willing to employ me, I am not coerced by him or anybody else. . . . Its ef-
> fect on my freedom is not different from that of any natural calamity.[61]

Shall citizens, therefore, not join bucket brigades or construct levees, because fires and floods are natural calamities? This narrow view of liberty indicates a denial of civic duties and a rejection of all responsibilities one has
not consented to.

Moreover, the evolution of labor law demonstrates that not all voluntary
contracts are equally free. American law once regarded contracts of indentured servitude as voluntary.[62] Southern state courts once treated annual
contracts between sharecroppers and planters as voluntary.[63] State and federal courts invalidated laws for the eight-hour day, against child labor,
against blacklisting, and against "yellow dog" contracts as infringements
on the liberty of the employment contract.[64] Denying that extreme economic
inequalities undermine the liberty of contract leads to the absurd conclusion
that an individual may voluntarily enter into subordinate status.

One may also raise doubts about the absolute inviolability of property
rights. Economic liberals treat property too abstractly, as the product of individual initiative and enterprise. Society, however, has not always been
under the rule of law, and the history of forced labor, the conquest of the
New World, and the plunder of war taint property rights. Even David
Hume recognized this:

> It is confessed that private justice, or the abstinence from the properties of oth-
> ers, is a most cardinal virtue. Yet reason tells us that there is no property in
> durable objects, such as land or houses, when carefully examined in passing
> from hand to hand, but must in some period have been founded on fraud and
> injustice. . . . The questions with regard to private property have filled infinite
> volumes of law and philosophy . . . and in the end we may safely pronounce
> that many of the rules they established are uncertain, ambiguous, and arbi-
> trary.[65]

Hume thus dismissed these objections with a wave of his hand. Should such
a tenuous right override all others?

Further complicating the issue is that the judiciary has stretched the concept of property well beyond the original concept as Locke and Hume understood it. Hume wrote of durable objects, and Locke spoke of property as
the acorns one gathered and the water one dipped from a stream. Until the
nineteenth century, property was tangible—land, livestock, currency, and
the like. But during the *Lochner* era the courts developed the concept of

substantive due process under the Fourteenth Amendment, which expanded the concept of property to include increasingly abstract and intangible forms. The "good will" of a business, the right to engage in business activity per se, and, by implication, the right to earn profits, became property rights.[66] This new conception of property right justified the extensive use of strike injunctions, with dire consequences for strikers' due process rights and their freedoms of speech, of assembly, of press, and other liberties and rights. If the right to property is stretched too far, it will overtrump not only the right to strike but political and civil rights as well.

This final point reveals the principal deficiency of economic liberalism: its failure to offer a satisfactory theory of citizenship. Individuals exercise their liberty in their private spheres; the state stands outside and against the private sphere as a source of coercion and potential monopoly. Economic liberals conceive of the desirable society as one characterized by free government. But *self*-government involves the public side of liberty, requiring the recognition of *citizenship* rights. Hayek raised vehement criticisms of majority rule and legislative law, and preferred the judiciary as the source of the rule of law. Indeed, the property rights objection to the right to strike parallels certain objections to universal voting rights. Economic liberals continue to fear that citizenship rights will encroach on property rights.

Rights-Based Liberalism and the Right to Strike

During the postwar era, a variety of progressive social movements sparked interest in equal rights as a justification for social reform and state intervention.[67] Inspired by the heady gains of the black civil rights movement, other social movements in the United States adopted the discourse of equal rights to promote their agendas. This new awareness of equal rights spawned a student free speech movement, a women's rights movement, and a gay rights movement, as well as movements promoting greater constitutional protections for accused persons, for mental patients, and for the disabled. An international revival of rights discourse accompanied this renewed interest in equal rights among American liberals, who envisaged their activism as part of this broader struggle for human rights, rather than simply a form of interest-group politics. An international human rights movement promoted the creation of the United Nations, which drew up the 1948 Universal Declaration of Human Rights, the 1966 International Covenant of Civil and Political Rights, and the 1966 International Covenant of Economic, Social and Cultural Rights.[68] In 1950 T. H. Marshall published *Citizenship and Social Class,* which provided the intellectual foundation for what he termed "social citizenship rights," that is, those advocated by the latter covenant. "Rights talk" became the lingua franca of

reform. With this commitment to equal rights, one might have expected renewed interest in wage-earners' rights to engage in concerted activity. Instead, the theory of equal rights developed during this period provided no
foundation for the right to strike, and may actually have weakened it.

These new social movements sparked the interest of Anglo-American
philosophers, political theorists, and legal theorists, who set about revising
the theory of rights to respond to the criticisms raised by utilitarians and
positivists. Jeremy Bentham had assailed proclamations of rights as sancti-
monious bombast. "Natural rights is simple nonsense," he declared; "natural and prescriptible rights (an American phrase) rhetorical nonsense, nonsense on stilts."[69] The only rights worth having are *positive* rights affirmed
by law and backed by force. David Hume had argued that natural rights
lack ontological status; because they cannot be verified empirically, one
ought more accurately to refer to them as advantages or interests.[70] Logical
positivists regarded statements about natural rights as statements of prefer-
ences masquerading as statements of fact. Utilitarianism and positivism had
reduced natural rights to a cipher, or worse, to a fallacy.

H. L. A. Hart, John Rawls, and Ronald Dworkin have attempted to recon-
ceptualize rights, in light of these criticisms, by establishing rights discourse
on the firmest and least controversial grounds possible.[71] To avoid the ontological criticisms raised against the concept of natural right, theorists now
refer to *moral* rights, or *individual* rights. To meet the challenge of logical
positivism, Hart denied that asserting a right is a statement of fact, so that an
assertion of one's rights is neither "true" nor "false" in the same way that a
statement of fact may be true or false. Rather, it states a moral *claim,* and as
such affirms a *rule* of behavior that establishes "when one person's actions
may appropriately be made the subject of coercive legal rules."[72]

Rawls similarly establishes his theory of rights on the firmest and least controversial grounds. Rawls avoids any teleological notions as grounds for a
theory of rights, and instead proposes the famous "original position," in
which rational persons, unaware of their future places in society, but concerned about advancing their future interests and purposes, must agree on
certain principles of justice. The preference for "an equal right to the most extensive basic liberty compatible with a similar liberty for others" as the first
principle of justice follows directly from the assumptions of the fairness of the
original position and the rationality of those who must agree on these rules.

Dworkin builds upon this theory of rights to respond to legal positivism
and utilitarianism. Rights, he argues, are *demands* that others provide a
moral justification for limiting one's freedom: "Individual rights are political trumps held by individuals. Individuals have rights when, for some reason, a collective goal is not sufficient justification for denying them what
they wish, as individuals, to have or do, or not a sufficient justification for
imposing some loss or injury upon them."[73] A right establishes a standard

with which one may overrule statutory and common law.[74] As just entitlements, individual rights trump, or override, the greater good of the community. Thus, the right to strike (in the strong sense) would override the industrial pluralists' concerns about industrial peace and inconvenience to the public, the Keynesian liberals' goals of economic growth and wage stabilization, and the economic liberals' norms of market efficiency and spontaneous social order.

Modern rights theory is especially concerned with justifying *equal* rights and with resolving the tension between equality and liberty. This demands that the relationship between liberty and equality have a rational, logical coherence. Thus, Hart argued that insofar as individuals are freely choosing human beings, "it follows that there is at least one natural right, the equal right of all men to be free."[75] Rawls justifies equal rights with his famous thought experiment, which, on the ground of individual rational choice, establishes an equal right to liberty as his first principle. Dworkin establishes the right to equality as his paramount value: "The most fundamental of rights is a distinct conception of the right to equality, which I call the right to equal concern and respect."[76] This becomes the Archimedean point for the development of his political theory of rights.

The egalitarian turn in rights theory reflected postwar demands for equal rights, as expressed by the civil rights movement and similar social struggles. Liberal rights theorists, however, also had to respond to the historical tension between liberty and equality in American political development. During the *Lochner* era, the federal judiciary cobbled together the concept of a right to liberty per se, based on the Fourteenth Amendment's due process clause. This provided a bulwark for employers' property rights and liberty of contract against state legislatures attempting to regulate economic interests, and against wage earners exercising their right to strike. As a result, John Dewey rejected earlier rights-based liberalism as doctrinaire, abstract, and a justification for the status quo.

> The earlier doctrine of "natural rights," superior to legislative action, has been given a definitely economic meaning by the courts, and used by judges to destroy social legislation passed in the interest of a real, instead of a purely formal, liberty of contract. . . . Beneficiaries of the established economic regime band themselves together in what they call Liberty Leagues to perpetuate the harsh regimentation of millions of their fellows. . . . They hold that beneficial social change can come about in but one way, the way of concrete private economic enterprise, socially undirected, based upon and resulting in the sanctity of private property—that is to say, freedom from social control.[77]

Consequently, when progressive liberals returned to rights-based liberalism in the postwar era, they had to rethink this relationship between liberty and equality. Rights-based liberals do not want to share the same agenda as the economic liberals discussed above. Instead, they embrace rights in order to promote social equality and government activism in the name of social justice. Thus, Dworkin argues that the right to liberty as such is not fundamental; individuals have equal rights to specific liberties, but not to liberty per se: "Individual rights to distinct liberties must be recognized when the fundamental right to treatment as an equal can be shown to require those rights."[78] Dworkin does not want his formula "rights are trumps" to shield property rights against claims for equal rights.

As previously noted, liberty of contract and the right to property also provided the grounds for economic liberals' arguments against the right to strike. Does rights-based liberalism then provide a possible defense of this right?

Although in the future liberal rights theory may defend the right to strike, rights-based liberals have offered no arguments supporting this right, and certain essential characteristics of the right to strike make it difficult to square with rights-based liberalism. Thus, the right to strike conflicts with other rights. All rights, at their peripheries, compete with the rights of others, but the right to strike at its core *always* and *necessarily* collides with other peoples' rights, especially the property rights of employers and the liberty of contract of strikebreakers. Although rights-based liberals refuse to grant these rights the same primacy that economic liberals give them, neither do they dismiss them as irrelevant.

How does one decide a case in which two rights *necessarily* conflict? Other than declaring "rights are trumps," or that they are moral claims, or entitlements to just treatment, rights-based liberals provide little guidance for determining which right takes precedence. Can one right overtrump another? Beyond asserting "the right to equal concern and respect" as the fundamental right, modern rights theorists have failed to provide a relative ordering of rights.[79]

Rights-based liberalism also leaves unresolved another difficulty. The right to strike (if there is such a right) is essentially a *collective* right. Contemporary liberal rights theories, however, only consider the moral and legal dimensions of rights, thus constructing rights on an individualistic basis: "A political right is an individuated political aim"[80] (Dworkin). "Rights are typically conceived of as *possessed* or *owned by* or *belonging to* individuals"[81] (Hart). "If X has a right to R, he may have (or do) R, or not, as he prefers"[82] (Benn and Peters). "Each person possesses an inviolability founded on justice that even the welfare of society as a whole cannot override"[83] (Rawls). In some sense, all rights are collective. Rights consist of social rules that establish a framework of powers, immunities, forbearances, and duties among individuals. Rights also invoke a series of correlative, corresponding, and mutual duties within a society. Thus, Robinson Crusoe could not have spoken meaningfully of having rights, at least until he met Friday. But a *collective* right is something else. Rights are collective in a nontrivial sense because they have always been extended on a group basis. From the barons at Runnymede in 1215 to the artisans of the 1830s to disabled Americans in 1992, groups, rather than individuals as such, have promoted their justice claims with the discourse of rights.

There remains an even more fundamental reason to regard the right to strike as a collective right, however. Only a group can meaningfully exercise the right to strike. An individual cannot go on strike alone; he or she may *quit* work, but the right to quit is not problematic. By definition, a strike is a temporary collective work stoppage, and the right to strike means that a group of workers, involved in a labor dispute, has a just entitlement to suspend all work, and a just claim to return to their jobs when they have resolved the dispute. The right to strike asserts a group claim. However, as Mary Ann Glendon argues, modern American rights talk does not recognize the social dimension of personhood and cannot recognize the claims of communities, families, labor unions, and so on, except insofar as they behave as special interest groups, "that is, collections of self-seeking individuals pursuing limited, parallel aims."[84] Sandel raises a similar criticism of rights-based liberalism:

> We cannot regard ourselves as independent in this way without great cost to the loyalties and convictions whose moral force consists partly in the fact that living by them is inseparable from understanding ourselves as the particular persons we are—as members of this family or community or nation or people, as bearers of this history, as sons and daughters of that revolution, as citizens of this republic.[85]

Rights-based liberalism cannot provide an adequate justification for the right to strike because it offers no satisfactory theory of collective rights.[86]

Although rights-based liberalism does not share economic liberalism's commitment to unfettered markets and private property rights, both versions of modern American liberalism reveal significant similarities. Hayek's aversion to collectivism parallels Dworkin's view that "individuals have rights when, for some reason, a collective goal is not sufficient justification for denying them what they wish, as individuals, to have or do." Neither economic liberalism nor rights-based liberalism offers an adequate conception of citizenship; even with rights-based liberalism, the citizen is very private and alienated from the state. The citizen stands apart from civil society; civil society does not enrich the individual but rather threatens his or her rights. Individuals are not part of larger political enterprises and do not share fundamental common purposes. Entirely missing is the civic dimension; citizenship is a pallid abstraction, defined as a framework of rights, but disconnected from acting in concert with other citizens to shape a common destiny. Upon such grounds one cannot justify the right to strike.

Modern American liberalism presents a paradox. On the one hand, extension of workers' rights is historically associated with liberal political development in the United States.[87] Modern American liberalism, however, provides no stalwart justification for this right, and, in some cases, has seen fit to limit this right. Industrial pluralists give priority to labor peace and uninterrupted production. Keynesian liberals give precedence to economic growth and wage-price stability. Economic liberals give preference to individual liberty, economic efficiency, and natural order. Rights-based liberals support equal rights among individuals over collective rights. The right to strike fits oddly into liberal democratic theory and vision. Indeed, it does not fit.[88]

10

"Something of slavery still remains"
The Right to Strike as a Citizenship Right

At the beginning of the twenty-first century, the right to strike still remains insecure and contested, disengaged from other social struggles, and subject to judicial erosion. The state defends only a limited range of collective action, leaves strikers vulnerable to job loss and unions exposed to decertification, and provides inadequate protection from employers who break the law. Strengthening the right to strike demands more than a few patches on the National Labor Relations Act, because the vulnerability of this right stems from the NLRA's foundations in modern American liberalism. Although most modern American liberals concede the right to strike as a necessary component of free collective bargaining, none unequivocally champions this right as worthy of a democratic society. Consequently, the NLRA affirms the right to strike as a commercial right rather than as a citizenship right. This has disengaged the right to strike from broader social policy concerns. Few today propose strengthening the right to strike in order to improve the lives of the working poor, as Senator Robert Wagner did in 1935. Moreover, the equivocal support for the right to strike has permitted its judicial erosion. Because the right to strike has no firm constitutional foundation, it lacks the urgency of civil rights and civil liberties. The legislative construction of this right upon the commerce powers and the absence of a coherent conception of collective rights have permitted the weakening of this right.

In this chapter I explain why the right to strike should be a citizenship right. The right to strike has political significance that transcends its utility as a commercial right and justifies the inconvenience to society. Like all rights, it must be balanced by its bearers' duties and by concern for the common good. But it must also be accorded more respect than it currently receives. The public philosophy of nineteenth-century worker republicanism provides a more secure foundation for the right to strike. Prior to the emergence of pure-and-simple unionism, labor leaders grasped the importance of labor liberty for sustaining citizenship and civil society. The right to strike is one element of labor liberty. The Free Labor Amendment, which establishes labor liberty as a citizenship right, provides a more stalwart constitutional anchor for the right to strike.

I address three possible objections to the right to strike as a citizenship right based on nineteenth-century worker republicanism. These criticisms include (1) that the right to strike promotes social strife; (2) that nineteenth-century worker republicanism is an anachronism; and (3) that nineteenth-century worker republicanism promoted exclusionary, nativist, racist, and sexist attitudes that have no place in a multicultural society.

Citizenship Rights

In his celebrated essay "Citizenship and Social Class," T. H. Marshall provided concise definitions of citizenship and citizenship rights. "Citizenship," he asserted, "is a status bestowed on those who are full members of a community. All who possess the status are equal with respect to the rights and duties with which the status is endowed."[1] Unlike modern liberal theories of rights, which view rights as *"owned by* or *belonging to* individuals,"[2] Marshall's conception does not regard rights merely as demands that individuals may make on the state for protection against arbitrary treatment and oppression. Instead, he emphasized the collective dimension of citizenship rights. Citizenship rights enable all (and especially the poor and oppressed) to share in the life of the community and to participate as full members of a polity. Marshall stated: "Citizenship requires . . . a direct sense of community membership based on loyalty to a civilization which is a common possession."[3] It is this social dimension of rights, the individual's attachments and commitments to the community, that the liberal theory of rights ignores.[4]

Marshall fully appreciated the role of employment rights in the expansion of citizenship and in British political development. The early British state, through the Statute of Laborers, the Statute of Artificers, and the Elizabethan Poor Law, treated workers as second-class citizens, unworthy of full membership in society. Wage earners had no right to choose their occupations or their employers, and the threat of the workhouse and the loss of what rights they had hung over those who could not find work. Hence, the recognition of employment rights represented an important expansion of the rights of British citizens: "The change from servile to free labour has been described . . . as a 'high water mark in the development both of economic and political society.' "[5] Likewise, the legalization of trade unionism "created a secondary system of industrial citizenship."[6]

Since then, Judith Shklar elaborated on similar themes in American citizenship. Shklar noted how one's activities in civil society, and particularly as a wage earner, are constitutive of American citizenship: "To be a recognized and active citizen at all he must be an equal member of the polity, a voter, but he must also be independent, which has all along meant that he must be an 'earner,' a free remunerated worker, one who is rewarded for the actual work he has done, neither more nor less."[7] Those who are deprived of their jobs lose not only their incomes but also their standing in civil society, eventually falling into the underclass. Shklar argued that work is so important to American citizenship that it establishes a right to work: "The right to earn should not be based upon personal responses, such as loss of self-respect, but on the loss of public respect, the reduction of standing and demotion to second-class citizenship, to which the public ethos, overtly and traditionally, condemns them."[8] The right to work creates a just expectation for remunerative and respectable employment, to secure one's standing as a full, contributing member of civil society.

Marshall included collective bargaining rights as an important component of employment rights, since they protect the right to work, extend political rights into the civil sphere, and contribute to social citizenship rights, such as the right to economic security. The right to strike is an essential component of collective bargaining rights: "Strikes usually involve breach of contract or the repudiation of agreements. Appeal is made to some allegedly higher principle—in reality, though this may not be expressly asserted, to the status rights of industrial citizenship."[9]

Although Shklar remained silent about the right to engage in concerted activities, her views have important implications for the right to strike. Shklar argued for employment rights as guarantees against losing one's standing as a citizen through job loss. The right to strike is consequent to this right. A strike is a temporary collective cessation of work, a transitory suspension of the employment contract; its purpose is not to destroy the employer but to protest. The right to strike establishes a just expectation that strikers may return to their jobs after the resolution of a labor dispute. Strikers should not be disenfranchised for exercising their rights and registering a complaint. The NLRA's protection of strikers' statutory rights, however, does not adequately protect their rights as citizens, because it permits their permanent replacement by strikebreakers.

By contrast, the liberal "right to work" as embodied in the Labor Management Relations Act and in state laws establishes very different rights that prohibit mandatory union membership and protect individual workers' right to refrain from collective action. Thus, Section 8(a)(3) prohibits the closed shop, and Section 8(b)(1)(A) and 8(b)(2) prohibit unions from forcing employees to join a union. Furthermore, Section 14(b) of the LMRA permits states to pass "right to work" laws that prohibit the union shop; twenty-one states currently have such laws. The LMRA thus guarantees the individual right to refuse membership in a civil association. This conception of the right to work celebrates the lone rights bearer, standing apart from, and often in opposition to, civil society. The liberal conception of the right to work establishes no expectation that the state will foster full employment of citizens and protect citizens from job loss as a matter of right.

Liberal rights talk thus encounters the problem of fitting the square peg of collective rights into the round hole of individual rights. Within the liberal framework, collective rights are suspect. The framework of citizenship rights, in contrast, acknowledges the social dimension of personhood that is missing in liberal rights discourse. Marshall argued that "citizenship requires a bond of a different kind, a direct sense of community membership based on loyalty to a civilization which is a common possession."[10] The political and social elements of citizenship manifest these allegiances. Shklar likewise emphasized the need for inclusion in order to repudiate the discriminatory practices that denied American citizenship to women, blacks, and the working poor. The fact that citizens exercise these rights collectively and publicly further demonstrates the collective nature of citizenship rights.

This collective dimension, moreover, is characteristic of other citizenship rights, and not only the right to strike. Consider the right to vote. Extension of the franchise has brought new citizens into the political community on a group basis: white male wage earners in the 1820s, white women in 1920, southern blacks in 1965. The act of voting, furthermore, connects the individual with the larger community in an act of collective decision making; notwithstanding the secret ballot, one can only exercise the right to vote as part of a collective activity. Finally, one is called upon to consider issues from a public-regarding point of view. Although public choice theory applies the individual rational actor model to the voting process, the fact that citizens vote at all demonstrates that they bring a civic awareness to the voting process.[11]

The right to education likewise demonstrates the collective dimension of citizenship rights. This right ensures that all individuals share in the common heritage of the community. The traditional justification for providing a public education as a matter of right maintains that the goal is not simply to enhance the human capital of the workforce but to foster the development of democratic character.[12] The process is fundamentally social and public; the experience of the common school is essential to public education.[13]

Racially segregated education violated the citizenship rights of blacks not only because it provided unequal educational opportunities but because it excluded black children from the common school—it denied them full and equal membership in the community.

The right to strike, by protecting groups of workers against job losses as a result of a labor dispute, recognizes the social side of persons. Job loss isolates the individual, cutting him or her off from one of the primary forms of sociality. Strikebreaking further disrupts sociality by destroying civic institutions and undermining community solidarity. As a citizenship right, the right to strike recognizes as legitimate the claims that wage earners' organizations make on their members, not as a contractual agreement but in virtue of the loyalties and allegiances that persons must show to sustain civic institutions. An emphasis on citizenship rights regards wage earners' organizations as more than pressure groups seeking private advantage at the workplace. As civic institutions they provide wage earners with a form of self-government and a voice in the workplace. The right to strike protects these institutions from annihilation during a labor dispute.

Retrieving Civic Republican Discourse

Michael Sandel has recently called for the revival of the civic republican tradition in American politics, as an alternative to modern American liberalism:

> The republican tradition, with its emphasis on community and self-government, may offer a corrective to our impoverished civic life. Recalling the republican conception of freedom as self-rule may prompt us to pose questions we have forgotten to ask: What economic arrangements are hospitable to self-government? How might our political discourse engage rather than avoid the moral and religious convictions people bring to the public realm? And how might the public life of a pluralist society cultivate in citizens the expansive self-understanding that civic engagement requires? If the public philosophy of our day leaves little room for civic considerations, it may help to recall how earlier generations of Americans debated such questions.[14]

The retrieval of this earlier civic discourse would enrich our understanding of collective action and bestow a deeper appreciation of the corresponding responsibilities that accompany the rights of citizenship. Critics of the liberal conception of rights, such as Mary Ann Glendon and Lawrence Mead, point out that liberal rights talk often ignores the corresponding obligations that rights create for the rights bearer. Rights talk may devolve into mere assertion of self-interest.[15] The strike then becomes a means for a powerful group of workers to press their economic advantage at the expense of the vulnerable. This exposes strikers to the criticism that they ignore the costs to the community: the social disruption, public inconvenience, and higher prices that may result.

Most strikes involve issues more complex than wages and benefits. More often, they include issues of job security, job control, safety, management authority, employee-employer relations, union recognition, plant closings, and issues that affect the community. But liberal rights talk has impoverished public discourse on these issues. Modern American liberalism has defined the strike as a bargaining tool and has confined collective bargaining largely to wages and working conditions; consequently, the only meaningful items that employees may strike over are their private economic interests.

A distinctive feature of republican rights talk, on the other hand, is its concern for public virtue and the common good. Rights and virtues go hand in hand, presupposing and reinforcing one another. Republican rights are not licenses for unencumbered citizens to do what they want without restrictions, but appeals that they take part in the community as full members. To justify their actions, persons must appeal to the public good, which may include one's rights and interests, but is not reducible to them. Civic republican discourse calls on strikers to provide public reasons for strikes and to consider their obligations to the common good. Nineteenth-century strike leaders realized this when they demanded living wages for their followers. Degrading living and working conditions, they contended, subvert republican institutions.

Liberal rights talk is so ingrained in our public discourse that it is difficult to grasp the right to strike as a citizenship right. However, a careful reading of early American labor writings demonstrates that the movement's leaders regarded the rights of wage earners, including the right to engage in collective action, as essential for defending their standing as American citizens. Their discourse was not simply a strident, one-dimensional assertion of their rights, but a more subtle discussion of civic virtues, citizen responsibilities, and the cooperative commonwealth. Although we seldom encounter this kind of discourse today, the California farm workers' strike and the Memphis sanitation workers' strike illustrate the capacity of the working poor to transcend the dominant rights discourse and affirm their common humanity, their membership in the larger community, and their dedication to nonviolence. In both cases, strikers effectively communicated that more was at stake than just the terms of employment, that their efforts were part of a larger struggle for human dignity and freedom. Strikers appealed to higher principles and to the American political tradition to defend their actions.

The retrieval of civic republican discourse would strengthen the right to strike in two important ways. First, it would ground the defense of the right to strike in a traditional American political discourse. Often, progressives posit a European-style social democratic labor politics as an alternative to American liberal labor politics. This European-style social democratic discourse, however, remains mostly foreign to American political life. There is another cultural tradition, however, neither purely liberal nor entirely social democratic, that progressives may draw on, a tradition that emphasizes American themes and values. Shklar demonstrated the central importance of labor liberty to our understanding of American citizenship, as well as the continuing significance of this principle.[16] Sandel has also suggested the value of reviving this civic strand in American political discourse as a way to revitalize American democracy. The American labor movement should also draw on this tradition, as it did frequently in the nineteenth century and infrequently in the early twentieth.

Second, the retrieval of civic republican discourse would provide a stronger constitutional foundation for the right to strike. The weakness of the modern American liberal right to strike results from its weak constitutional foundations. The U.S. Constitution makes no mention of the right to strike, and the Supreme Court has rejected attempts to derive the right to strike from First Amendment rights.[17] Instead, the legal right to strike is a *statutory* right, derived from congressional powers to regulate interstate commerce. Nineteenth-century worker-republican discourse, however, suggests that a more substantial right to strike may be derived from the Thirteenth Amendment, the one part of the Constitution that articulates the link between free labor and citizenship. Under a system of chattel slavery, there is no right to strike; "strikes" are slave rebellions that threaten the state. Moreover, the Thirteenth Amendment—the "Free Labor" Amendment— prohibits not only chattel slavery but all forms of involuntary servitude. Employment systems that compromise free employment relations, such as the open shop system and the sharecropper system, also severely constrain the right to strike. Denial of the right to strike smacks of involuntary servitude and denies the spirit of this amendment.

Grounding the right to strike in the Free Labor Amendment will require a more expansive reading of this amendment. Thus far, the Supreme Court has adopted a truncated interpretation of the rights of free labor, accepting the liberal position that individual labor contracts are consistent with labor liberty, and insisting that involuntary servitude must involve physical or legal coercion or restraint. In *United Automobile Workers v. Wisconsin Employment Relations Board,* Justice Robert H. Jackson observed "nothing in the [Wisconsin] statute or the order [to a union to cease and desist from intermittent work stoppages] makes it a crime to abandon work individually . . . or collectively. Nor does either undertake to prohibit or restrict any employee from leaving the service of the employer."[18] The Court has responded only in passing to labor unions' claims that their right to strike rests on the Free Labor Amendment, perfunctorily dismissing their claims as "without merit."[19] Neither opinion seriously addressed the right to strike nor engaged unionists' arguments that the Free Labor Amendment confers workers' rights to organize and to strike.

From the late nineteenth century until the passage of the LMRA in 1947, by contrast, labor unionists insisted that their rights to organize and to strike were constitutional rights resting upon this amendment, and that, in the absence of these rights, the individual worker's liberty of contract would not protect workers against involuntary servitude. Union leaders argued that yellow dog contracts compromised labor liberty, and Andrew Furuseth, president of the Seamen's Union, urged Senators Norris and Wagner to establish their labor laws on this amendment.[20]

Granted, a new labor law regime grounded in the Thirteenth Amendment would require a fundamental shift in the Supreme Court. However, *If the Workers Took a Notion* has challenged the notion of a hegemonic judiciary single-handedly ordaining the boundaries of the right to strike. Other factors in American political development, including the presidency, commissions, administrative agencies, and the labor movement's own discourse of rights, have also shaped this right. Moreover, the current NLRA regime fostered a fundamental shift in the Court—the famous "switch in time that saved nine"—that overturned precedents far more formidable than those standing in the way of using the Free Labor Amendment to ground the right to strike.

Objections and Responses

This argument for a more robust right to strike as a citizenship right, and for the retrieval of worker-republican discourse, raises a variety of reasonable objections. First, some may object that a more protected right to strike would intensify industrial conflict and social strife. Second, some may argue that nineteenth-century worker republicanism is anachronistic, and that advocating a return to this public philosophy is mere nostalgia. Third, others may assert that nineteenth-century worker republicanism expressed exclusionary, nativist, racist, and sexist sentiments that have no place in a pluralistic polity.

A Stronger Right to Strike Would Mean More Strikes

The first objection maintains that there exists a strong public interest in averting strikes, and that a more stalwart right to strike would increase strike activity. Strikes not only create inconvenience and nuisance for the public; in some cases, they cause genuine suffering. In addition, strikes increase social discord, which is reason enough to be suspicious of any measure that could increase their frequency. The costs to the public and the violence associated with strikes are legitimate public concerns. Sumner Slichter, for example, repudiated AFL president William Green's assertion that "the right to strike distinguishes the free worker from the slave. The right to strike involves the foundation of our free economy." This "amount[s] to a claim that the right to strike is superior to all other rights," because it concedes no rights to the community.[21] Since the end of the nineteenth century, the peaceful resolution of labor disputes has been one of the primary goals of federal labor relations policy.

Granted, civil peace is a matter of concern, and there may sometimes be better means of adjusting labor disputes than resorting to a work stoppage. This objection, however, exaggerates the social costs of a strike. Arthur Kornhauser estimated that between 1933 and 1954, a period of relatively high strike activity, the total amount of working time lost due to strikes amounted to less than one-fifth of the time lost to unemployment during 1933.[22] Since 1946, the highest U.S. strike rate occurred in 1959, when the number of work days idle due to work stoppages as a percentage of all working time peaked at 0.5 percent.[23] Since the late 1980s, this figure has plummeted to about 0.02 percent. True, a total accounting of strike costs would have to include losses resulting from interruptions in commercial activity and external costs—costs that are very difficult to measure. But percent days lost annually due to strikes provides a benchmark and helps to keep the costs of strikes in perspective. Strikers and their employers, moreover, bear the brunt of these costs, in lost wages, lost jobs, and lost revenues, and the fear of these losses acts as a restraint in most cases. No one favors strikes, least of all the participants.

Still, no matter what the economic cost, picket-line violence, sabotage, looting, vigilantism, threats, and discord weaken civil society and leave wounds that take years to heal. Apart from actual violence, strikes generate antagonism and pit groups against one another. Is this not reason enough to avert strikes?

This criticism assumes that strikers are the cause of violence and discord, and that the only way to avert strikes is to suppress them. The historical record, however, indicates that most strike violence is limited and generally in reaction to strikebreaking and the use of armed force on behalf of employers. According to the *Report Submitted to the National Commission on the Causes and Prevention of Violence,* "The precipitating causes have been attempts by pickets and sympathizers to prevent a plant from being reopened by strikebreakers, or attempts of company guards, police, or even National Guardsmen to prevent such interference."[24] Violence occurred in the Homestead strike of 1892, for example, after a boatload of several hundred Pinkerton guards attempted to seize the Carnegie Steel plant. The Pullman strike likewise remained peaceful until the deployment of U.S. Army regulars to Chicago. The report further notes that the greatest strike violence has occured in those cases where employers have refused to recognize a union or sought its demise. Other federal government investigations concur with this general point. The 1915 report by the Commission on Industrial Relations concluded that industrial feudalism, autocratic management, strikebreaking, and attacks on workers' rights caused the labor violence during the early part of the twentieth century. The 1937 La Follette Committee hearings further documented employers' refusal to bargain and their use of industrial spies, armed guards, and strikebreakers.

Strike leaders realize that they occupy a very tenuous position and that any act of violence weakens public support and may provide a pretext for authorities to suppress a strike. Strike discipline requires maintaining peace during the work stoppage. In the past, however, antiunion employers have hired agents provocateurs to foment striker violence. Many believed, for example, that provocateurs ignited the bomb in the 1886 Haymarket incident, perhaps the most notorious act of strike violence in U.S. history. As the *Report Submitted to the National Commission on the Causes and Prevention of Violence* noted, "The use of employer agents, disguised as union members or union officials for advocating violence within the union, testifies to the advantage such practices gave the employer."[25] Strike leaders such as Cesar Chavez and Eugene Debs, by contrast, espoused nonviolence during strikes to add moral legitimacy to their causes.

Not only has the suppression of strikes and strikebreaking caused the violence associated with strikes, but affirming the right to strike has diminished social discord. The greatest strike-related violence occurred between 1877 and 1937, cresting just before World War I, during the height of the open shop movement. Since the Supreme Court affirmed the NLRA, however, strike-related violence has declined.[26] Strengthening the right to strike has not yet increased industrial strife.

However, the NLRA, as the Supreme Court has interpreted it, does create an adversarial process. In *NLRB v. Insurance Agents/International Union* (1960), the Court affirmed that "the parties—even granting the modification of views that may come from a realization of economic interdependence—still proceed from contrary and to an extent antagonistic viewpoints and concepts or self-interest."[27] According to current law, both employers and unions have economic weapons in reserve, and the role of the state is merely to be a referee in this contest. This equates strikebreaking with strikes. Current labor law prohibits NLRB intervention in the substance of collective bargaining, turns collective bargaining into a tug-of-war between contending interests, leads to delay, and places burdens on grieving workers and unions. Moreover, by permitting employers to hire strikebreakers, current labor law also makes it too easy for management to bargain in bad faith and to goad workers into strikes in order to establish a union-free employment system.[28] This has led to longer, more extensive, and more bitter conflicts. A more robust right to strike would alter the balance of power between workers and employers, but it would not increase industrial strife. Indeed, as Sweden demonstrates, more legal protections for the right to strike might lead to a lower strike rate.[29]

Averting strikes does not call for suppression but for fair and expeditious mechanisms for adjusting labor disputes. Addressing the underlying causes of employee discontent, providing fair and prompt means for resolving workplace disputes, and strengthening employment rights provides a more effective and democratic solution. This would require more authority and greater administrative capacities than the NLRB currently exercises. Early advocates of nineteenth-century worker republicanism, for example, advocated state intervention in the form of compulsory arbitration. Although the modern labor movement repudiated compulsory arbitration as a violation of voluntarism, the labor movement made significant gains under systems of quasi-compulsory arbitration during World Wars I and II, and public employee unions have thrived under compulsory arbitration. Although national labor relations policy does not support this level of NLRB intervention, the president's emergency powers are elastic enough to permit this kind of intervention in major strikes on an ad hoc basis. The presidency is well equipped to press the existing institutional boundaries of authority relations, and the expansion of the right to strike in the past has accompanied such expansion in presidential authority.[30]

Nineteenth-Century Worker Republicanism Is Obsolete

The second objection contends that nineteenth-century worker republicanism is out of date, an anachronism. This nineteenth-century worker republicanism emerged during the Jacksonian era, when artisan journeymen's associations dominated the labor movement. From the late 1860s through the early 1890s, the National Labor Union, the Knights of Labor, and others adhered to the principles of nineteenth-century worker republicanism to defend their declining standing under industrialization. Today, Americans live and work in a postindustrial, service- and information-based economy. Nineteenth-century worker-republican discourse, moreover, thrived during the era of the early American republic, in the context of a benign republic. The rise of the modern American liberal state, however, undermined the structural and institutional foundations of worker republicanism. Desire for the revival of the public philosophy of a bygone era is little more than nostalgia for a simpler past.

This criticism presupposes that past discourses are not available for appropriation outside of their original political-economic contexts, and that the lessons of the past were only lessons for the past. Discourses, however, are not the same as doctrines. A doctrine suggests an unwavering system of rules and beliefs, an orthodoxy with little room for revision. But a discourse connotes an ongoing conversation, a set of shared concerns, a way of defining problems and setting the limits of what counts as a possible solution. Over time, discourses evolve, often accepting ideas that were once rejected. Adapting worker-republican discourse to the concerns of wage earners today would no doubt require revision of these ideas, but that should not discredit it.

Nineteenth-century worker republicanism was itself an adaptation of old ideas to new social circumstances and a modern political system. Classical republican discourse originally expressed an aristocratic disdain for working people. Aristotle, for example, argued that mechanics and artisans could not by nature become citizens because the degrading influence of manual labor and the dependency that manual workers experienced made them unsuitable for self-rule. Classical republicanism further emphasized the need for small, manageable political units, much smaller than the original United States. Jefferson's adaptation of republican discourse celebrated the hardworking, small yeoman farmer as the ideal American republican, but rejected the urban laboring classes as unfit for self-rule. Although civic republican discourse originated in an entirely different social and political context, the nineteenth-century American labor movement still could draw upon it to express their aspirations.

Other discourses have adapted to changing social circumstances. Liberalism arose in the early modern era as a new middle class began to challenge the aristocratic privileges of the ancien regime. Classic liberalism, with its principles of a limited state, free market economics, and laissez-faire policies, gave way to modern liberalism, which has fostered an activist state, a mixed economy, and the Keynesian welfare state. Conservatism developed in response to the Enlightenment, the French Revolution, and the commercialization of society. Conservatives today reject aristocratic values and embrace capitalist values. Socialists once advocated the nationalization of industry and the expansion of the state; now socialists accept private property and market systems.

Although modern American liberalism overshadowed the civic republican tradition, this latter discourse represents a homegrown public philosophy that resonates with traditional American values. Civic republican discourse remained part of the American political tradition through the Progressive Era and well into the civil rights period. Thus, in "The Ethics of Democracy" John Dewey asserted:

There is no need to beat about the bush in saying that democracy is not a reality what it is in name until it is industrial, as well as civil and political. . . . All industrial relations are to be regarded as subordinate to human relations, to the law of personality. . . . They are to become the material of an ethical realization; the form and substance of a community of good (though not necessarily of goods) wider than any now known.[31]

Similarly, Cesar Chavez recognized the slavelike servitude that farm workers endured and sought full citizenship for Mexican American workers by demanding their rights to organize and engage in collective action.

In some ways, a modern version of worker-republican discourse would better harmonize with today's labor market than would a reformed version of liberal labor relations. The liberal regime of industrial relations—characterized by worker self-organization into industrial unions, collective bargaining over wages and working conditions, and interest-group politics—developed toward the end of the industrial era, during the 1930s and '40s. These institutions and administrative procedures served the industrial workforce well, but they have failed to spread into the new economic sectors such as services and information technologies. At the lower end of the new labor market, organizers cannot withstand the employment-application screening process, antiunion communications, and appropriate bargaining unit challenges—all legal under current labor law, but effective weapons that low-wage employers such as Wal-Mart use to combat unionization. At the upper end of the new labor market, highly trained employees reject pure-and-simple unionism as unprofessional and somewhat demeaning of their autonomy. A modern version of worker republicanism that values autonomy at work, dignity, and craft pride would better reflect the values of professional employees today. At the same time, it would protect the citizenship rights of low-wage workers to organize and engage in collective action.

A modern version of worker republicanism would also better harmonize with the principles of new business management. During the early twentieth century, management experts developed techniques of scientific management, which applied the principles of industrial engineering to the workforce, and by the mid-twentieth century scientific management was integrated into the liberal model of employment relations. The principles of scientific management, including the separation of execution from control, limiting worker autonomy, and bureaucratizing management, now appear to stifle the modern corporation. Modern employment management techniques today call for greater employee autonomy, initiative, control, and knowledge, and reject the assembly-line techniques that Charlie Chaplin lampooned in *Modern Times*. W. Edwards Deming, for example, recommends the use of quality circles and other total quality management techniques that integrate management functions into the execution of work.[32] Employees must have more autonomy as creative problem-solvers, quality-control specialists, and team-workers. Nineteenth-century worker-republican support for self-rule at the workplace, craft pride, the craft community, work as a source of personal satisfaction and dignity, and rejection of hierarchy presaged many of the principles that management experts now promote.

Management experts do not propose, however, that employees have a right to strike. If employers would actually treat employees as team members, with equal respect and the freedom to participate in the governance of the firm, rather than as wage costs, many of the sources of discontent inherent in the wage system would disappear, reducing the incidence of work stoppages. But it is utopian to believe that greater employee independence, participation, and creativity will lead inevitably to cooperation between employers and employees and never to strife. If the Damoclean sword of permanent replacement hangs over the workforce, participation at the workplace will be spurious.

Even if civic republican discourse is available for today's labor market and workplace, some might still ask what institutional arrangements, short of a cooperative commonwealth, could foster a modern version of worker-republican discourse and strengthen the right to strike. One suggestion is to expand the authority and administrative capacities of the NLRB, to warrant greater involvement in the substance of collective bargaining, and perhaps to develop compulsory arbitration procedures. In addition, a modern version of worker republicanism would require a wider and broader form of collective bargaining. According to the Current Population Survey conducted by the Bureau of Labor Statistics and the Census Bureau, collective bargaining agreements covered only 14.3 percent of the American workforce in 2003—a proportion too low to revive worker republicanism. Moreover, collective bargaining agreements cover a relatively narrow range of issues concerning wages and working conditions, and they generally exclude the right to manage and the core of entrepreneurial control of the firm. A new workers' republicanism at the very least would call for restoration of Senator Robert Wagner's vision of collective bargaining as "a cooperative venture guided by intelligence, rather than a mere test of relative strength."[33] Wagner supported extending collective bargaining to the working poor, and espoused an expansive form of collective bargaining as a system of industrial democracy and cooperative management. He predicated workers' rights to organize, bargain collectively, and engage in collective action on the commerce powers out of political expediency. A new Wagner Act, founded upon the Free Labor Amendment, would more firmly establish collective rights, including the right to engage in an expansive form of collective bargaining. A more robust right to strike, moreover, would encourage workers to press the boundaries of collective bargaining, so institutional changes and enhanced citizenship rights would reinforce one another.

Nineteenth-Century Worker Republicanism Excluded Most Workers

The third objection contends that nineteenth-century worker-republican discourse promoted the rights and interests of a minority of American workers—native-born white males—and fostered certain racist and sexist assumptions that have no place in a modern, liberal, and pluralistic society.[34] Rogers Smith argues that American political actors, including labor leaders, have always promoted civic ideologies that intermingled liberal, civic republican, and ascriptive elements.[35] Robert Wiebe, writing about the Jacksonian era, notes:

> Democracy's radical new principle was self-rule; people ruled themselves collectively, people ruled themselves individually. . . . Self-defined authority gave *white men* the mandate to rule collectively; self-directed work gave them the freedom to strike out individually. From one trunk came community self-government, from the other economic self-determination.[36]

This view of American democracy actively and consciously excluded Native Americans, women, and blacks, and increasingly the new immigrants who arrived during the Gilded Age.

Furthermore, male workers in the nineteenth century countenanced explicitly masculine notions of work, and the cult of manliness permeated the workplace. Eugene Debs constantly dwelled on masculinity: "When a man surrenders his honest convictions without resistance, his loyalty to principle, he ceases to be a man."[37] During the Pullman strike, Debs announced:

> The great lesson of the Pullman strike is found in the fact that it arouses widespread sympathy. This fellow-feeling for the woes of others—this desire to help the unfortunate . . . should be accepted as at once the hope of civilization and the supreme glory of manhood.[38]

Free white workers in the nineteenth century also displayed little commitment to black freedom. During the 1840s and '50s, free white workers in the North expressed deep ambivalence toward slavery, condemning the institution as inimical to freedom but refusing to advocate black equality. Abraham Lincoln, for example, feared the expansion of the slave system into the Midwest and Southwest, because it would limit opportunities for wage earners to establish themselves as independent farmers and tradesmen on the frontier.[39] Moreover, between 1830 and 1860, nearly every northern state passed laws denying to blacks the right to vote and creating unequal employment opportunities.[40] In 1834, striking white artisans in Philadelphia rioted against the employment of free black artisans.[41] White workers struck over fifty times between 1882 and 1900 to oppose the employment of blacks in traditionally white occupations.[42]

Some early labor leaders also expressed nativist and anti-immigrant themes, attacking Chinese immigrants as unfit for American citizenship. In the 1870s, the party manifesto of the Workingmen's Party declared: "To an American, death is preferable to life on par with the Chinaman. . . . Treason is better than to labor beside a Chinese slave."[43] In 1884, the Democratic Party endorsed Chinese exclusion in order to appeal to the labor vote.

> [The Chinese] come to this country not to partake in the responsibilities of citizenship; they come here with no love of our institutions; they do not hold intercourse with the people of the United States except for gain; they do not homologate in any degree with them. On the contrary, they are parasites when they come, parasites while they are here, and parasites when they go.[44]

Eugene Debs also disparaged new immigrant workers, regarding them as poor material for American citizenship: "The Dago works for small pay, and lives far more like a savage or a wild beast, than the Chinese."[45]

Thus, in the past, some advocates of nineteenth-century worker republicanism have also espoused ascriptive notions of American citizenship that privileged native-born white males, who represented their ideal of free labor and the citizenship standing it confers. Does this mean that worker republicanism is essentially inegalitarian and undemocratic? Is it so intertwined with ascriptive notions of American citizenship that it is irredeemable for today's labor movement, or unavailable to women and to nonwhites? These questions raise serious objections to the proposal that American workers should consider the right to strike a citizenship right supported by the principles of worker republicanism, and a full treatment of these questions would go beyond the scope of this book. Still, here are at least some tentative responses.

First, critics need to make a stronger case that worker republicanism logically and necessarily promotes ascriptive notions of American citizenship. A strong historical connection is apparent: white men were free workers who espoused these principles; some early labor leaders expressed illiberal and unrepublican beliefs. Such strong historical connections raise questions, but they do not establish logical connections. Instead, these connections suggest that those who expressed these views had not fully reconciled their beliefs and their principles. Rogers Smith demonstrates that various groups and elites have drawn on multiple traditions of American citizenship to gain political advantage, for example, but he recognizes that this has led to an extremely inconsistent set of citizenship laws.

Some nineteenth- and twentieth-century liberal labor leaders and reformers also expressed inconsistent and unreconciled beliefs on this topic. Samuel Gompers declared:

> Unless protective measures were taken, it was evident the whole [cigar] industry would soon be "Chinaized". . . . This was an element in deciding the cigar-makers to give early and hearty endorsement to the movement for a national organization of labor unions, for the help of all wage earners was needed in support of Chinese exclusion.[46]

Gompers and Herman Guttstadt, another AFL official, authored a pamphlet stating their position on Chinese exclusion, *Meat vs. Rice: American Manhood vs. Asiatic Coolieism: Which Shall Survive?* Exclusionary craft unionism that promoted the interests of "old labor" became the strategy of the AFL. Herbert Hill, former legal counsel for the NAACP, has painstakingly documented the continuation of racial exclusion by AFL-CIO unions, even after the passage of the National Labor Relations Act, and their resistance to equal employment opportunity and affirmative action, even beyond the 1960s, which he blames for much of the institutional racism that persists today in the American labor market.[47] Although liberal labor leaders in the past have expressed ascriptive attitudes and tolerated unequal employment opportunities, that does not mean that modern liberalism logically and necessarily promotes ascriptive notions of American citizenship.

Second, strikebreaking has been a more serious cause than worker republicanism itself of ethnic divisions and racial strife. Employers in the late nineteenth and early twentieth centuries discovered that employing strikebreakers from different racial and ethnic groups than the striking workers weakened labor solidarity and provided a wedge strategy for dividing the labor movement. This contributed to ascriptive beliefs and inflamed working-class prejudices. Ronald Takaki observes that one of the first such incidents involved the employment of Chinese immigrants to break a strike by shoe factory workers in 1870 in North Adams, Massachusetts. He quotes a writer for *Scribner's Monthly*: "If for no other purpose than the breaking up of the incipient steps toward labor combinations and 'Trade Unions' . . . the advent of Chinese labor should be hailed with a warm welcome." The "heathen Chinese," the writer concluded, could be the "final solution" to the labor problem in America.[48] Stephen Norwood has written about employers' exploitation of blacks as strikebreakers, commenting that their employment in the 1904 national pack-inghouse workers' strike and the 1905 Chicago teamsters' strike were "critically important to forging an identity for African Americans as a 'scab race,' a perception widely held by the white public and in the labor movement until the 1930s."[49] Strikebreaking was a greater source of division than worker republicanism, and strengthening the right to strike would curtail this strategy in the future.

Third, the historical record also presents counterexamples of labor organizations, leaders, and reformers who transcended boundaries of race, ethnicity, and gender. For example, the largest labor organization that proclaimed nineteenth-century worker republicanism, the Knights of Labor, pursued a racially and ethnically inclusive strategy as a matter of policy. So did the early United Mine Workers, which formed in 1890 out of a combination of the National Progressive Union of Miners and Mine Laborers and local assemblies of the Knights of Labor. Many CIO unions also opened their membership to African Americans, realizing that inclusion was the best strategy against strikebreaking. In addition, labor leaders and reformers who made invidious statements about immigrants, such as Debs and Henry George, came to recognize immigration reform as a red herring that distracted the labor movement from more important goals.[50]

Finally, more recent labor leaders and reformers have presented their case for collective action on grounds reminiscent of worker republicanism, suggesting that worker republicanism is available for appropriation by groups other than white male workers. During the Memphis sanitation workers' strike, Martin Luther King Jr. acknowledged the connection between degraded work and second-class citizenship, and recognized that full membership in American society called for dignity at work as well as collective action. In his speech "I Have Seen the Promised Land," King asserted: "Whenever the slaves get together, something happens in Pharaoh's court. When the slaves get together, that's the beginning of the getting out of slavery." King thus encouraged the sanitation strikers to exercise their "right to protest for right." Likewise, Cesar Chavez frequently spoke of "La Causa" and his dream to improve the lives of farm workers and ultimately to end the system of migrant labor that employed Mexican Americans as well as legal and illegal Mexican nationals.

> Farm laborers acknowledged that we had allowed ourselves to become victims in a democratic society—a society where majority rule and collective bargaining are supposed to be more than academic theories or political rhetoric. And by addressing this historical problem, we created confidence, pride, and hope in an entire people's ability to create the future.[51]

King and Chavez recognized that demeaning work and low wages abetted second-class citizenship for black sanitation workers and Mexican American farm workers, and that exercising the right to strike promoted self-rule and full membership in society. William Sylvis and George McNeill would have agreed.

Notes

1. "An inevitable and irresistible conflict"

1. Julius Getman, *The Betrayal of Local 14* (Ithaca: ILR Press, an imprint of Cornell University Press, 1998).

2. Getman, *Betrayal of Local 14*, 213.

3. United States Bureau of Labor Statistics, *Compensation and Working Conditions* (Washington, D.C.: GPO, December, 2004).

4. Seymour Martin Lipset, *The First New Nation: The United States in Historical and Comparative Perspective* (New York: Basic Books, 1963), 178–82; Stanley Aronowitz, *False Promises: The Shaping of American Working Class Consciousness* (New York: McGraw-Hill, 1973), 259; Philip Taft and Philip Ross, "American Labor Violence: Its Causes, Character, and Outcomes," in *Violence in America*, ed. Hugh Graham and Ted Gurr (New York: Bantam, 1969), 281; Walter Korpi, *The Democratic Class Struggle* (London: Routledge and Kegan Paul, 1983), 175–76; Walter Korpi and Michael Shalev, "Strikes, Power, and Politics in Western Nations, 1900–1976," *Political Power and Social Theory* 1 (1980): 323; Paul K. Edwards, *Strikes in the United States, 1881–1974* (New York: St. Martin's, 1984), 219–53.

5. Korpi and Shalev, 323; Walter Korpi and Michael Shalev, "Strikes, Industrial Relations, and Class Conflict in Western Nations," *British Journal of Sociology* 30 (1979): 164–87.

6. Korpi, *Democratic Class Struggle*, 165.

7. Arthur M. Ross and Paul T. Hartman, *Changing Patterns of Industrial Conflict* (New York: John Wiley, 1960).

8. Michael Goldfield, *The Decline of Organized Labor in the United States* (Ithaca: Cornell University Press, 1987), 39–54; Richard B. Freeman and James L.

Medoff, *What Do Unions Do?* (New York: Basic Books, 1984), 221–45; and Thomas A. Kochan, Harry C. Katz, and Robert B. McKersie, *The Transformation of American Industrial Relations* (New York: Basic Books, 1986), 48–50.

9. Rajib N. Sanyal, "The Withering Away of the Strike: The Ross-Hartman Thesis Thirty Years Since," *Labor Studies Journal* 15, no. 4 (1990): 56; Bureau of Labor Statistics, *Compensation and Working Conditions*, various years.

10. Sanyal, "Withering Away of the Strike," 58.

11. See, e.g., Mike Davis, *Prisoners of the American Dream: Politics and Economy in the History of the U.S. Working Class* (London: Verso, 1986), 136–49; Kim Moody, *An Injury to All: The Decline of American Unionism* (London: Verso, 1988), 127–64; Thomas Byrne Edsall, *The New Politics of Inequality* (New York: Norton, 1984), 151–78; Desmond King, *The New Right: Politics, Markets, and Citizenship* (Chicago: Dorsey, 1987), 154–55.

12. Korpi and Shalev, "Strikes, Industrial Relations, and Class Conflict," 164–87; Korpi and Shalev, "Strikes, Power, and Politics in Western Nations," 301–34; Edward Shorter and Charles Tilly, *Strikes in France, 1830–1968* (Cambridge: Cambridge University Press, 1974), 317; Douglas A. Hibbs Jr., *The Political Economy of Industrial Democracies* (Cambridge: Harvard University Press, 1987), 62. Others suggest that increasing global competition accounts for the decline in U.S. strike rates. See, e.g., William B. Gould, *Agenda for Reform: The Future of Employment Relationships and the Law* (Cambridge: MIT Press, 1996), 181. However, no other country has experienced such a dramatic decline in its strike rates. Canada, which is exposed to much of the same international economic pressures as the United States, has actually experienced an *increase* in its strike rates. See Paul Weiler, "Striking a New Balance: Freedom of Contract and the Prospects for Union Representation," *Harvard Law Review* 98 (1984). Moreover, global competition affects at most 20 percent of U.S. firms, but the strike rate remains low in industries not exposed to global competition, such as transportation, construction, retail, services, and so forth, as well as in manufacturing.

13. Brian Smart, "The Right to Strike and the Right to Work," *Journal of Applied Philosophy* 2 (1985): 31–40; J. L. McFarlane, *The Right to Strike* (Harmondsworth, England: Penguin, 1981). For a criticism of this view, see H. B. Acton, "Strikes, Trade Unions, and the State," in *The Morality of Politics*, ed. Bhiku Parekh and B. N. Berki (London: Allen Unwin, 1972), 136–48: "One does not have to be a totalitarian to question the wisdom of including striking among the human rights" (148). Also see Friedrich A. Hayek, *The Constitution of Liberty* (Chicago: University of Chicago Press, 1960), 267–84, for the classic liberal critique of the right to strike.

14. Ann Freemantle, *Papal Encyclicals in Their Historical Context* (New York: New American Library, 1956), 167–95, 228–35.

15. Vatican Council (2nd, 1962–1965), *The Teachings of the Second Vatican Council: Complete Texts of the Constitutions, Decrees, and Declarations* (Westminster, Md.: Newman Press, 1966), 524. For fuller discussions of workers' rights in Catholic social thought, see Michael Joseph Schuck, *That They Be One: The Social Teaching of the Papal Encyclicals, 1740–1989* (Washington, D.C.: Georgetown University Press, 1991).

16. National Council of Churches of Christ, *The Right to Strike and the General Welfare* (New York: Council Press, 1967), 4. See also Walter Rauschenbusch, *Christianity and the Social Crisis* (New York: Harper and Row, 1964 [1902]).

17. National Council of Churches, *Right to Strike*, 11–14. See also Rauschenbusch, *Christianity and the Social Crisis*, 327: "The working class is now engaged in a great historic class struggle which is ever more conscious and bitter. Their

labor is all they have. Individually they are helpless. Their only hope for wrestling better wages and conditions from the other side is in union of action."

18. T. H. Marshall and Tom Bottomore, *Citizenship and Social Class* (London: Pluto, 1991 [1950]), 12, 26, 40.

19. Maurice Cranston, *What Are Human Rights?* (London: Bodley Head, 1973), 77.

20. International Labour Organization, *Freedom of Association and Collective Bargaining* (Geneva: ILO, 1981), 61–78. According to ILO case number 1543, U.S. employers who hire permanent striker replacements impair this right to strike.

21. *Stapleton v. Mitchell,* 1945, 60 F Supp. 51, p. 61.

22. Keith David Ewing, *The Right to Strike* (Oxford: Clarendon, 1991), 2, 150–52. Interestingly, the right to strike has also eroded in Britain, under the Employment (Consolidation) Act of 1978, which permits employers to terminate strikers en masse, and the 1982 amendments, which permit employers to hire crossovers. Thus, the striker replacement strategy became common in Britain under Thatcher at about the same time it became common in the United States under Reagan. Rupert Murdoch, for example, used this strategy in the 1985 *London Post* strike and the 1994 *New York News* strike. Similar modern liberal principles inform the law of labor disputes in both countries.

23. Michael J. Sandel, *Liberalism and the Limits of Justice* (Cambridge: Cambridge University Press, 1982), 179; Michael J. Sandel, *Democracy's Discontent: America in Search of a Public Philosophy* (Cambridge: Harvard University Press, 1996), 6.

24. Milton R. Konvitz, "An Empirical Theory of the Labor Movement: W. Stanley Jevons," *Philosophical Review* 57 (January 1948): 75.

25. John R. Hicks, *The Theory of Wages,* 2nd ed. (London: Macmillan, 1964 [1932]).

26. Alvin Hansen, "Cycles of Strikes," *American Economic Review* 11 (March 1921): 616–21; Albert Rees, "Industrial Conflict and Business Fluctuations," *Journal of Political Economy* 60 (October 1952): 371–82; Orley Aschenfelter and George E. Johnson, "Bargaining Theory, Trade Unions, and Industrial Strike Activity," *American Economic Review* 59 (March 1969): 35–48; David Card, "Strikes and Bargaining: A Review of the Recent Empirical Literature," *American Economic Association, Papers and Proceedings, 102nd Meeting* 80 (May 1990): 410–15.

27. 254 U.S. 481.

28. *NLRB v. Insurance Agents,* 1960, 316 U.S., 489.

29. Shorter and Tilly, *Strikes in France,* iv.

30. Korpi and Shalev, "Strikes, Power and Politics in Western Nations," 324–25; Hibbs, *Political Economy of Industrial Democracies,* 62.

31. Max Weber, "Politics as a Vocation," in *From Max Weber: Essays in Sociology,* trans. and ed. H. H. Gerth and C. Wright Mills (New York: Oxford University Press, 1969 [1946]), 78.

32. Hicks, *Theory of Wages,* 146.

33. Mancur Olson, *The Logic of Collective Action: Public Goods and the Theory of Groups* (Cambridge: Harvard University Press, 1965), 71.

34. Robert Blauner, *Alienation and Freedom: The Factory Worker and His Industry* (Chicago: University of Chicago Press, 1964), 122.

35. See Freeman and Medoff, *What Do Unions Do?*.

36. Sean Wilentz, *Chants Democratic: New York City and the Rise of the American Working Class, 1788–1850* (Oxford: Oxford University Press, 1984), 87–97.

37. Claus Offe, "Two Logics of Collective Action," in Claus Offe, *Disorganized Capitalism: Contemporary Transformations of Work and Politics* (Cambridge: MIT Press, 1985), 187–200.

38. Archibald Cox, "Strikes, Picketing, and the Constitution," *Vanderbilt Law Review* 4 (1951): 574.

39. 310 U.S. 88.

40. Quoted by Sidney Fine, "Frank Murphy, the Thornhill Decision, and Picketing as Free Speech," *Labor History* 6 (spring 1965): 376.

41. 316 U.S. 708.

42. See, e.g., *Hopkins v. Oxley Stove Co.*, 1897; *Teamsters Local 695, AFL v. Vogt, Inc.*, 354 U.S. 284 (1957), and *Teamsters Local 309 v. Hanke*, 339 U.S. 470 (1950); James Gray Pope, "Labor and the Constitution: From Abolition to Deindustrialization," *Texas Law Review* 65 (May 1987): 1118. The Supreme Court has, on the other hand, ruled that picketing and boycotting to protest civil rights violations *do* constitute protected speech under the Constitution. See *NAACP v. Claiborne Hardware*, 486 U.S. 886 1982. Modern American liberalism remains ambivalent about strikes as protected forms of expression.

43. Herbert G. Gutman, *Work, Culture, and Society in Industrializing America: Essays in American Working-Class and Social History* (New York: Knopf, 1976); Alan Dawley, *Class and Community: The Industrial Revolution in Lynn* (Cambridge: Harvard University Press, 1976); Leon Fink, *Workingmen's Democracy: The Knights of Labor and American Politics* (Urbana: University of Illinois Press, 1983); Leon Fink, *In Search of the Working Class: Essays in American Labor History and Political Culture* (Urbana: University of Illinois, 1994); Eric Foner, *Free Soil, Free Labor, Free Men: The Ideology of the Republican Party before the Civil War* (Oxford: Oxford University Press, 1970); Bruce Laurie, *Working People of Philadelphia, 1800–1850* (Philadelphia: Temple University Press, 1980); David Montgomery, *Beyond Equality: Labor and the Radical Republicans, 1862–1872* (Urbana: University of Illinois Press, 1981 [1967]); David Montgomery, *Citizen Worker: The Experience of Workers in the United States with Democracy and the Free Market during the Nineteenth Century* (Cambridge: Cambridge University Press, 1993); Wilentz, *Chants Democratic*.

44. Judith Shklar, *American Citizenship: The Quest for Inclusion* (Cambridge: Harvard University Press, 1992), 63–101.

45. Edwin E. Witte, *The Government in Labor Disputes* (New York: Arno, 1969 [1932]), 17, noted that past labor leaders have made a similar case for a constitutional right to strike based on the Thirteenth Amendment's prohibition of involuntary servitude. The Supreme Court, however, generally regards the employee's liberty of contract as sufficient to maintain labor liberty.

46. John R. Commons et al., eds., *A Documentary History of American Industrial Society* (Cleveland: Arthur H. Clark, 1910), vols. 3 and 4; Edwin E. Witte, "Early American Labor Cases," *Yale Law Journal* 35 (1925–26): 825–37; Richard B. Morris, "Criminal Conspiracy and Early Labor Combinations in New York," *Political Science Quarterly* 52, no. 1: 51–85.

47. Edward Berman, *Labor and the Sherman Act* (New York: Russell and Russell, 1930); Felix Frankfurter and Nathan Greene, *The Labor Injunction* (Gloucester, Mass.: Peter Smith, 1963 [1928]); William E. Forbath, *Law and the Shaping of the American Labor Movement* (Cambridge: Harvard University Press, 1989), 59–97; Holly J. McCammon, " 'Government By Injunction': The U.S. Judiciary in the Late 19th and Early 20th Centuries," *Work and Occupations* 20 (May 1993): 174–204.

48. John R. Commons, *The Legal Foundations of Capitalism* (New York: Macmillan, 1932 [1924]), especially 307–12.

49. John R. Commons et al., *History of Labour in the United States*, vol. 1 (New York: Macmillan, 1918), 3–21; Selig Perlman, *A Theory of the Labor Movement* (New York: Macmillan, 1928), 157–58.

50. Louis Hartz, *The Liberal Tradition in America: An Interpretation of American Political Thought since the Revolution* (New York: Harcourt, Brace, 1955) is the classic treatment of this thesis. Jean Heffer and Jeanine Rovet, eds., *Why Is There No Socialism in the United States?* (Paris: Ecole des Hautes Etudes en Sciences Sociales, 1988) provides a wide variety of contemporary essays on this topic.

51. Hartz, *Liberal Tradition in America*, 6–7, 14–20; see also Seymour Martin Lipset, *The First New Nation: The United States in Historical and Comparative Perspective* (New York: Basic Books, 1963), 173–78.

52. Werner Sombart, *Why Is There No Socialism in the United States?* (New York: M. E. Sharpe, 1976 [1906]); Commons et al., *History of Labour in the United States*, vols. 1, 3; Perlman, *Theory of the Labor Movement*, 155; Seymour Martin Lipset, "The Failure of the American Socialist Movement," in Heffer and Rovet, *Why Is There No Socialism in the United States?*, 23.

53. Perlman, *Theory of the Labor Movement*, 157–61.

54. Commons et al., *History of Labour in the United States*, vols. 1, 3; Lipset, "Failure of the American Socialist Movement," 25; Gwendolyn Mink, *Old Labor and New Immigrants in American Political Development: Union, Party, and State, 1875–1920* (Ithaca: Cornell University Press, 1986), 113–18; Amy Bridges, "Becoming Americans: The Working Classes in the United States before the Civil War," in Ira Katznelson and Aristide R. Zolberg, *Working-Class Formation: Nineteenth Century Patterns in Western Europe and the United States* (Princeton: Princeton University Press, 1986), 157–96; Martin Shefter, "Trade Unions and Political Machines: The Organization and Disorganization of the American Working Class in the Late Nineteenth Century," in Katznelson and Zolberg, *Working-Class Formation*, 197–276.

55. Commons et al., *History of Labour in the United States*, vols. 1, 9. See also Forbath, *Law and the Shaping of the American Labor Movement*, 37–56; Victoria C. Hattam, *Labor Visions and State Power: The Origins of Business Unionism in the United States* (Princeton: Princeton University Press, 1993); and Theodore J. Lowi, "Why Is There No Socialism in the United States? A Federal Analysis," in Heffer and Rovet, *Why Is There No Socialism in the United States?*, 69–85, offers another explanation: federalism provides "the key to the liberal victory over socialism" (77). The fragmentation of the state into many states discouraged the formation of a nationwide, class-based political movement. The weakness of the federal government and the institutionalization of property law at the state level meant "there was no national regime to topple, no national apparatus worth seizing" (84).

56. Karen Orren, *Belated Feudalism: Labor, the Law, and Liberal Development in the United States* (Cambridge: Cambridge University Press, 1991), 122–28.

57. Orren, *Belated Feudalism*, 3.

58. Orren, *Belated Feudalism*, 209.

59. Alan Dawley, "Farewell to 'American Exceptionalism,' " in Heffer and Rovet, ed., *Why Is There No Socialism in the United States?*; Sean Wilentz, "Against Exceptionalism: Class Consciousness and the American Labor Movement, 1790–1920," *International Labor and Working Class History* 26 (1984): 1–24; Aristide Zolberg, "How Many Exceptionalisms?" in Katznelson and Zol-

berg, *Working-Class Formation,* 397–454; Kim Voss, *The Making of American Labor: The Knights of Labor and Class Formation in the Nineteenth Century* (Ithaca: Cornell University Press, 1993), 89–101.

60. Comparison with early European labor movements, furthermore, has led historians to conclude that the early American labor movement was not so different from its European counterparts, and, in many ways, was more developed. In the United States, Britain, and France, the labor movement originated with associations of skilled artisans during the early stages of industrialization. All of them espoused a modified version of eighteenth-century bourgeois radicalism that promoted not the overthrow of the state and the system of private property but the rights of self-governing, free workers in a republic. Fink, *Workingmen's Democracy,* 3–6; Fink, *In Search of the Working Class,* 178; Wilentz, *Chants Democratic,* 243–45; Voss, *Making of American Labor,* 4–9.

61. Gabriel Kolko, *The Triumph of Conservatism: A Reinterpretation of American History, 1900–1916* (Chicago: Quadrangle Books, 1967 [1963]); James Weinstein, *The Corporate Ideal and the Liberal State, 1900–1918* (Boston: Beacon, 1968); Ronald Radosh, *American Labor and United States Foreign Policy* (New York: Random House, 1969).

62. E.g., Kolko, *Triumph of Conservatism,* concludes that "Progressivism was not the triumph of small businesses over trusts, as has often been suggested, but the victory of big businesses in achieving the rationalization of the economy that only the federal government could provide" (284).

63. Kolko, *Triumph of Conservatism,* 164; Weinstein, *Corporate Ideal;* Daniel R. Fusfeld, *The Rise and Repression of Radical Labor, 1877–1918,* 3rd ed. (Chicago: Charles H. Kerr, 1985), 62–64. On the other hand, the new American state at times continued to exercise repression against the more mainstream labor movement. For example, *Buck's Stove and Range Company v. American Federation of Labor* (36 Washington Law Reporter 822, 1908) affirmed contempt rulings against Gompers and other AFL leaders, and the federal government supported the suppression of the 1919 steelworkers' organizing strikes. See chapter 4.

64. "In [AFL-CIO leaders'] eyes, labor unions are meant to function as junior partners of the large corporations, and the leaders naturally seek only those gains that are acceptable to the system's top men, men from the corporate community who depend for their profits on Cold War politics; the union leaders see the chance for limited gains disappearing if they offer challenges to corporate foreign policy," Radosh, *American Labor and United States Foreign Policy,* 28–29. Also see Michael Goldfield, "Worker Insurgency, Radical Organization, and New Deal Labor Legislation," *American Political Science Review* 83 (December 1989): 1276; Christopher L. Tomlins, *The State and the Unions: Labor Relations, Law, and the Organized Labor Movement in America, 1880–1960* (Cambridge: Cambridge University Press, 1985), 145–47.

65. Katherine Van Wezel Stone, "The Post-War Paradigm in American Labor Law," *Yale Law Journal* 90 (June 1981): 1511–80; Duncan Kennedy, "Critical Labor Law Theory: A Comment," *Industrial Relations Law Journal* 4 (1981): 503–6; Karl Klare, "Judicial Deradicalization of the Wagner Act and the Origins of Modern Legal Consciousness, 1937–1941," *Minnesota Law Review* 62 (1977–78): 265; Karl Klare, "Labor Law as Ideology: Towards a New Historiography of Collective Bargaining Law," *Industrial Relations Law Journal* 4 (1981): 450–82; Staughton Lynd, "Government Without Rights: The Labor Law Vision of Archibald Cox," *Industrial Relations Law Journal* 4 (summer 1981): 483–95; James Atleson, *Values and Assumptions in American Labor Law* (Amherst: Univer-

sity of Massachusetts Press, 1982); Roberto Mangabeira Unger, *The Critical Legal Studies Movement* (Cambridge: Harvard University Press, 1983), 1–14.

66. Archibald Cox and John Dunlop, "Regulation of Collective Bargaining by the National Labor Relations Board," *Harvard Law Review* (1950); John Dunlop, *Industrial Relations Systems* (1958). For a general statement of this perspective, see Derek C. Bok and John T. Dunlop, *Labor and the American Community* (New York: Simon and Schuster, 1970); Stone, "Post-War Paradigm," 1511–15.

67. Kennedy, "Critical Labor Law Theory," 503.

68. Klare, "Labor Law as Ideology," 452–461.

69. Klare, "Judicial Deradicalization of the Wagner Act"; Stone, "Post-War Paradigm," 1526–30.

70. Tomlins, *State and the Unions*, 245, 328.

71. Theda Skocpol, "Bringing the State Back In: Strategies of Analysis in Current Research," in *Bringing the State Back In*, ed. Peter B. Evans, Dietrich Rueschmeyer, and Theda Skocpol (New York: Cambridge University Press, 1985), 3–37; Gross, *Broken Promises*.

72. Forbath, *Law and the Shaping of the American Labor Movement*, 135.

73. Hattam, *Labor Visions and State Power*, ix.

74. Stephen Skowronek, *Building a New American State: The Expansion of National Administrative Capacities, 1877–1920* (Cambridge: Cambridge University Press, 1982).

2. "Something of freedom is yet to come"

1. Robert Wiebe, *Self-Rule: A Cultural History of American Democracy* (Chicago: University of Chicago Press, 1995).

2. See also Edwin Emil Witte, "Early American Labor Cases," *Yale Law Journal* 35 (1926): 825–37; Richard B. Morris, "Criminal Conspiracy and Early Labor Combinations in New York," *Political Science Quarterly* 52 (March 1937): 51–85; Sean Wilentz, "Conspiracy, Power, and the Early Labor Movement: The People v. James Melvin et al., 1811," *Labor History* 24 (1983): 572–79; Christopher L. Tomlins, *The State and the Unions: Labor Relations, Law, and the Organized Labor Movement in America, 1880–1960* (Cambridge: Cambridge University Press, 1985), 32–59; Christopher L. Tomlins, "Criminal Conspiracy and Early Labor Combination: Massachusetts, 1824–1849," *Labor History* 28 (summer 1987): 370–86; Victoria Hattam, *Labor Visions and State Power: The Origins of Business Unionism in the United States* (Princeton: Princeton University Press, 1993), 30–75; and Christopher L. Tomlins, *Law, Labor, and Ideology in the Early American Republic* (Cambridge: Cambridge University Press, 1993), 101–219. Tomlins and Wilentz have uncovered seven additional conspiracy cases.

3. Quoted by Tomlins, *Law, Labor, and Ideology*, 123. The conspiracy doctrine in British law has a statutory basis, dating back to Edward I's Ordinance of Conspirators (1293) and the seventeenth-century Statutes of Artificers and Laborers. By the early nineteenth century, the statutory basis had been forgotten in U.S. courts, and U.S. judges accepted the common law basis.

4. *Commonwealth v. Hunt*, 1842, 4 Metc., Mass., 111, 38 Am. Dec. 346.

5. Hattam, *Labor Visions and State Power*, 36.

6. Tomlins, *Law, Labor, and Ideology*.

7. Wilentz, "Conspiracy, Power, and the Early Labor Movement," 572–79.

8. Bruce Laurie, *Working People of Philadelphia, 1800–1850* (Philadelphia: Temple University Press, 1980), 90–92.

9. Alan Dawley, *Class and Community: The Industrial Revolution in Lynn* (Cambridge: Harvard University Press, 1976), 78–89.

10. Tomlins, "Criminal Conspiracy and Early Labor Combination."

11. Witte, "Early American Labor Cases."

12. Sean Wilentz, *Chants Democratic: New York and the Rise of the American Working Class, 1788–1850* (Oxford: Oxford University Press, 1984), 288.

13. Wilentz, *Chants Democratic,* 377–81.

14. Laurie, *Working People of Philadelphia.*

15. Herbert G. Gutman, *Work, Culture, and Society in Industrializing America: Essays in American Working-Class and Social History* (New York: Knopf, 1976), 319.

16. Jerry M. Cooper, *The Army and Civil Disorder: Federal Military Intervention in Labor Disputes, 1877–1900* (Westport, Conn.: Greenwood Press, 1980), 18.

17. Quoted by Kim Voss, *The Making of American Exceptionalism: The Knights of Labor and Class Formation in the Nineteenth Century* (Ithaca: Cornell University Press, 1993), 24.

18. Judith Shklar, *American Citizenship: The Quest for Inclusion* (Cambridge: Harvard University Press, 1991), 83.

19. William Sylvis, "Speech Delivered at Boston, January 1867," in *The Life, Speeches, Labors and Essays of William H. Sylvis,* ed. James C. Sylvis (Philadelphia: Claxton, Remson and Haffelfinger, 1872), 184. All Sylvis quotations are from this book.

20. Wiebe, *Self-Rule,* 23–31.

21. David Montgomery, *Beyond Equality: Labor and the Radical Republicans, 1862–1872* (Urbana: University of Illinois Press, 1981 [1967]), 14–25; Wiebe, *Self-Rule,* 31–40.

22. David Brody, *In Labor's Cause: Main Themes on the History of the American Worker* (New York: Oxford University Press, 1993), 11.

23. Robert J. Steinfeld, *The Invention of Free Labor: The Employment Relation in English and American Law and Culture, 1350–1870* (Chapel Hill: University of North Carolina Press, 1991).

24. Quoted by Eric Foner, *Free Soil, Free Labor, Free Men: The Ideology of the Republican Party before the Civil War* (New York: Oxford University Press, 1970), 42.

25. Foner, *Free Soil, Free Labor, Free Men,* 40–65.

26. Quoted by Foner, *Free Soil, Free Labor, Free Men,* 20.

27. Montgomery, *Beyond Equality,* 335–86.

28. Dawley, *Class and Community,* 50–58; Wilentz, *Chants Democratic,* 363–89.

29. Orestes A. Brownson, *The Laboring Classes (1840) with Brownson's Defence of the Article on the Laboring Classes* (Delmar, N.Y.: Scholars' Facsimiles and Reprints, 1978), 13.

30. George E. McNeill, *The Labor Movement: The Problem of To-Day* (Boston: A. M. Bridgeman, 1886), 454.

31. Marcus Cunliffe, *Chattel Slavery and Wage Slavery: The Anglo-American Context* (Athens: University of Georgia Press, 1979).

32. Quoted by Cunliffe, *Chattel Slavery and Wage Slavery,* 12.

33. Quoted by Wilentz, *Chants Democratic,* 333.

34. Quoted by Montgomery, *Beyond Equality,* 251–52.

35. Quoted by Leon Fink, *Workingmen's Democracy: The Knights of Labor and American Politics* (Urbana: University of Illinois Press, 1983), 4.

36. Aristotle, *The Politics of Aristotle,* trans. Ernest Barker (Oxford: Oxford University Press, 1948), 123–26.

37. Edward P. Thompson, *The Making of the English Working Class* (New York: Vintage, 1966), chap. 5; Eric Foner, *Tom Paine and Revolutionary America* (London: Oxford University Press, 1976).

38. Foner, *Tom Paine,* 90–100.

39. For a discussion of the producerist ideology of the early American labor movement, see Hattam, *Labor Visions and State Power,* chap. 3.

40. William Leggett, "The Corporation Question," *Democratick Editorials: Essays in Jacksonian Political Economy,* ed. Lawrence H. White (Indianapolis: Liberty Press, 1984 [1837]), 343.

41. Quoted by Richard T. Ely, *The Labor Movement in America* (New York: Thomas Y. Crowell, 1886), 147.

42. See "Platform of Principles of the National Labor Union, 1868," in Sylvis, 284–85.

43. Sylvis, "Address Delivered at Buffalo, New York, January 1864," 111.

44. John R. Commons et al., *Documentary History of American Industrial Society* (Cleveland: Arthur H. Clarke, 1910), vol. 6, 44–45.

45. Sylvis, "The Aristocracy of Intellect," 445.

46. Leggett, "Right Views Among the Right Sort of People," *Democratick Editorials,* 265.

47. Sylvis, "Address Delivered at Chicago Convention, January 9, 1865," 129–30.

48. Ira Steward, "A Reduction of Hours an Increase of Wages," 1865, in Commons et al., *Documentary History,* vol. 9, 297.

49. Sylvis, "Platform of Principles of the National Labor Union, adopted Friday, September, 25, 1868," 284.

50. Sylvis, "Address Delivered at Chicago Convention, January 9, 1865," 171–72.

51. Quoted by S. M. Jelley, *The Voice of Labor* (Philadelphia: H. J. Smith, 1888), 198.

52. Sylvis, "Address Delivered at Chicago Convention, January 9, 1865," 156.

53. Brownson, *Laboring Classes,* 21.

54. McNeill, *Labor Movement,* 469.

55. Sylvis, "Platform of Principles of the National Labor Union, adopted Friday, September 15, 1868," 286.

56. McNeill, *Labor Movement,* 462.

57. Michael Sandel, *Democracy's Discontent: America in Search of a Public Philosophy* (Cambridge: Belknap Press of Harvard University Press, 1996), 7.

58. John Rawls, *A Theory of Justice* (Cambridge: Harvard University Press, 1973), 30. See also John Rawls, "Justice as Fairness: Political Not Metaphysical," *Philosophy & Public Affairs* 14 (1985): 223–51.

59. Friedrich A. Hayek, *The Constitution of Liberty* (Chicago: University of Chicago Press, 1960), 283.

60. Hayek, *Constitution of Liberty,* 231.

61. Rawls, *Theory of Justice,* 272.

62. McNeill, *Labor Movement,* 455, quoting from his 1877 editorial.

63. Quoted by Wilentz, *Chants Democratic,* 242.

64. Sylvis, "Address Delivered at Buffalo, New York, January 1864," 104.

65. George McNeill, "The Philosophy of the Labor Movement" (Washington, D.C.: American Federation of Labor, 1926 [1893]), 2.

66. Ira Steward, "The Power of the Cheaper over the Dearer," Commons et al., *Documentary History,* vol. 9, 306–29.

67. Andrew C. Cameron, "The Address of the National Labor Congress to the Workingmen of the United States," Commons et al., *Documentary History,* vol. 6, 151.

68. Sylvis, "Address Delivered at Buffalo, New York, January 1864," 101.

69. McNeill, *Labor Movement,* 456.

70. Sylvis, "Address Delivered at Buffalo, New York, January 1864," 118.

71. On the Knights of Labor and the cooperative movement, see Commons et al., *History of Labour in the United States* (New York: Macmillan, 1935–36), vol. 2, 430–38.

72. Nick Salvatore, *Eugene V. Debs: Citizen and Socialist* (Urbana: University of Illinois Press, 1982), 151.

73. Sylvis, "Address Delivered at Boston, January 1867," 198–99.

74. For one possible institutional plan, see McNeill, *Labor Movement,* 508–31.

75. Fink, *Workingmen's Democracy,* 14.

76. McNeill, *Labor Movement,* 531.

77. "Combination, as we have been using or applying it, makes war upon the effects, leaving the cause undisturbed, to produce, continually, like effects. If wages are reduced, combination may force an advance; but they will go down again, because the *cause* of the reduction remains. . . . The cause of all these evils is the WAGES SYSTEM." William Sylvis, "Secret Circular to the Officers and Members of the several and subordinate Unions," 266.

78. Quoted in Commons et al., *Documentary History,* vol. 6, 385.

79. Steward, "A Reduction of Hours an Increase of Wages," 284–301. See also George Gunton, *Wealth and Progress: A Critical Examination of the Labor Problem* (New York: Appleton, 1887), for a more systematic treatment.

80. William Sylvis made the same point at the 1865 Chicago convention of the National Labor Union: "As civilization advances and workingmen become more enlightened, they will see that they have a right to a voice in the fixing of the 'wages fund,' and that ten per cent of what they produce is hardly a fair or just proportion to be set aside for their benefit" (164).

81. Steward, "Reduction of Hours," 285.

82. Steward, "Reduction of Hours," 291, 294–95.

83. Quoted by Montgomery, *Beyond Equality,* 260.

84. For a presentation of the National Labor Unions 1866 Baltimore Program, see Andrew C. Cameron in Commons et al., *Documentary History,* vol. 9, 126–68.

85. Montgomery, *Beyond Equality,* 305–11, 323–34.

86. For the history of the great upheaval, see Commons et al., *History of Labour in the United States,* vol. 2, 356–94.

87. Denunciations of strikes also occurred. The 1866 Baltimore Congress of the National Labor Unions regarded strikes as injurious and ill-advised, to be used as a *dernier* (last) resort. These denunciations were not directed against the right to strike, however. Instead, they were recognitions that strikes often ended in defeat, harming both the strikers and their organization. Labor leaders never denounced the right to strike as such. Thus, when Susan B. Anthony called for restoring the

resolution deprecating strikes at the 1868 New York Congress of the National Labor Union, while a massive strike by bricklayers was taking place, the National Labor Union instead issued a resounding resolution proclaiming the right to strike: "Resolved, that this congress recognizes in its platform the right of the workingmen and workingwomen of this nation to strike, when all other just and equitable concessions are refused. Adopted unanimously." In Commons et al., *Documentary History*, vol. 9, 208.

88. Commons et al., *History of Labour in the United States*, vol. 1, 3–21; Selig Perlman, *A Theory of the Labor Movement* (New York: Macmillan, 1928), 3–10, 154–207.

89. Wiebe, *Self-Rule*, 23–40.

90. Gwendolyn Mink, *Old Labor and New Immigrants in American Political Development: Union, Party, and State, 1875–1920* (Ithaca: Cornell University Press, 1986), 45–68.

91. Stephen Skowronek, *Building a New American State: The Expansion of National Administrative Capacities, 1877–1920* (Cambridge: Cambridge University Press, 1982), 21–22.

92. Ira Katznelson, *City Trenches: Urban Politics and the Patterning of Class in the United States* (Chicago: University of Chicago Press, 1981), 62.

93. See Richard Franklin Bensel, *The Political Economy of American Industrialization* (New York: Cambridge University Press, 2001), 233–52. The Civil War draft, however, did divide wage earners from others. The New York City draft riot of 1863, the largest civil disturbance of the nineteenth century, began as a spontaneous work stoppage.

94. Theodore J. Lowi, "Why Is There No Socialism in the United States? A Federal Analysis," in *Why Is There No Socialism in the United States?*, ed. Jean Heffer and Jeanine Rovet (Paris: Ecole des Hautes Etudes et Sciences Sociales, 1988), 69–85; Amy Bridges, "Becoming American: The Working Classes in the United States before the Civil War," in *Working Class Formation*, ed. Ira Katznelson and Aristide R. Zolberg (Princeton: Princeton University Press, 1986), 157–96.

95. Alexis De Tocqueville, *Democracy in America* (New York: Knopf, 1946), vol. 1, 55.

96. See, for example, Sean Wilentz, "Artisan Republican Festivals and the Rise of Class Conflict in New York City, 1787–1737," in *Working-Class America: Essays on Labor, Community, and American Society*, ed. Daniel J. Walkowitz (Urbana: University of Illinois Press, 1983); Wilentz, *Chants Democratic*, 87–97.

97. Weibe, *Self-Rule*, 22–23; Shklar, *American Citizenship*, chap. 2.

98. See, for example, Walter Dean Burnham, *The Current Crisis in American Politics* (New York: Oxford University Press, 1982), 50. See also Martin P. Wattenberg, *Where Have All the Voters Gone?* (Cambridge: Harvard University Press, 2002), 6.

99. Michael J. Sandel, *Democracy's Discontent: America in Search of a Public Philosophy* (Cambridge: Harvard University Press, 1996), 3.

3. "A nation of mock citizens"

1. Samuel Gompers, *Seventy Years of Life and Labor: An Autobiography*, vol. 1 (New York: Augustus M. Kelley, 1967 [1925]), 89–105, 134–63, 288–310, 403–27.

2. William E. Forbath, *Law and the Shaping of the American Labor Movement* (Cambridge: Harvard University Press, 1989).

3. Holly J. McCammon, " 'Government by Injunction': The U.S. Judiciary in the Late 19th and Early 20th Centuries," *Work and Occupations* 20, no. 2 (May 1993): 175.

4. Victoria C. Hattam, *Labor Visions and State Power: The Origins of Business Unionism in the United States* (Princeton: Princeton University Press, 1993), 204.

5. Jerry M. Cooper, "The Army and Industrial Workers: Strikebreaking in the Late Nineteenth Century," in *Soldiers and Civilians: The U.S. Army and the American People,* ed. Garry D. Ryan and Timothy K. Neuringer (Washington, D.C.: National Archives and Records Administration, 1987), 259; Burton C. Hacker, "The United States Army as a National Police: The Federal Policing of Labor Disputes, 1877–1896," *Military Affairs* 33, no. 1 (April 1969): 259; Arthur A. Ekrich Jr., "The American Liberal Tradition and Military Affairs," in *Bayonets in the Streets: The Use of Troops in Civil Disorders,* ed. Robin Higham (Manhattan, Kans.: Sunflower University Press, 1969), 143; John K. Mahon, "The Domestic Use of Armed Force: A Summary," in Higham, 224; Jerry M. Cooper, "The Army as Strikebreaker: The Railroad Strikes of 1877–1894," *Labor History* 18, no. 2 (spring 1977): 178–98; William Riker, *Soldiers of the States* (New York: Arno, 1979 [1957]), 47–63; Martha Derthick, *The National Guard in Politics* (Cambridge: Harvard University Press, 1967), 16–19. Historians disagree about the exact number of National Guard unit deployments because not all interventions were documented.

6. Alexis de Tocqueville, *Democracy in America,* vol. 1 (New York: Knopf, 1946), 57.

7. Robert Wiebe, *Self-Rule: A Cultural History of American Democracy* (Chicago: University of Chicago Press, 1995), 23–39.

8. David Montgomery, "Labor and the Republic in Industrial America, 1860–1920," *Le Mouvement Social* 11 (June–July 1980): 201–15, esp. 204–6.

9. Paul Krause, *The Battle for Homestead, 1880–1982: Politics, Culture, and Steel* (Pittsburgh: University of Pittsburgh Press, 1992), 347–48.

10. John R. Commons, *A Sociological View of Sovereignty* (New York: Augustus Kelley, 1965 [1899–1900]), 45.

11. Max Weber, "Politics as a Vocation," in *From Max Weber: Essays in Sociology,* ed. H. H. Gerth and C. Wright Mills (New York: Oxford University Press, 1959 [1946]), 78.

12. Lt. William Wallace, "The Army and the Civil Power," *Journal of Military Service Institutions of the United States* 17, no. 77 (September 1895): 255.

13. Riker, *Soldiers of the States,* 50–51; Jeremy Brecher, *Strike!* (Boston: South End Press, 1972), 44–45.

14. Leon Wolff, *Lockout, The Story of the Homestead Strike of 1892: A Study of Violence, Unionism, and the Carnegie Steel Empire* (New York: Harper and Row, 1965), 69.

15. Jerold S. Auerbach, *Labor and Liberty: The La Follette Committee and the New Deal* (Indianapolis: Bobbs-Merrill, 1966), 101.

16. Quoted by Auerbach, *Labor and Liberty,* 100, 107.

17. The Labor Bureau eventually became the Bureau of Labor Statistics within the Department of Labor, which Congress established as a separate cabinet-level department in 1913.

18. Karen Orren, *Belated Feudalism: Labor, Law, and Liberal Development in the United States* (Cambridge: Cambridge University Press, 1991), 191.

19. Gerald G. Eggert, *Railroad Labor Disputes: The Beginnings of Federal Strike Policy* (Ann Arbor: University of Michigan Press, 1967), 98–102.

20. United States Strike Commission, *Report on the Chicago Strike, June–July 1894* (Washington, D.C.: GPO, 1895).

21. Martin Shefter, "Trade Unions and Political Machines: The Organization and Disorganization of the American Working Class in the Late Nineteenth Century," in *Working-Class Formation: Nineteenth Century Patterns in Western Europe and the United States,* ed. Ira Katznelson and Aristide Zolberg (Princeton: Princeton University Press, 1986). Also see Amy Bridges, "Becoming Americans: The Working Classes in the United States before the Civil War," in Katznelson and Zolberg, 157–90.

22. David Montgomery, *Beyond Equality: Labor and the Radical Republicans, 1862–1872* (Urbana: University of Illinois Press, 1981), 230–60.

23. Michael Sandel, *Democracy's Discontent: America in Search of a Public Philosophy* (Cambridge: Harvard University Press, 1996), 185–89.

24. Eric Foner, *A Short History of Reconstruction, 1863–1877* (New York: Harper and Row, 1990), 238–47.

25. Walter Dean Burnham, "The Changing Shape of the American Political Universe," in Burnham, *The Current Crisis in American Politics* (New York: Oxford University Press, 1982), 48.

26. Gwendolyn Mink, *Old Labor and New Immigrants in American Political Development: Union, Party, and State, 1875–1920* (Ithaca: Cornell University Press, 1986).

27. John Garraty, *Labor and Capital in the Gilded Age* (Boston: Little, Brown, 1968), summarizes the four volumes of testimony that the Blair Committee gathered in the early 1880s.

28. Melvyn Dubofsky, *The State and Labor in Modern America* (Chapel Hill: University of North Carolina Press, 1994), 13.

29. Cooper, "Army and Industrial Workers."

30. Ekrich, "American Liberal Tradition and Military Affairs"; Mahon, "Domestic Use of Armed Force."

31. 71 U.S. 2. Darwin Kelley, *Milligan's Fight against Lincoln* (New York: Exposition Press, 1973), 95–103; Ekrich, "American Liberal Tradition and Military Affairs," 143.

32. Jerry M. Cooper, *The Army and Civil Disorders: Federal Military Intervention in Labor Disputes, 1877–1900* (Westport, Conn.: Greenwood Press, 1980), 144.

33. See 1877 Secretary of War George Washington McCrary's statement below.

34. Herbert Gutman, "The Workers' Search for Power: Labor in the Gilded Age," in *The Gilded Age: A Reappraisal,* ed. H. Wayne Morgan (Syracuse, N.Y.: Syracuse University Press, 1963). See also Herbert Gutman, *Work, Culture, and Society in Industrializing America* (New York: Vintage, 1977), and Shefter, "Trade Unions and Political Machines," 157–90.

35. Wallace, "Army and the Civil Power," 235.

36. Wallace, "Army and the Civil Power," 257.

37. Robert V. Bruce, *1877: Year of Violence* (Chicago: Ivan R. Dee, 1959). See also Riker, *Soldiers of the States,* 47–53; Cooper, *Army and Civil Disorders;* and Cooper, "Army as Strikebreaker," 179–96.

38. Riker, *Soldiers of the States,* 44–49.

39. Quoted by Brecher, *Strike!,* 11.

40. Bruce, *1877: Year of Violence,* 180.

41. Riker, *Soldiers of the States,* 48.

42. Bruce, *1877: Year of Violence,* 93–95.

43. Cooper, "Army as Strikebreaker," 183–84.

44. Quoted by Hacker, "United States Army as a National Police," 260.

45. Derthick, *National Guard in Politics,* 16.

46. Riker, *Soldiers of the States,* 53.

47. Bruce, *1877: Year of Violence,* 311.

48. Stephen Skowronek, *Building a New American State: The Expansion of National Administrative Capacities, 1877–1920* (Cambridge: Cambridge University Press, 1982), 92–94.

49. Quoted by Cooper, *Army and Civil Disorder,* 13.

50. Quoted by Bruce, *1877: Year of Violence,* 232.

51. Quoted by Bruce, *1877: Year of Violence,* 225–26.

52. Wallace, "Army and the Civil Power," 264.

53. See George E. McNeill, *The Labor Movement: The Problem of To-Day* (Boston: A. M. Bridgeman, 1886); ; Leon Fink, "Class Conflict American-Style," *In Search of the Working Class: Essays in American Labor History and Political Culture* (Urbana: University of Illinois, 1994), 15–32; Leon Fink, *Workingmen's Democracy: The Knights of Labor and American Politics* (Urbana: University of Illinois, 1983), 3–17, 219–33; Kim Voss, *The Making of American Exceptionalism: The Knights of Labor and Class Formation in the Nineteenth Century* (Ithaca: Cornell University, 1993), 72–101, 185–225.

54. Joshua Freeman et al., *Who Built America? Working People and the Nation's Economy, Politics, Culture, and Society* (New York: Pantheon Books, 1992), 118.

55. Brecher, *Strike!,* 31.

56. The Federation of Organized Trades and Labor Unions was a forerunner of the American Federation of Labor. Wage earners could hold memberships in both a FOTLU affiliate and the Knights, because the latter was not a trade union.

57. Voss, *Making of American Exceptionalism,* 78; Brecher, *Strike!,* 39.

58. Fink, *Workingmen's Democracy,* 189–95.

59. Henry David, *The History of the Haymarket Affair: A Study in the American Social-Revolutionary and Labor Movements* (New York: Collier Books, 1963), 163–94.

60. In 1895, Illinois governor John Altgeld pardoned the three remaining men convicted of the bombing. See John Peter Altgeld, "Reasons for Pardoning Fielden, Neebe, and Schwab, the So-Called Anarchists," June 26, 1895, in *The Mind and Spirit of John Peter Altgeld: Selected Writings and Addresses,* ed. Henry C. Christman (Urbana: University of Illinois, 1960), 62–104.

61. Fink, *Workingmen's Democracy,* 194–97.

62. David, *History of the Haymarket Affair,* 41–42.

63. Quoted in Eric Foner, *The Story of American Freedom* (New York: Norton, 1998), 124.

64. Voss, *Making of American Exceptionalism,* 78–79.

65. Forbath, *Law and the Shaping of the American Labor Movement,* 73–78; Melvyn Dubofsky, "The Federal Judiciary, Free Labor, and Equal Rights," in *The Pullman Strike and the Crisis of the 1890s: Essays on Labor and Politics,* ed. Richard Schneirov, Shelton Stromquist, and Nick Salvatore (Urbana: University of Illinois Press, 1999), 159.

66. See, for example, Almont Lindsey, *The Pullman Strike: The Story of a Unique Experiment and of a Great Labor Upheaval* (Chicago: University of Chi-

cago Press, 1942); Cooper, *Army and Civil Disorder*, 144–64; Eggert, *Railroad Labor Disputes*, 152–91; Nick Salvatore, *Eugene V. Debs: Citizen and Socialist* (Urbana: University of Illinois, 1982), 126–39.

67. Cooper, *Army and Civil Disorder*, 165–72.

68. Skowronek, *Building a New American State*, 20.

69. John Peter Altgeld, "Address on Labor Unrest and the Pullman Strike," New York, October 17, 1896, in Christman, *Mind and Spirit of John Peter Altgeld*, 130–48.

70. Lindsey, *Pullman Strike*, 185, 214.

71. United States Strike Commission, *Report on the Chicago Strike*, xx.

72. Quoted by Lindsey, *Pullman Strike*, 164.

73. Christman, *Mind and Spirit of John Peter Altgeld*, 153.

74. Quoted by Eggert, *Railroad Labor Disputes*, 173.

75. Quoted by Lindsey, *Pullman Strike*, 163.

76. *In re Debs* 158 U.S. 564 (1895).

77. Quoted by Lindsey, *Pullman Strike*, 174.

78. Quoted by Brecher, *Strike!*, 85.

79. Gompers, *Seventy Years of Life and Labor*, 413.

80. United States Strike Commission, *Report on the Chicago Strike*, 170.

81. Quoted by Salvatore, *Eugene V. Debs*, 153–54.

82. See below, chap. 4. See also Daniel Fusfeld, *The Rise and Repression of Radical Labor, 1877–1918* (Chicago: Charles H. Kerr, 1980).

83. Samuel Gompers, *Labor and the Employer*, comp. and ed. Hayes Robbins (New York: Dutton, 1920 [1899]), 290–91.

84. Gompers, *Labor and the Employer*, 33.

85. See, e.g., Gompers, *Labor and the Employer*, 202, 224, 233.

86. Gompers, *Labor and the Employer*, 235.

87. The Arbitration Act of 1888 provided the president with this authority, although he refused to set up the U.S. Strike Commission to adjudicate the dispute.

88. United States Strike Commission, *Report on the Chicago Strike*, xlvi.

4. "The very instruments of democracy are often used to oppress them"

1. Felix Frankfurter and Nathan Greene, *The Labor Injunction* (Gloucester, Mass.: Peter Smith, 1963 [1928]), 66–74.

2. Holly J. McCammon, "Government by Injunction: The United States Judiciary in the Late Nineteenth and Early Twentieth Centuries," *Work and Occupations* 20, no. 2 (May 1993): 174–204; William E. Forbath, *Law and the Shaping of the American Labor Movement* (Cambridge: Harvard University Press, 1989), 193; Frankfurter and Greene, *Labor Injunction*.

3. Forbath, *Law and the Shaping of the American Labor Movement*, 193, 197.

4. *Duplex Printing v. Deering* 254 U.S. 443 (1921). The Court further weakened Section 20 in *American Steel Foundries v. Tri-City Trades Council* (1921), *United Mine Workers v. Coronado Co.* (1922), *Red Jacket Consolidated Coal & Coke Co. v. Lewis* (1922; allowed to stand on appeal, 1927), *Bedford Cut Stone Co. v. Journeymen Stone Cutters' Association* (1927), and other decisions. 254 U.S. 443 (1921); 257 U.S. 184 (1921); 259 U.S. 344 (1922); 275 U.S. 518 (1927); 274 U.S.

37 (1927). See Edward Berman, *Labor and the Sherman Act* (New York: Russell and Russell, 1969 [1930], 99–179.

5. Edward Berman, *Labor Disputes and the President of the United States* (New York: Longmans Green, 1924), 42–44; Jerry M. Cooper, *The Army and Civil Disorder: Federal Military Intervention in Labor Disputes, 1877–1900* (Westport, Conn.: Westport Press, 1980), 181–93.

6. Ex parte Milligan 71 U.S. 2 (1866). Darwin Kelley, *Milligan's Fight against Lincoln* (New York: Exposition Press, 1973), 95–103; Arthur A. Ekrich Jr., "The American Liberal Tradition and Military Affairs," in *Bayonets in the Streets: The Use of Troops in Civil Disorders*, ed. Robin Higham (Manhattan, Kans.: Sunflower University Press, 1969), 143.

7. Cooper, *Army and Civil Disorder*, 187.

8. *In re Boyle* (Idaho, 1899).

9. See George G. Suggs Jr., *Colorado's War on Militant Unionism: James H. Peabody and the Western Federation of Miners* (Norman: University of Oklahoma Press, 1990).

10. Berman, *Labor Disputes and the President*, 60–62. See also *Theodore Roosevelt: An Autobiography* (New York: Charles Scribner's, 1921), 480.

11. Suggs, *Colorado's War on Militant Unionism*, 96–99.

12. Quoted by Suggs, *Colorado's War*, 133–34.

13. *In re Moyer* (Colorado, 1904).

14. *Moyer v. Peabody* 212 U.S. 78 (1909).

15. David Alan Corbin, *Life, Work, and Rebellion in the Coal Fields: The Southern West Virginia Miners, 1880–1922* (Urbana: University of Illinois Press, 1981), 87–101.

16. Quoted by Corbin, *Life, Work, and Rebellion*, 99.

17. Robert Rankin, *When Civil Law Fails: Martial Law and Its Legal Basis in the United States* (Durham, N.C.: Duke University Press, 1939), 85.

18. Leon Stein and Philip Taft, eds., *Massacre at Ludlow* (New York: Arno, 1971), provides contemporary reports of the Colorado strike, including those of the Colorado Adjutant General's Office, the U.S. Commission on Industrial Relations, and Congress. See also H. M. Gitelman, *Legacy of Ludlow: A Chapter in American Industrial Relations* (Philadelphia: University of Pennsylvania Press, 1988).

19. Berman, *Labor Disputes and the President*, 79–85.

20. Colorado Adjutant General's Office, *The Military Occupation of the Coal Strike Zone of Colorado by the Colorado National Guard, 1913–1914* (Denver: Smith-Brook Printing Company), 30–31, in Stein and Taft, *Massacre at Ludlow*.

21. George P. West, *United States Commission on Industrial Relations: Report on the Colorado Strike, Washington, D.C., 1915* (Chicago: Barnard and Miller Printers), 126–33, in Stein and Taft, *Massacre at Ludlow*.

22. Quoted by Graham Adams, *Age of Industrial Violence: The Activities and Findings of the United States Commission on Industrial Relations* (New York: Columbia University Press, 1966), 159.

23. Gitelman, *Legacy of Ludlow*, 18–20.

24. West, *Report on the Colorado Strike*, 132.

25. Philip Taft and Philip Ross, "American Labor Violence: Its Causes, Character, and Outcome," in *Violence in America: Historical and Comparative Perspectives: A Report Submitted to the National Commission on the Causes and Prevention of Violence*, ed. Hugh Davis Graham and Ted Robert Gurr (New York: Bantam, 1969), 320–21.

26. Paul K. Edwards, *Strikes in the United States, 1881–1974* (New York: St. Martin's, 1981), 13–15.

27. The 1912 Lawrence, Massachusetts, textile workers' strike and the 1913 Patterson, New Jersey, silk workers' strike are among the best-known examples of this strategy.

28. Adams, *Age of Industrial Violence,* 1–25.

29. United States Commission on Industrial Relations, *Final Report and Testimony Submitted to Congress,* vol. 11 (Washington, D.C.: GPO, 1916), 158.

30. Richard T. Ely, *The Labor Movement in America* (New York: Thomas Y. Crowell, 1886); George E. McNeill, *The Labor Movement: The Problem of To-Day* (Boston: A. M. Bridgeman, 1886).

31. Seth Low, "The National Civic Federation and Industrial Peace," *Annals of the Academy of Political and Social Science* 44 (November 1912): 10–17.

32. Marguerite Green, *The National Civic Federation and the American Labor Movement, 1900–1925* (Washington, D.C.: Catholic University Press, 1956), 41.

33. David Montgomery, *The Fall of the House of Labor: The Workplace, the State, and American Labor Activism, 1865–1925* (New York: Cambridge University Press, 1987), 263.

34. "The purpose of the Act is to promote peaceful settlements of disputes by providing legal remedies for the invasion of employees' rights" (*NLRB v. Fansteel Metallurgical Corporation,* 306 U.S. 240, 1939).

35. Green, *National Civic Federation and the American Labor Movement,* 10; John R. Commons, *Myself* (New York: Macmillan, 1934), 81–87.

36. See, e.g., Samuel Gompers, *Labor and the Common Welfare,* ed. Hayes Robbins (New York: Dutton, 1919), 39; Samuel Gompers, *Labor and the Employer,* ed. Hayes Robbins (New York: Dutton, 1920 [1899]), 235.

37. See, e.g., Commons, *Myself,* 173–74.

38. Green, *National Civic Federation,* 69.

39. The 1947 Taft-Hartley Act specifically prohibits the NLRB from making substantive rulings in labor disputes. The Federal Conciliation and Mediation Service, a relatively minor agency, provides voluntary mediation on request.

40. Gabriel Kolko, *The Triumph of Conservatism: A Reinterpretation of American History, 1900–1916* (Chicago: Quadrangle Books, 1967), 164; James Weinstein, *The Corporate Ideal and the Liberal State, 1900–1918* (Boston: Beacon, 1968), 9–23.

41. John R. Commons, *The Legal Foundations of Capitalism* (New York: Macmillan, 1924), 307; John R. Commons, *The Economics of Collective Action* (Madison: University of Wisconsin Press, 1970).

42. Marcus Alonzo Hanna, "Every man who works with his hands is a human being" (Chicago: Public Policy Publishers, 1902).

43. David Montgomery, *Workers' Control in America: Studies in the History of Work, Technology, and Labor Struggles* (Cambridge: Cambridge University Press, 1979), 97–101.

44. Gitelman, *Legacy of Ludlow,* 51–67.

45. *Theodore Roosevelt: An Autobiography,* 464–79; Berman, *Labor Disputes and the President,* 46–59.

46. Berman, *Labor Disputes and the President,* 55–56; Gwendolyn Mink, *Old Labor and New Immigrants in America Political Development: Union, Party, and State, 1875–1920* (Ithaca: Cornell University Press, 1986), 177.

47. *Theodore Roosevelt: An Autobiography,* 466.

48. *Theodore Roosevelt: An Autobiography,* 377.

49. So controversial was the report that John R. Commons wrote a minority report.

50. Montgomery, *Fall of the House of Labor*, 361.

51. Melvin Dubofsky, *The State and Labor in Modern America* (Chapel Hill: University of North Carolina Press, 1994), 140.

52. Montgomery, *Workers' Control in America*, 96.

53. Alexander Bing, *War-Time Strikes and Their Adjustment* (New York: Arno, 1971 [1921]), 7.

54. Alvin H. Hansen, "Cycles of Strikes," *American Economic Review* 11 (1921): 616–21; Albert Rees, "Industrial Conflict and Business Fluctuations," *Journal of Political Economy* 60 (1952): 371–82; David Card, "Strikes and Bargaining: A Review of the Recent Empirical Literature," *American Economic Association, Papers and Proceedings, 102nd Meeting* 80 (1990): 410–15.

55. Montgomery, *Workers' Control in America*, 95–97.

56. Montgomery, *Fall of the House of Labor*, 375, 370.

57. Bing, *War-Time Strikes*, 1.

58. Taft and Ross, "American Labor Violence," 286–87.

59. Melvyn Dubofsky, *We Shall Be All: A History of the Industrial Workers of the World* (Urbana: University of Illinois Press, 1988), 380.

60. *Whitney v. California* 274 U.S. 357 (1927)

61. Dubofsky, *We Shall Be All*, 394–444; Daniel R. Fusfeld, *The Rise and Repression of Radical Labor, 1877–1918* (Chicago: Charles H. Kerr, 1985), 58–60; Montgomery, *Fall of the House of Labor*, 393–95.

62. United States Department of Labor, Bureau of Labor Statistics, *National War Labor Board: A History of its Formation and Activities, Together with its Awards and Documents of Importance in the Record of its Development* (Washington, D.C.: GPO, 1922), 34–35; Bing, *War-Time Strikes*, 154; Gitelman, *Legacy of Ludlow*, 230.

63. United States Department of Labor, *National War Labor Board*, especially 7–26.

64. For a summary of union density statistics, see Edwards, *Strikes in the United States, 1881–1974*, 260.

65. Bing, *War-Time Strikes*, 73–81; Montgomery, *Workers' Control in America*, 127–33; Berman, *Labor Disputes and the President*, 146–48.

66. David Brody, *Labor in Crisis: The Steel Strike of 1919* (Urbana: University of Illinois Press, 1987), 72–73; Corbin, *Life, Work, and Rebellion*, 176–90.

67. Montgomery, *Fall of the House of Labor*, 386; Dubofsky, *State and Labor*, 70.

68. Montgomery, *Fall of the House of Labor*, 392–94.

69. Quoted by Dubofsky, *State and Labor*, 77.

70. The following account is based primarily on Brody's *Labor in Crisis*; Commission of Inquiry, Interchurch World Movement, *Report on the Steel Strike of 1919* (New York: Harcourt, Brace and Howe, 1920); and Commission of Inquiry, Interchurch World Movement, *Public Opinion and the Steel Strike: Supplementary Reports of the Investigators* (New York: Harcourt, Brace, 1921).

71. Brody, *Labor in Crisis*, 115–28.

72. Brody, *Labor in Crisis*, 134, 154.

73. George Soule, "Civil Rights in Western Pennsylvania," in Commission of Inquiry, Interchurch World Movement, *Public Opinion and the Steel Strike*, 163–223. The Interchurch World Movement, a short-lived ecumenical organization

composed of the foremost Protestant leaders of the day, was established in the aftermath of World War I to promote education and social reform.

74. Soule, "Civil Rights in Western Pennsylvania," 178.

75. Commission of Inquiry, Interchurch World Movement, *Report on the Steel Strike*, 239. See also Soule, "Civil Rights in Western Pennsylvania," for the full report on this topic.

76. Corbin, *Life, Work, and Rebellion*, xiii.

77. Montgomery, *Fall of the House of Labor*, 387–88.

78. Corbin, *Life, Work, and Rebellion*, 198.

79. Berman, *Labor and the Sherman Act*, 118–39.

80. Corbin, *Life, Work, and Rebellion*, 199–224, provides a detailed account of this conflict.

81. Corbin, *Life, Work, and Rebellion*, 216.

82. Corbin, *Life, Work, and Rebellion*, 223–24.

83. Robert K. Murray, *The Harding Era: Warren G. Harding and His Administration* (Minneapolis: University of Minnesota Press, 1969), 238–64.

84. Eugene A. Trani and David L. Wilson, *The Presidency of Warren G. Harding* (Lawrence: University of Kansas Press, 1977), 100.

85. Irving Bernstein, *The Lean Years: A History of the American Worker, 1920–1932* (Boston: Houghton-Mifflin, 1960), 84.

86. Bernstein, *Lean Years*, 89.

87. Gwendolyn Mink argues that organized labor's decision to support Wilson in the 1912 presidential election institutionalized a partisan split in the labor movement, between old labor (primarily English, Irish, and German skilled workers associated with AFL unions) and new immigrants (unskilled immigrant workers from southern and eastern Europe and from China). See Mink, *Old Labor and New Immigrants*, 213–28.

5. "Let the toilers assemble"

1. 211 U.S. 78 (1925); 283 U.S. 697 (1931).

2. Irving Bernstein, *The Lean Years: A History of the American Worker, 1920–1933* (Boston: Houghton-Mifflin, 1960), 201.

3. Bernstein, *Lean Years*, 404.

4. *Bedford Cut Stone Co. v. Journeymen Stone Cutters' Association of North America*, 274 U.S. 37 (1927), 65.

5. Felix Frankfurter and Nathan Greene, *The Labor Injunction* (Gloucester, Mass.: Peter Smith, 1963 [1928]), 81.

6. See chap. 3, pp. 135–36.

7. The 1932 Norris–La Guardia Anti-Injunction Act was technically not a New Deal statute. However, the Congress that passed it was essentially the same Congress that passed the early New Deal legislation in 1933, and Felix Frankfurter, who helped draft the statute, was a New Deal appointment to the Supreme Court.

8. National Labor Relations Board, *Legislative History of the National Labor Relations Act 1935*, vol. 2 (Washington, D.C.: GPO, 1949), 3273, 3278. Sheldon Leader makes the case that the freedom of association implies the right to strike. See *Freedom of Association: A Study in Labor Law and Political Theory* (New Haven: Yale University Press, 1992), 180–210.

9. Quoted by Jerold Auerbach, *Labor and Liberty: The La Follette Committee and the New Deal* (Indianapolis: Bobbs-Merrill, 1966), 78.

10. Quoted by Auerbach, *Labor and Liberty*, 105–37; for a popular account of private strikebreaking forces, see Edward Levinson, *I Break Strikes* (New York: Arno: 1969 [1935]).

11. Donald Richberg, *Industrial Disputes and the Public Interest* (Berkeley: Institute for Industrial Relations, University of California, 1947), 59–60.

12. Auerbach, *Labor and Liberty*, 78.

13. Quoted by Sidney Fine, "Frank Murphy, the Thornhill Decision, and Picketing as Free Speech," *Labor History* 6 (spring 1965): 99.

14. See James A. Gross, *The Reshaping of the National Labor Relations Board: National Labor Policy in Transition, 1937–1947* (Albany: State University of New York Press, 1981).

15. Gross, *Reshaping of the National Labor Relations Board*, 151–86.

16. Quoted by Gross, *Reshaping*, 242.

17. David Saposs, who wrote the Interworld Church Committee's report on civil liberties violations during the 1919 steel strike, served as the director of the NLRB's economic research division during the years when it provided research support for the La Follette investigators.

18. David Brody, *In Labor's Cause: Main Themes on the History of the American Worker* (New York: Oxford University Press, 1993), 179–82.

19. This characterization of the compulsory arbitration model is an ideal type. In practice, strikes occur all the time under compulsory arbitration. Australia, for example, relies on this process for the adjustment of labor disputes, but has one of the highest strike rates among Western industrialized democracies. Critics point to the prevalence of strikes under compulsory arbitration as an indication that this process fails to secure industrial peace.

20. See, for example, "Platform of Principles of the National Labor Union, 1868," in *The Life, Speeches, Labors and Essays of William H. Sylvis*, ed. James C. Sylvis (Philadelphia: Claxton, Remson and Haffelfinger, 1872), 284–85.

21. John Dickinson, "The Recovery Program," in *America's Recovery Program*, ed. Clair Wilcox, Herbert Fraser, and Patrick Murphy Malin (London: Oxford University Press, 1934), 29.

22. Stanley Vittoz, *New Deal Labor Policy and the American Industrial Economy* (Chapel Hill: University of North Carolina Press, 1987); Colin Gordon, *New Deals: Business, Labor, and Politics in America, 1920–1930* (Cambridge: Cambridge University Press, 1994), 166.

23. Vittoz, *New Deal Labor Policy*, 95; Gordon, *New Deals*, 87–127.

24. Leo Wolman, "Labor under the NRA," in *America's Recovery Program*, ed. Wilcox et al., 94–97.

25. Irving Bernstein, *The New Deal Collective Bargaining Policy* (Berkeley: University of California Press, 1950), 58.

26. Irving Bernstein, *The Turbulent Years: A History of American Workers, 1933–1939* (Boston: Houghton-Mifflin, 1969), 172–73.

27. Quoted by Sidney Lens, *The Labor Wars: From the Molly Maguires to the Sitdowns* (Garden City, N.Y.: Doubleday, 1973), 246.

28. Melvyn Dubofsky and Warren Van Tine, *John L. Lewis: A Biography* (New York: Quadrangle Books, 1977), 184–87.

29. Dubofsky and Van Tine, *John L. Lewis*, 222–79.

30. Quoted by Gordon, *New Deals*, 208.

31. Quoted by Harold S. Roberts, *Compulsory Arbitration: Panacea or Millstone?* (Honolulu: University of Hawaii Press, 1965), 94.

32. Donald R. Richberg, "Before the Arbitration Board: Wages of Firemen and Hostlers, Western Railroads," pamphlet (Chicago, November 10, 1927), 38–39.

33. James A. Gross, *The Making of the National Labor Relations Board* (Albany: State University of New York Press, 1974), 21–33, discusses attempts by the early NLB to adjust the content of wage agreements.

34. Vittoz, *New Deal Labor Policy,* 139.

35. Gross, *Making of the National Labor Relations Board,* 76–88.

36. 10 F. Supp. 55 (1935).

37. 295 U.S. 549–550 (1935).

38. See, for example, Roberts, *Compulsory Arbitration.*

39. Nelson Lichtenstein, *Labor's War at Home: The CIO in World War II* (Cambridge: Cambridge University Press, 1982), contains a detailed account of the National War Labor Board, and the interaction of arbitration, wage and price controls, and labor unrest during World War II.

40. Friedrich A. Hayek, *The Constitution of Liberty* (Chicago: University of Chicago Press, 1960), 282–83.

41. Quoted by Leon Keyserling, "The Wagner Act: Its Origin and Current Significance," *George Washington Law Review* 29 (1960): 217.

42. Quoted by Paul A. Abodeely, *Compulsory Arbitration and the NLRB: A Study of Congressional Intent and Administration Policy* (Philadelphia: University of Pennsylvania, Wharton School of Finance and Commerce, Industrial Research Unit, 1968), 10.

43. United States National Labor Relations Board, *Legislative History of the National Labor Relations Act,* vol. 2 (Washington, D.C.: GPO, 1935), 2373–74.

44. 301 U.S. 1 (1937).

45. Quoted in Roberts, *Compulsory Arbitration,* 129.

46. Sumner Slichter, *Trade Unions in a Free Society* (Cambridge: Harvard University Press, 1947), 12.

47. Brinkley observes that the idea of the state that emerged during the late 1930s proposed that "Americans would have to accept the inevitable conflict and instability in their economic lives. And they would have to learn to rely on the state to regulate that conflict and instability." Alan Brinkley, "The New Deal and the Idea of the State," in *The Rise and Fall of the New Deal Order,* ed. Steve Fraser and Gary Gerstle (Princeton: Princeton University Press, 1989), 93.

48. Bernstein, *Turbulent Years,* 173.

49. The 1947 Taft-Hartley amendments added a list of unfair labor practices by labor unions to the NLRA.

50. What constitutes bargaining in bad faith remains controversial, since the NLRA does not require employers and employees to reach agreement. See, for example, Frederick U. Reel, "The Duty to Bargain and the Right to Strike," *George Washington Law Review* 29 (1960): 479–89; Archibald Cox, "The Duty to Bargain in Good Faith," *Harvard Law Review* 71 (1958): 1401–42.

51. See, e.g., Abodeely, *Compulsory Arbitration and the NLRB,* 1–10.

52. Quoted by Charles J. Morris, "The Role of Interest Arbitration in a Collective Bargaining System," in *The Future of Labor Arbitration in America,* ed. Joy Correge, Virginia A. Hughes, and Morris Stone (New York: American Arbitration Association, 1976), 208.

53. Quoted by Reel, "Duty to Bargain and the Right to Strike," 480.

54. Slichter, *Trade Unions in a Free Society,* 22. Herbert R. Northrup, *Compulsory Arbitration and Government Intervention in Labor Disputes* (Washington, D.C.: Labor Policy Association, 1966), 183.

55. Keyserling, "Wagner Act," 216–217.

56. Title 29, Chapter 7, Subchapter II, Section 1, United States Code.

57. Alvin Hansen, *Full Recovery or Stagnation?* (New York: Norton, 1938), 24–25.

58. Keyserling, "Wagner Act," 218–20.

59. Keyserling, "Wagner Act," 312–18. On social Keynesianism, see Margaret Weir, *Politics and Jobs: The Boundaries of Employment Policy in the United States* (Princeton: Princeton University Press, 1992), 28–41; Theda Skocpol, "The Limits of the New Deal System and the Roots of Contemporary Welfare Dilemmas," in *The Politics of Social Policy in the United States,* ed. Margaret Weir, Ann Shola Orloff, and Theda Skocpol (Princeton: Princeton University Press, 1988), 298–302.

60. Keyserling, "Wagner Act," 206.

61. 306 U.S. 257–58 (1939).

62. These procedures include NLRB-supervised representation elections, investigations of unfair labor practice complaints, and private grievance mediation.

63. Michael J. Sandel, *Democracy's Discontent: America in Search of a Public Philosophy* (Cambridge: Harvard University Press, 1996), 3–24. See also Michael J. Sandel, *Liberalism and the Limits of Justice* (Cambridge: Cambridge University Press, 1982).

64. 198 U.S. 45 (1905); 208 U.S. 161 (1908); 236 U.S. 1 (1915); 261 U.S. 523 (1923).

65. Title 29, Chapter 7, Subchapter II, Section 1, United States Code.

66. 301 U.S. 41 (1937).

67. 300 U.S. 379 (1937).

68. Auerbach, *Labor and Liberty,* 55.

69. Auerbach, *Labor and Liberty,* 108–97.

70. Sandel, *Democracy's Discontent,* 274.

6. "Get down to the type of job you're supposed to be doing"

1. Katherine Van Wezel Stone, "The Post-War Paradigm in American Labor Law," *Yale Law Journal* 90, no. 7 (June 1981): 1511–80; Christopher Tomlins, *The State and the Unions: Labor Relations, Law, and the Organized Labor Movement in America, 1880–1960* (Cambridge: Cambridge University Press, 1985), 282–316; Michael Goldfield, *The Decline of Organized Labor in the United States* (Chicago: University of Chicago Press, 1987), 32–33; Joel Rogers, "Divide and Conquer: Further Reflections on the Distinctive Character of American Labor Laws," *Wisconsin Law Review* no. 1 (1990): 8–11.

2. Stone, "Post-War Paradigm," 1545.

3. Tomlins, *The State and the Unions,* 245.

4. American Federation of Labor, *Conference of the Representatives of National, International, and the American Federation of Labor on Provisions of the Taft-Hartley Act* (Washington, D.C.: AFL, 1947); Harry A. Millis and Emily Clark Brown, *From the Wagner Act to Taft-Hartley: A Study of National Labor Policy and Labor Relations* (Chicago: University of Chicago Press, 1950), 271.

5. On the end of the New Deal era, see Alan Brinkley, *The End of Reform: New Deal Liberalism in Recession and War* (New York: Knopf, 1995).

6. Howell John Harris, *The Right to Manage: Industrial Relations Policies of American Business in the 1940s* (Madison: University of Wisconsin Press, 1982), 42.

7. Sumner Slichter, *Trade Unions in a Free Society* (Cambridge: Harvard University Press, 1947), 5.

8. Robert Lekachman, *The Age of Keynes* (New York: Random House, 1966), 287–89; Edwin Amenta and Theda Skocpol, "Redefining the New Deal: World War II and the Development of Social Provision in the United States," in *The Politics of Social Policy in the United States,* ed. Margaret Weir, Ann Shola Orloff, and Theda Skocpol (Princeton: Princeton University Press, 1988), 94; Margaret Weir, "The Federal Government and Unemployment: The Frustration of Policy Innovation from the New Deal to the Great Society," in *Politics of Social Policy,* ed. Weir, Orloff, and Skocpol, 171–80.

9. Richard Titmuss, "War and Social Policy," in Titmuss, *Essays on the Welfare State* (New Haven: Yale University Press, 1950), 82.

10. Jerold S. Auerbach, *Labor and Liberty: The La Follette Committee and the New Deal* (Indianapolis: Bobbs-Merrill, 1966), 108–97.

11. James Gross, *The Reshaping of the NLRB: National Labor Policy in Transition, 1937–1947* (Albany: State University of New York Press, 1981), 151–86.

12. Nelson Lichtenstein, *Labor's War at Home: The CIO in World War II* (Cambridge: Cambridge University Press, 1982), 8–25.

13. Irving Bernstein, *The Turbulent Years: A History of American Workers, 1933–1939* (Boston: Houghton-Mifflin, 1969), 686–99; Walter Galenson, *The CIO Challenge to the AFL: A History of the American Labor Movement, 1935–1941* (Cambridge: Harvard University Press, 1960), 3–24.

14. Bert Cochran, *Labor and Communism: The Conflict That Shaped American Unions* (Princeton: Princeton University Press, 1977), 124–25.

15. Philip Murray, "Industrial Council Program," excerpted from "Report to the Fourth Constitutional Convention of the Congress of Industrial Organizations," Detroit, November 17, 1941, in Clinton S. Golden and Harold J. Ruttenberg, *The Dynamics of Industrial Democracy* (New York: Harper and Brothers, 1942), 343–47; Philip Murray, "How to Speed Up Steel Production: A Plan to Achieve Total Steel Output to Aid National Defense" (Pittsburgh: Steel Workers Organizing Committee, 1941).

16. Walter Reuther, *Five Hundred Plans a Day* (Washington, D.C.: American Council on Public Affairs, 1940); Victor Reuther, *The Brothers Reuther* (Boston: Houghton Mifflin, 1976), 220–34; Nelson Lichtenstein, *The Most Dangerous Man in Detroit: Walter Reuther and the Fate of American Labor* (New York: Basic Books, 1995), 161–95.

17. Quoted by David Milton, *The Politics of U.S. Labor: From the Great Depression to the New Deal* (New York: Monthly Review Press, 1982), 139.

18. David Brody, *In Labor's Cause: Main Themes on the History of the American Worker* (New York: Oxford University Press, 1993), 179–82.

19. On wartime mobilization and the retreat from social reform, see Brinkley, *End of Reform,* 175–200.

20. Melvyn Dubofsky, *The State and Labor in Modern America* (Chapel Hill: University of North Carolina Press, 1994), 176.

21. U.S. Civilian Production Administration, *Industrial Mobilization for War: History of the War Production Board and Predecessor Agencies, 1940–1945* (Washington, D.C.: GPO, 1947), 82; Lichtenstein, *Labor's War at Home,* 48.

22. Thomas A. Kochan, Harry C. Katz, and Robert B. McKersie, *The Transformation of American Industrial Relations* (New York: Basic Books, 1986), 32.

23. U.S. Civilian Production Administration, *Industrial Mobilization for War,* 247–65.

24. Ibid., 282.

25. Brinkley, *End of Reform,* 201–26; Harris, *Right to Manage,* 60–67; Lichtenstein, *Labor's War at Home,* 67–109; Joel Seidman, *American Labor from Defense to Reconversion* (Chicago: University of Chicago Press, 1953), chaps. 5–6; Joshua Freeman, "Delivering the Goods: Industrial Unionism in World War II," in *The Labor History Reader,* ed. Daniel J. Laeb (Urbana: University of Illinois Press, 1985), 393–406.

26. Seidman, *American Labor from Defense to Reconversion,* 81–83.

27. After A. Philip Randolph, president of the Brotherhood of Sleeping Car Porters, threatened a march on Washington to protest racial discrimination in defense industry employment, President Roosevelt created the Fair Employment Relations Administration, an agency, to be sure, with a social policy goal, but institutionally separate from the NLRB and the National War Labor Board. See Joseph F. Wilson, *Tearing Down the Color Bar: A Documentary History and Analysis of the Brotherhood of Sleeping Car Porters* (New York: Columbia University Press, 1989).

28. The closed shop, which the LMRA outlawed, permits the employment of union members only. The union shop, which the LMRA allowed but which right-to-work states prohibit, permits the employment of nonmembers, but requires all new hires to become members within a specified period. Maintenance of membership prohibits members from quitting during the contract period. Dues checkoff automatically deducts union dues from the payroll. The agency shop requires nonmembers to reimburse the union for the costs of collective bargaining.

29. United States National War Labor Board, *Reports of Decisions of the National War Labor Board* vol. 1 (Washington, D.C.: Bureau of National Affairs, 1942), xv.

30. Lichtenstein, *Labor's War at Home,* 78–81.

31. Quoted by Freeman, "Delivering the Goods," 388.

32. Lichtenstein, *Labor's War at Home,* 81.

33. Seidman, *American Labor from Defense to Reconversion,* 106.

34. Freeman, "Delivering the Goods," 387.

35. Seidman, *American Labor from Defense to Reconversion,* 112.

36. Quoted by Melvyn Dubofsky and Warren Van Tine, *John L. Lewis: A Biography* (New York: Times Books, 1977), 418.

37. Seidman, *American Labor from Defense to Reconversion,* 129–30.

38. Dubofsky and Van Tine, *John L. Lewis,* 419.

39. Dubofsky and Van Tine, *John L. Lewis,* 415–40.

40. Seidman, *American Labor from Defense to Reconversion,* 141.

41. Millis and Brown, *From the Wagner Act to Taft-Hartley,* 354–56.

42. Dubofsky and Van Tine, *John L. Lewis,* 432–36.

43. Seidman, *American Labor from Defense to Reconversion,* 132–35.

44. Freeman, "Delivering the Goods," 396; Paul K. Edwards, *Strikes in the United States, 1881–1974* (New York: St. Martin's, 1981), 138.

45. Seidman, *American Labor from Defense to Reconversion,* 132–35.

46. George Lipsitz, *Class and Culture in Cold War America: "A Rainbow at Midnight"* (South Hadley, Mass.: Bergen and Harvey, 1982), 37–86.

47. U.S. Civilian Production Administration, *Industrial Mobilization for War*, 502.

48. Lipsitz, *Class and Culture in Cold War America*, 37.

49. Brinkley, *End of Reform*, 237–40.

50. Quoted by Brody, *In Labor's Cause*, 205.

51. U.S. Civilian Production Administration, *Industrial Mobilization for War*, 945–59.

52. Reuther, *Brothers Reuther*, 246–48.

53. Quoted by Lichtenstein, *Most Dangerous Man in Detroit*, 230.

54. Harris, *Right to Manage*, 60.

55. Harris, *Right to Manage*, 181

56. Harris, *Right to Manage*, 58–89.

57. R. Alton Lee, *Truman and Taft-Hartley: A Question of Mandate* (Lexington: University of Kentucky Press, 1966), 22–26.

58. Quoted by David Brody, "The Uses of Power I: Industrial Background," in *Workers in Industrial America: Essays on the Twentieth Century Struggle* (New York: Oxford University Press, 1982), 176.

59. Quoted by Robert H. Zeiger, *American Workers, American Unions, 1920–1985* (Baltimore: Johns Hopkins University Press, 1986), 105.

60. Martin Halpern, *UAW Politics in the Cold War Era* (Albany: State University of New York Press, 1988), 53.

61. William Serrin, *The Company and the Union: The "Civilized Relationship" of the General Motors Corporation and the United Automobile Workers* (New York: Knopf, 1973), 161.

62. Executive Order 9599, August 16, 1945.

63. Reuther, *Brothers Reuther*, 304–6.

64. Reuther, *Brothers Reuther*, 251.

65. This also foreshadowed features in the LMRA that shield management rights and Supreme Court decisions that deny the right to strike over issues relating to "the core of entrepreneurial control." See *Fibreboard Paper Products Corp. v. NLRB* 379 U.S. 203 (1964); *First National Maintenance Corp. v. NLRB* 452 U.S. 666 (1981).

66. Lee, *Truman and Taft-Hartley*, 34–38.

67. Dubofsky and Van Tine, *John L. Lewis*, 465.

68. *United States v. United Mine Workers of America* 330 U.S. 258 (1947).

69. Brinkley, *End of Reform*, 259–71; Alan Brinkley, "The New Deal and the Idea of the State," in *The Rise and Fall of the New Deal Order, 1930–1980*, ed. Steve Fraser and Gary Gerstle (Princeton: Princeton University Press, 1989), 100–112.

70. Slichter, *Trade Unions in a Free Society*, 5. See also Sumner Slichter, *The Challenge of Industrial Relations: Trade Unions, Management, and the Public Interest* (Ithaca: Cornell University Press, 1947).

71. Slichter, *Trade Unions in a Free Society*, 36.

72. Slichter, *Trade Unions in a Free Society*, 16–17.

73. Slichter, *Trade Unions in a Free Society*, 28–31.

74. The LMRA also bans strikes in violation of other provisions of the LMRA (such as its ban on closed shop agreements, and its striker replacement provisions, Section 8[b]), strikes during the sixty-day notification (cooling off) period (Section 8[d]), and holds labor organizations legally liable for unauthorized ("wildcat") strikes (Section 303).

75. It is debatable whether this really does "equalize" the rights of employers and employees. Workers who engage in an unfair labor practice, such as an illegal boycott, lose important rights, namely, their rights to their jobs. An employer who engages in an unfair labor practice, such as illegally firing a striker, loses no rights, and only has to reinstate the striker and compensate her for lost wages.

76. The rationale for this was that the earlier boards combined prosecutor, judge, and jury in a single body. See Gross, *Reshaping of the National Labor Relations Board,* 264; James Gross, *Broken Promises: The Subversion of U.S. Labor Relations Policy, 1947–1994* (Washington, D.C.: Catholic University Press, 1995), 11–71.

77. Gross, *Reshaping,* 264.

78. Gross, *Reshaping,* 267; Tomlins, *The State and the Unions,* 154.

79. Quoted by Mark Rosenberg, "The Political Economy of the Wagner Act: Power, Symbol, and Workplace Cooperation," *Harvard Law Review* 106 (1993): 1413.

80. Quoted by Leon H. Keyserling, "The Wagner Act: Its Origin and Current Significance," *George Washington Law Review* 29 (1960): 216.

81. Keyserling, "Wagner Act," 221.

82. Thomas A. Kochan, *Collective Bargaining and Industrial Relations: From Theory to Policy and Practice* (Homewood, Ill.: Richard D. Irwin, 1980), 166. *Fibreboard Paper Products Corp. v. NLRB,* 379 U.S. 203 (1964).

83. See Harris, *Right to Manage,* 81–83, 123.

84. Nor does the scope of collective bargaining even cover all employment issues that directly affect the employee. Workplace discipline and the introduction of new production technologies are two such issues that remain largely under the control of the employer.

85. Brody, *In Labor's Cause*; Brody, "Uses of Power," 200–213.

86. *Boys Market, Inc. v. Retail Clerks Local 770,* 398 U.S. 235 (1970).

87. See Cochran, *Labor and Communism,* and Halpern, *UAW Politics in the Cold War Era.*

88. Slichter, *Trade Unions in a Free Society,* 11–22; Robert Dubin, "Constructive Aspects of Industrial Conflict," in *Industrial Conflict,* ed. Arthur Kornhauser, Robert Dubin, and Arthur M. Ross (New York: McGraw-Hill, 1954), 37–47; this theme runs throughout *Industrial Conflict.*

89. Slichter, *Trade Unions in a Free Society,* 20.

90. Slichter, *Challenge of Industrial Relations,* 138, and *Trade Unions in a Free Society.*

91. Clinton S. Golden and Virginia D. Parker, eds., *Causes of Industrial Peace under Collective Bargaining* (New York: Harper and Brothers, 1955 [1949]), 40–54.

92. Golden and Parker, *Causes of Industrial Peace.* For more on the ideology of free collective bargaining, see discussion of industrial pluralists in chapter 9.

93. Frederick Harbison, "Collective Bargaining and American Capitalism," in *Industrial Conflict,* ed. Kornhauser et al., 270–79.

7. "Let us stand with a greater determination"

1. Ira Katznelson, *City Trenches: Urban Politics and the Patterning of Class in the United States* (Chicago: University of Chicago Press, 1981), 6.

2. For a different interpretation that focuses on the changing nature of rights consciousness during the 1960s, see Nelson Lichtenstein, *State of the Union: A Century of American Labor* (Princeton: Princeton University Press, 2002), 185–211.

3. Joseph F. Wilson, *Tearing Down the Color Bar: A Documentary History and Analysis of the Brotherhood of Sleeping Car Porters* (New York: Columbia University Press, 1989), 126–27, 282.

4. Rebecca M. Blank and Alan S. Blinder, "Macroeconomics, Income Distribution, and Poverty," in *Fighting Poverty: What Works and What Doesn't*, ed. Sheldon H. Danziger and Daniel H. Weinberg (Cambridge: Harvard University, 1986), 180.

5. Margaret Weir, *Politics and Jobs: The Boundaries of Employment Policy in the United States* (Princeton: Princeton University Press, 1992), 91.

6. William Julius Wilson, *The Truly Disadvantaged: The Inner City, the Underclass, and Public Policy* (Chicago: University of Chicago Press, 1987), 31.

7. Quoted by Weir, *Politics and Jobs*, 90.

8. Quoted by Herbert Hill, *Black Labor and the American Legal System: Race, Work, and the Law* (Madison: University of Wisconsin Press, 1985), 33.

9. Sean Wilentz, *Chants Democratic: New York City and the Rise of the American Working Class, 1788–1850* (New York: Oxford University Press, 1984), 158–66, 337–39.

10. David Montgomery, "Strikes in Nineteenth-Century America," *Social Science History* 4 (1980): 82.

11. Herbert Gutman, "Class, Status, and Community Power in Nineteenth-Century American Industrial Cities: Patterson, New Jersey; A Case Study," in Gutman, *Work, Culture and Society in Industrializing America: Essays in American Working-Class and Social History*, 4th ed. (New York: Alfred A. Knopf, 1977), 234–60; Herbert Gutman, "The Workers' Search for Power: Labor in the Gilded Age," in Gutman, *Power and Culture: Essays on the American Working Class* (New York: Pantheon, 1987), 75–86.

12. Steve Fraser, "The 'Labor Question,' " in *The Rise and Fall of the New Deal Order, 1930–1980*, ed. Gary Gerstle and Steve Fraser (Princeton: Princeton University Press, 1989), 55–56.

13. Jane Addams, *Twenty Years at Hull-House* (New York: New American Library, 1960 [1910]), 155–58.

14. Addams, *Twenty Years at Hull-House*, 166.

15. Richard A. Lester, *As Unions Mature* (Princeton: Princeton University Press, 1958), 29–33; Robert Dubin, "Constructive Aspects of Industrial Conflict," in *Industrial Conflict*, ed. Arthur Kornhauser, Robert Dubin, and Arthur M. Ross (New York: McGraw-Hill, 1954), 44–47; Frederick H. Harbison, "Collective Bargaining and American Capitalism," in *Industrial Conflict*, ed. Kornhauser, Dubin, and Ross, 270–79.

16. James Gross, *Reshaping of the National Labor Relations Board: National Labor Policy in Transition* (Albany: State University of New York Press, 1981), 267.

17. Hill, *Black Labor and the American Legal System*, 140–41.

18. David Brody, *In Labor's Cause: Main Themes in the History of the American Worker* (New York: Oxford University Press, 1993), 221–50.

19. *Fibreboard Paper Products Corp. v. NLRB* 379 U.S. 206 (1964); *NLRB v. First National Maintenance Corp.* 452 U.S. 666 (1981); see also James G. Pope, "Labor and the Constitution: From Abolition to Deindustrialization," *Texas Law Review* 65 (1987): 1071–1136.

20. Barry Bluestone and Bennett Harrison, *The Deindustrialization of America: Plant Closings, Community Abandonment, and the Dismantling of Basic Industry* (New York: Basic Books, 1982), 49–81.

21. William Julius Wilson, *When Work Disappears: The World of the New Urban Poor* (New York: Knopf, 1996), 25–50.

22. J. Joseph Huthmacher, *Senator Robert F. Wagner and the Rise of Urban Liberalism* (New York: Atheneum, 1968), 192–95; Leon H. Keyserling, "The Wagner Act: Its Origin and Current Significance," *George Washington Law Review* 29 (1960): 218–20.

23. Quoted by Irving Bernstein, *The New Deal Collective Bargaining Policy* (Berkeley: University of California Press, 1950), 124.

24. Jerold S. Auerbach, *Labor and Liberty: The La Follette Committee and the New Deal* (Indianapolis: Bobbs-Merrill, 1966), 177–96.

25. Hill, *Black Labor and the American Legal System,* 97.

26. Michael B. Katz, *In the Shadow of the Poorhouse: A Social History of Welfare in America* (New York: Basic Books, 1986), 238–39; David M. Gordon, Richard Edwards, and Michael Reich, *Segmented Work, Divided Workers: The Historical Transformation of Labor in the United States* (Cambridge: Cambridge University Press, 1982), 185–215; Theda Skocpol, "The Limits of the New Deal System and the Roots of Contemporary Welfare Dilemmas," in *The Politics of Social Policy in the United States,* ed. Margaret Weir, Ann Shola Orloff, and Theda Skocpol (Princeton: Princeton University Press, 1988), 302.

27. Andrew Hacker, *Two Nations: Black and White, Separate, Hostile, Unequal* (New York: Ballantine Books, 1992), 116.

28. Richard C. Kearney, *Labor Relations in the Public Sector* (New York: Marcel Dekker, 1984), 217–21. Nine states (Alaska, Hawaii, Minnesota, Montana, Oregon, Pennsylvania, Rhode Island, Vermont, and Wisconsin) permit a limited right to strike for public employees. The 1947 Labor Management Relations Act (Taft-Hartley Act) forbids federal employees to strike.

29. Hill, *Black Labor and the American Legal System,* 100–106.

30. Quoted by Hill, *Black Labor and the American Legal System,* 106.

31. Quoted by James T. Patterson, *America's Struggle against Poverty, 1900–1985* (Cambridge: Harvard University Press, 1986), 112.

32. Robert Dahl, *Who Governs? Democracy and Power in an American City* (New Haven: Yale University Press, 1961); Nelson Polsby, *Community Power and Political Theory* (New Haven: Yale University Press, 1963); David Truman, *The Governmental Process: Political Interests and Public Opinion* (New York: Knopf, 1951); Floyd Hunter, *Community Power Structure: A Study of Decision-Makers* (Chapel Hill: University of North Carolina Press, 1953).

33. Richard A. Cloward and Lloyd E. Ohlin, *Delinquency and Opportunity: A Theory of Delinquent Gangs* (New York: Free Press, 1960). For a current example, see Wilson, *When Work Disappears.*

34. Peter Bachrach and Morton S. Baratz, "Two Faces of Power," *American Political Science Review* 56 (1962): 947–52.

35. John R. Logan and Harvey L. Molotch, *Urban Fortunes: The Political Economy of Place* (Berkeley: University of California Press, 1987).

36. Wilson, *When Work Disappears,* 46–48.

37. Donald H. Grubbs, *Cry from the Cotton: The Southern Tenant Farmers' Union and the New Deal* (Chapel Hill: University of North Carolina Press, 1971), 17–29.

38. Nicholas Lehman, *The Promised Land: The Great Black Migration and How It Changed America* (New York: Alfred A. Knopf, 1991), 5–6.

39. Grubbs, *Cry from the Cotton*. Violence against STFU strikers helped to instigate the La Follette Civil Liberties Committee investigations. The committee held hearings on the conflict in Delano, California, in an attempt to eliminate the exclusion of farm workers from the NLRA. These investigations proved too controversial even for the La Follette Committee, which was unable to alter this feature of the NLRA. See Auerbach, *Labor and Liberty*, 53, 177–96.

40. Wilson, *When Work Disappears*, 26–30; Stanley Lieberson, *A Piece of the Pie: Blacks and White Immigrants since 1880* (Berkeley: University of California Press, 1980), 358.

41. Daniel Bell, *The Coming of Post-Industrial Society: A Venture in Social Forecasting* (New York: Basic Books, 1973), 129.

42. Quoted by Daniel Patrick Moynihan, *Maximum Feasible Misunderstanding: Community Action in the War on Poverty* (New York: Basic Books, 1969), 81; emphasis added.

43. James L. Sundquist, *Politics and Policy: The Eisenhower, Kennedy, and Johnson Years* (Washington, D.C.: Brookings Institute, 1968), 111–54.

44. Quoted by Patterson, *America's Struggle against Poverty*, 140. Emphasis added.

45. Quoted by Moynihan, *Maximum Feasible Misunderstanding*, 81.

46. Quoted in Derek C. Bok and John T. Dunlop, *Labor and the American Community* (New York: Simon and Schuster, 1970), 441.

47. Bok and Dunlop, *Labor and the American Community*, 442–50.

48. Patterson, *America's Struggle against Poverty*, 142–54.

49. Moynihan, *Maximum Feasible Misunderstanding*, 25.

50. T. H. Marshall and Thomas Bottomore, *Citizenship and Social Class* (London: Pluto Press, 1991 [1950]), 6–15.

51. Katz, *In the Shadow of the Poorhouse*, 234–39; Norman Furniss and Timothy Tilton, *The Case for the Welfare State: From Social Security to Social Equality* (Bloomington: University of Indiana Press, 1977), 179–83; Skocpol, "Limits of the New Deal System," in *Politics of Social Policy*, ed. Weir, Orloff, and Skocpol, 295–98.

52. Wilson, *When Work Disappears*, 155.

53. Michael R. Sosin, "Legal Rights and Welfare Change, 1960–1980," in *Fighting Poverty: What Works and What Doesn't*, ed. Sheldon H. Danziger and Daniel H. Weinberg (Cambridge: Harvard University Press, 1986), 261–64.

54. JOIN Community Union, "Welfare Bill of Rights" (Chicago: undated; unpublished typescript on file at Wisconsin State Historical Society Library, Madison, Wisconsin).

55. Frances Fox Piven and Richard A. Cloward, *Regulating the Poor: The Functions of Public Welfare* (New York: Random House, 1971), 220–30.

56. Frances Fox Piven and Richard A. Cloward, *Poor People's Movements: Why They Succeed, How They Fail* (New York: Random House, 1979), 275–78.

57. Sosin, "Legal Rights and Welfare Change," 272.

58. *King v. Smith* 392 U.S. 309 (1968); *Shapiro v. Thompson* 394 U.S. 618 (1969).

59. *Goldberg v. Kelly* 397 U.S. 254 (1970).

60. *Rosado V. Wyman* 397 U.S. 397 (1970).

61. Piven and Cloward, *Poor People's Movements*, 331–43.

62. See, e.g., Charles Murray, *Losing Ground: American Social Policy, 1950–1980* (New York, Basic Books, 1984).

63. Lawrence M. Mead, *Beyond Entitlement: The Social Obligations of Citizenship* (New York: Free Press, 1986).

64. Sosin, "Legal Rights and Welfare Change," 272–81.

65. Piven and Cloward, *Poor People's Movements,* 277.

66. Guida West, *The National Welfare Rights Movement: The Social Protest of Poor Women* (New York: Praeger, 1981), 366–77.

67. In "Was the Great Society a Lost Opportunity?" Ira Katznelson argues that the failure of the Great Society to achieve its social democratic prospects was a result of the politics and policies of the late 1940s. In *Rise and Fall of the New Deal Order,* ed. Fraser and Gerstle, 185–211.

68. Michael Goldfield, *The Decline of Organized Labor in the United States* (Chicago: University of Chicago Press, 1987), 206. The data comes from a 1982 Harvard PhD dissertation by Paula Voos.

69. Hill, *Black Labor and the American Legal System,* 37–62. See also Herbert Hill, "The AFL-CIO and the Black Worker: Twenty-Five Years after the Merger," Industrial Relations Research Institute Reprint: 1. Reprinted from *Journal of Intergroup Relations* 10 (1982).

70. Hill, "The AFL-CIO and the Black Worker," 12.

71. Gwendolyn Mink, *Old Labor and New Immigrants in American Political Development: Union, Party, State, 1875–1920* (Ithaca: Cornell University Press, 1986).

72. For a detailed account of this strike, see Joan Turner Beifuss, *At the River I Stand: Memphis, the 1968 Strike, and Martin Luther King* (New York: Carlson Publishing, 1989).

73. See Ronald B. Taylor, *Chavez and the Farm Workers* (Boston: Beacon Press, 1975).

74. Peter B. Levy, *The New Left and Labor in the 1960s* (Urbana: University of Illinois Press, 1994), 143; David J. Garrow, *Bearing the Cross: Martin Luther King and the Southern Christian Leadership Conference* (New York: Random House, 1986), 590.

75. Martin Luther King Jr., "I Have Seen the Promised Land," speech delivered in Memphis, Tennessee, April 3, 1968.

76. Quoted by Taylor, *Chavez and the Farm Workers,* 229, 164.

77. Taylor, *Chavez and the Farm Workers,* 167.

78. King, "I Have Seen the Promised Land."

79. John C. Hammerback and Richard J. Jensen, *The Rhetorical Career of Cesar Chavez* (College Station: Texas A&M University Press, 1998), 16–21.

80. Richard W. Etulain, ed., *Cesar Chavez: A Brief Biography with Documents* (New York: Palgrave, 2002), 39.

81. Beifuss, *At the River I Stand,* 345–49.

82. Taylor, *Chavez and the Farm Workers,* 247–49.

83. Wilson, *When Work Disappears.* Compare to Mead, *Beyond Entitlement.*

8. "Playing hardball"

1. U.S. Congress, Senate, *National Labor Relations Act of 1935,* Section 15, 74th Cong., 1st sess., S. 1958, as it appears in the National Labor Relations Board, *Legislative History of the National Labor Relations Act, 1935,* vol. 1 (Washington, D.C.: GPO, 1949), 1309.

2. During the 1990s, days idle due to strikes accounted for .01–.02% of available working time; during the 1970s, .08–.29%. United States Bureau of Labor

Statistics, *Compensation and Working Conditions* (Washington, D.C.: GPO, fall 2000).

3. Stephen H. Norwood, *Strikebreaking and Intimidation: Mercenaries and Masculinity in Twentieth-Century America* (Chapel Hill: University of North Carolina Press, 2002); Robert Michael Smith, *From Blackjacks to Briefcases: A History of Commercialized Strikebreaking and Unionbusting in the United States* (Athens: Ohio University Press, 2003).

4. Ruth A. Bandzac, "A Productive Systems Analysis of the 1983 Phelps Dodge Strike," *Journal of Economic Issues* 25 (1991): 1119.

5. Thomas Byrne Edsall, *The New Politics of Inequality* (New York: Norton, 1984), 120–78.

6. Thomas A. Kochan, Harry C. Katz, and Robert B. McKersie, *The Transformation of American Industrial Relations* (New York: Basic Books, 1986), 21–145; Peter Capelli and Robert B. McKersie, "Labor and the Crisis in Collective Bargaining," in *Challenges and Choices Facing American Labor,* ed. Thomas A. Kochan (Cambridge: MIT Press, 1986), 227–47; see also James Freeman and Richard Medoff, *What Do Unions Do?* (New York: Basic Books, 1984), 221–45; Michael Goldfield, *The Decline of Labor in the United States* (Chicago: University of Chicago Press, 1987), 189–217; and Mike Davis, *Prisoners of the American Dream: Politics and Economy in the History of the U.S. Working Class* (London: Verso, 1986), 126–38.

7. Kochan, Katz, and McKersie, *Transformation of American Industrial Relations,* 134–35.

8. Ruth A. Bandzak, "The Strike as Management Strategy," *Journal of Economic Issues* 26 (1992): 647–49; U.S. Congress, House, *Hearing before the Subcommittee on Labor and Human Resources on H.R. 5, Preventing Replacement of Economic Strikers,* 101st Cong., 2nd sess., 6 June 1990, 65; Herbert Northrup, *Operating during Strikes* (Philadelphia: University of Pennsylvania, Wharton School, 1980), provides detailed advice for employing permanent striker replacements.

9. Arthur B. Shostak and David Skocik, *The Air Traffic Controllers Controversy: Lessons from the PATCO Strike* (New York: Human Sciences Press, 1986).

10. Shostak and Skocik, *Air Traffic Controllers Controversy,* 103–22.

11. Kim Moody, *An Injury to All: The Decline of American Unionism* (London: Verso, 1988), 141; Bandzac, "Productive Systems Analysis," 1116.

12. Jonathan D. Rosenblum, *Copper Crucible: How the Arizona Miners' Strike of 1983 Recast Labor-Management Relations in America* (Ithaca: ILR Press, 1995); Bandzac, "Strike as Management Strategy," 649–53; Kochan, Katz, and McKersie, *Transformation,* 135–36.

13. Bandzac, "Productive Systems Analysis," 1120–21; Rosenblum, *Copper Crucible,* 91, 125.

14. Rosenblum, *Copper Crucible,* 60.

15. Quoted by Rosenblum, *Copper Crucible,* 125.

16. Norwood, *Strikebreaking and Intimidation,* 242.

17. Bandzac, "Productive Systems Analysis," 1119.

18. Michael H. LeRoy, "The Changing Character of Strikes Involving Permanent Striker Replacements, 1935–1990," *Journal of Labor Research* 16 (1995): 433–36.

19. Paul Weiler, "Striking A New Balance: Freedom of Contract and the Prospects for Union Representation," *Harvard Law Review* 98 (1984): 390;

William B. Gould, *Agenda for Reform: The Future of Employment Relationships and the Law* (Cambridge: MIT Press, 1993), 203.

20. *NLRB v. Mackay Radio and Telegraph Co.*, 304 U.S. 333 (1938); Hal Keith Gillespie, Comment, "The Mackay Doctrine and the Myth of Business Necessity," *Texas Law Review* 50 (1972): 782–90; Weiler, "Striking a New Balance," 387–94; Charles B. Craver, *Can Unions Survive? The Rejuvenation of the American Labor Movement* (New York: New York University Press, 1992), 132–33; Gould, *Agenda*, 184–85.

21. 304 U.S. 333 at 346–347 (1938).

22. Weiler, "Striking a New Balance," 388.

23. *NLRB v. Fleetwood Trailer Co.*, 389 U.S. 375 (1967); *Mastro Plastics Corp. v. NLRB*, 350 U.S. 270 (1956); *Laidlow v. NLRB*, 414 F2d 99 (D.C. Cir., 1969), 397 U.S. 920 (*cert. denied*, 1970).

24. *Belknap v. Hale*, 463 U.S. 49 (1983).

25. *NLRB v. Erie Resistor*, 373 U.S. 375 (1963); *NLRB v. Great Dane Trailers*, 388 U.S. 26 (1967); *NLRB v. Curtin Matheson Scientific, Inc.*, 494 U.S. 775 (1990); *Harter Equipment, Inc. and Local 825, International Union of Operating Engineers, AFL-CIO*, 280 NLRB No. 71 (1986).

26. *NLRB v. Allis Chalmers Mfg. Co.*, 388 U.S. 175 (1967); *Scofield v. NLRB*, 394 U.S. 423 (1969); *NLRB v. Granite State Board*, 409 U.S. 213 (1972); *Pattern Makers League of North America v. NLRB*, 473 U.S. 95 (1985).

27. *Trans World Airlines v. Independent Federation of Flight Attendants*, 489 U.S. 426 (1989).

28. "Is Greyhound Sending Labor Signals?" *New York Times*, October 27, 1990, 1.

29. *Chamber of Commerce of the United States et al. v. Reich*, 74 F.3d 1322 (D.C. Cir., 1996)

30. U.S. National Labor Relations Board, *Legislative History of the Wagner Act 1935*, vol. 1 (Washington, D.C.: GPO, 1949), 1346.

31. The 1959 Landrum-Griffin Act included an amendment to the NLRA altering the decertification procedures to permit economic strikers to participate in elections up to one year after the strike began.

32. See, e.g., International Association of Machinists, "The Truth about the Taft-Hartley Law and Its Consequences for the Labor Movement" (Washington, D.C.: 1948).

33. U.S. Congress, House, *Hearing before the Subcommittee on Labor and Human Resources on H.R. 5, Preventing Replacement of Economic Strikers*, 101st Cong., 2nd sess., June 6, 1990, 5.

34. Claus Offe, "Two Logics of Collective Action," in Offe, *Disorganized Capitalism: Contemporary Transformations of Work and Politics* (Cambridge: MIT Press, 1985), 187–88. Emphasis in original.

35. Offe, "Two Logics of Collective Action," 193.

36. Terry Moe, "Interests, Institutions, and Positive Theory," *Studies in American Political Development* 2 (New Haven: Yale University Press, 1987), 247–59; James A. Gross, *Broken Promises: The Subversion of U.S. Labor Relations Policy, 1947–1994* (Philadelphia: Temple University Press, 1995).

37. Frank W. McCullock and Tim Bornstein, *The National Labor Relations Board* (New York: Praeger, 1974), 51

38. "Reagan NLRB Tips toward Management," *Business Week*, July 6, 1981, 27.

39. Donald Dotson, letter, *American Bar Association Journal*, August 1980: 938.

40. Aaron Bernstein and Susan B. Garland, "Dotson's Exit: A Lot More than Politics," *Business Week,* November 9, 1987, 114; Gross, *Broken Promises,* 254; Peter D. Walther, "The NLRB Today," *Labor Law Journal* 36 (November 1985): 808.

41. "NLRB Rulings That Are Inflaming Labor Relations," *Business Week,* June 11, 1984, 122; Congress, House Committee on Education and Labor, *Cesar Chavez Workplace Fairness Act, Report Together with Minority and Additional Views,* 102nd Cong., 1st sess., 1991 (Washington, D.C.: GPO, 1991), 60, 64–65.

42. Michael Sandel, *Democracy's Discontent: America in Search of a Public Philosophy* (Cambridge: Harvard University Press, 1996), 4; see also Michael Sandel, *Liberalism and the Limits of Justice* (Cambridge: Cambridge University Press, 1982).

43. Sandel, *Liberalism,* 180, 183.

44. Archibald Cox, "The Duty to Bargain in Good Faith," *Harvard Law Review* 71 (1958): 1401–42; Frederick U. Reel, "The Duty to Bargain and the Right to Strike," *George Washington Law Review* 29 (1960): 179–89.

45. *NLRB v. Insurance Agents/International Union,* 361 U.S. 489, 496 (1960).

46. *American Shipbuilding Co. v. NLRB,* 380 U.S. 300 (1965).

47. Cox, "Duty to Bargain," 1414.

48. Ibid.

49. John Stuart Mill, *On Liberty* (New York: Norton, 1975 [1859]), 14.

50. *Radio Officers v. NLRB,* 347 U.S. 17 (1954).

51. Permanently replaced strikers retain certain "statutory rights" under the NLRA. After the strike, employers must rehire replaced workers first, as positions become available. These statutory rights, however, do not obligate the employer to create positions to rehire former strikers, and, as noted above, the employer may not terminate permanent replacements to make room for returning employees.

52. U.S. Congress, House, *Hearing before the Committee on Economic and Educational Opportunities on H.R. 1176, To Nullify Executive Order that Prohibits Federal Contracts with Employers Who Hire Permanent Replacement Workers during Strikes (Executive Order #12954),* 104th Cong., 1st sess., June 22, 1995 (Washington, D.C.: GPO, 1995), 44.

53. U.S. Congress, House, *Hearing before the Subcommittee on Labor and Human Resources on H.R. 5, Preventing Replacement of Economic Strikers,* 101st Cong., 2nd sess., June 6, 1990 (Washington, D.C.: GPO, 1990); U.S. Congress, House, *Hearing before the Subcommittee on Labor-Management Relations of the Committee on Education and Labor on H.R. 5, The Striker Replacement Bill,* 102nd Cong., 1st sess., March 6 and 13, 1991 (Washington, D.C.: GPO, 1991); "Should the Senate Approve S. 55, the Workplace Fairness Act?" *Congressional Digest* (June–July 1993), entire issue.

54. See, e.g., Weiler, "Striking a New Balance," 413.

55. U.S. Congress, House, *Hearing before the Subcommittee on Labor-Management Relations of the Committee on Education and Labor on H.R. 5, The Striker Replacement Bill,* 102nd Cong., 1st sess., March 6 and 13, 1991 (Washington, D.C.: GPO, 1991), 106.

56. See, e.g., testimony by John Irving, counsel for the U.S. Chamber of Commerce, United States Congress, House, *Hearing before the Subcommittee on Labor-Management Relations of the Committee on Education and Labor on H.R. 5,* 102nd Cong., 1st sess., June 27, 1991 (Washington, D.C.: GPO, 1991), 250–51; and Paul Huard, senior vice president for policy and communications for the National Association of Manufacturers, U.S. Congress, House, *Hearing before the*

Committee on Economic and Educational Opportunities on H.R. 1176, 104th Cong., 1st sess., June 22, 1995 (Washington, D.C.: GPO, 1995), 83.

57. 489 U.S. 426 at 438.

58. Martin Jay Levitt and Tim Conrow, *Confessions of a Union Buster* (New York: Crown, 1993), 118, 59, 245, 205.

59. See. e.g., Reed Larson, president, National Right to Work Committee, statement to United States Congress, House, *Hearing before the Committee on Economic and Educational Opportunities on H.R. 1176*, 104th Cong., 1st sess., June 22, 1995 (Washington, D.C.: GPO, 1995), 46–52.

60. For the relationship between employment rights and American citizenship, see Judith Shklar, *American Citizenship: The Quest for Inclusion* (Cambridge: Harvard University Press, 1991), pt. 2.

9. "We deplore strikes because of the inconvenience"

1. Among their essential works: Archibald Cox and John Dunlop, "The Regulation of Collective Bargaining by the National Labor Relations Board," *Harvard Law Review* 63 (1950): 389–433; Archibald Cox and John Dunlop, "The Duty to Bargain during the Term of an Existing Agreement," *Harvard Law Review* 63 (1950): 1097–1133; Archibald Cox, "The Right to Engage in Concerted Activities," *Industrial Relations Law Journal* 26 (1951); Archibald Cox, "The Duty to Bargain in Good Faith," *Harvard Law Journal* 71 (1958): 1401–42; Arthur Kornhauser, Robert Dubin, and Arthur M. Ross, eds., *Industrial Conflict* (New York: McGraw-Hill, 1954); Richard Lester, *As Unions Mature* (Princeton: Princeton University Press, 1958); Sumner Slichter, James J. Healy, and Robert E. Livernash, *The Impact of Collective Bargaining on Management* (Washington, D.C.: Brookings Institute, 1960); Clarke Kerr, John Dunlop, Frederick Harbison, and Charles Myers, *Industrialism and Industrial Man: The Problems of Labor and Management in Economic Growth* (Cambridge: Harvard University Press, 1960); John Dunlop, *Industrial Relations Systems* (New York: Holt, 1958); Arthur M. Ross and Paul T. Hartman, *Changing Patterns of Industrial Conflict* (New York: Wiley, 1960); John Dunlop and Neil W. Chamberlain, *Frontiers of Collective Bargaining* (New York: Harper and Row, 1967); Derek C. Bok and John T. Dunlop, *Labor and the American Community* (New York: Simon and Schuster, 1970); Milton Derber, *The American Idea of Industrial Democracy, 1865–1965* (Urbana: University of Illinois, 1970); Jack Barbash, *The Theory of Industrial Relations* (Madison: University of Wisconsin Press, 1984). For an overview, see Katherine Van Wezel Stone, "The Post-War Paradigm in American Labor Law," *Yale Law Journal* 90 (1981): 1511–80; Ronald W. Schatz, "From Commons to Dunlop: Rethinking the Field of Industrial Relations," *Industrial Democracy: The Ambiguous Promise,* ed. Nelson Lichtenstein and Howell John Harris (Cambridge: Cambridge University Press, 1993), 87–112.

2. Many began as mediators for the National War Labor Board, which helps to explain their orientation toward contract administration and mediation.

3. Kornhauser, Dubin, and Ross, eds., *Industrial Conflict,* provides one of the best examples of pluralist social theory in labor relations.

4. George C. Homans, "Industrial Harmony as a Goal," in Kornhauser, Dubin, and Ross, eds., *Industrial Conflict,* 48–58. For more criticisms of this view, see Stone, "The Post-War Paradigm in American Labor Law."

5. See Robert Dubin, "Constructive Aspects of Industrial Conflict," in Kornhauser, Dubin, and Ross, eds., *Industrial Conflict,* 37–47.

6. See Frederick Harbison, "Collective Bargaining and American Capitalism," in Kornhauser, Dubin, and Ross, ed., *Industrial Conflict,* 270–79.

7. See Dunlop, *Industrial Relations Systems.*

8. See Clinton S. Golden and Virginia D. Parker, eds., *Causes of Industrial Peace under Collective Bargaining* (New York: Harper and Brothers, 1955 [1949]), 40–54; Sumner Slichter, *Trade Unions in a Free Society* (Cambridge: Harvard University Press, 1947), 6–11.

9. Harbison, "Collective Bargaining and American Capitalism," in Kornhauser, Dubin, and Ross, ed., *Industrial Conflict,* 276.

10. Arthur A. Ross, "Conclusions," in Kornhauser, Dubin, and Ross, eds., *Industrial Conflict,* 532.

11. Bok and Dunlop, *Labor and the American Community,* 229.

12. Sumner Slichter, *The Challenge of Industrial Relations: Trade Unions, Management, and the Public Interest* (Ithaca: Cornell University Press, 1947), 127.

13. Martin Jay Levitt and Terry Conrow, *Confessions of a Union Buster* (New York: Crown, 1993); Stephen H. Norwood, *Strikebreaking and Intimidation: Mercenaries and Masculinity in Twentieth-Century America* (Chapel Hill: University of North Carolina Press, 2002), 236–47.

14. See Slichter, *Challenge of Industrial Relations,* 135; Slichter, *Trade Unions in a Free Society,* 26; Bok and Dunlop, *Labor and the American Community,* 232–33.

15. *United Steelworkers v. American Manufacturing Company* 363 U.S. 564 (1960); *United Steelworkers v. Warrior and Gulf Company* 363 U.S. 574 (1960); *United Steelworkers v. Enterprise Wheel and Car* 363 U.S. 593 (1960); see also *Textile Workers Union v. Lincoln Mills* 353 U.S. 448 (1957).

16. Stone, "Post-War Paradigm," 1569–74.

17. Thomas Geoghegan, *Which Side Are You On? Trying to Be for Labor When It's Flat on Its Back* (New York: Farrar, Straus, Giroux, 1991), 169.

18. Bok and Dunlop, *Labor and the American Community,* 231–32, make this argument. See also Slichter, *Trade Unions in a Free Society,* 31.

19. Michael H. LeRoy and John H. Johnson, "Death by Legal Injunction: National Emergency Strikes under the Taft-Hartley Act and the Moribund Right to Strike," *Arizona Law Review* 43, no. 1 (January 2001): 63–137.

20. Golden and Parker, *Causes of Industrial Peace under Collective Bargaining*; William F. Whyte, *Pattern for Industrial Peace* (New York: Harper, 1951); Lester, *As Unions Mature*; Ross and Hartman, *Changing Patterns of Industrial Conflict.*

21. A. H. Raskin and John T. Dunlop, "Two Views of Collective Bargaining," in *Challenges to Collective Bargaining,* ed. Lloyd Ulman (Englewood Cliffs, N.J.: Prentice-Hall, 1967), 156.

22. Marc Trachtenberg, "Keynes Triumphant: A Study in the Social History of Ideas," *Knowledge and Society: Studies in the Sociology of Culture Past and Present* 4 (1983): 17–86; Herbert Stein, *The Keynesian Revolution in America* (Chicago: University of Chicago Press, 1969).

23. Margaret Weir, *Politics and Jobs: The Boundaries of Employment Policy in the United States* (Princeton: Princeton University Press, 1992), 27–47; Edwin Amenta and Theda Skocpol, "Redefining the New Deal: World War II and the Development of Social Provision in the United States," in *The Politics of Social Policy in the United States,* ed. Margaret Weir, Ann Shola Orloff, and Theda Skocpol (Princeton: Princeton University Press, 1988), 87–93.

24. Robert Lekachman, *The Age of Keynes* (New York: Random House, 1966), 287–89; Weir, *Politics and Jobs*, 27–61.

25. Weir, *Politics and Jobs*, 45–51.

26. Ira Katznelson, "Was the Great Society a Lost Opportunity?" in *The Rise and Fall of the New Deal Order, 1930–1980* (Princeton: Princeton University Press, 1989), 199–204.

27. William Henry Beveridge, *Full Employment in a Free Society*, (New York: W. W. Norton, 1945), 29.

28. John Hicks, *The Crisis of Keynesian Economics* (Oxford: Basil Blackwell, 1974), 34–42.

29. Colin Crouch, "Inflation and the Political Organization of Interests," in *The Political Economy of Inflation*, ed. Fred Hirsch and John Goldthorpe (Cambridge: Harvard University Press, 1978), 217–39.

30. Nelson Lichtenstein, *The Most Dangerous Man in Detroit: Walter Reuther and the Fate of American Labor* (New York: Basic Books, 1995), 271–98.

31. John Kenneth Galbraith, *The New Industrial State* (Boston: Houghton Mifflin, 1967), 397.

32. See chapter 6.

33. Daniel Quinn Mills, *The Government, Labor, and Inflation* (Chicago: University of Chicago Press, 1975).

34. Melvin W. Reder, "The Public Interest in Wage Settlements," in *Frontiers of Collective Bargaining*, ed. John T. Dunlop and Neil W. Chamberlain (New York: Harper and Row, 1967), 156.

35. Mills, *Government, Labor, and Inflation*, 230–52.

36. Ibid., 230–51.

37. Ibid., 251.

38. Colin Crouch, "Conditions for Trade Union Wage Restraint," *The Politics of Inflation and Economic Stagnation: Theoretical Approaches and International Case Studies*, ed. Leon N. Lindberg and Charles S. Maier (Washington, D.C.: Brookings, 1985), 139.

39. Desmond S. King, *The New Right: Politics, Markets, and Citizenship* (Chicago: Dorsey, 1987), 49–90; Norman P. Barry, *The New Right* (London: Croom Helm, 1987), 1–55.

40. See, for example, William H. Hutt, *The Strike-Threat System: Economic Consequences of Collective Bargaining* (New Rochelle, N.Y.: Arlington House, 1973); Henry C. Simons, "Some Reflections on Syndicalism," in *Economic Policy for a Free Society* (Chicago: University of Chicago Press, 1948), 119–59; Arthur Shenfield, *What Right to Strike?* (London: Institute of Public Affairs, 1986). Classic texts stating the economic liberal case against collectivism include Friedrich A. Hayek, *The Road to Serfdom* (London: Routledge and Kegan Paul, 1944); Friedrich A. Hayek, *The Constitution of Liberty* (Chicago: Regnery, 1960); Friedrich A. Hayek, *The Fatal Conceit: The Errors of Socialism*, ed. W. W. Bartley III (Chicago: University of Chicago Press, 1989); and Milton and Rose Friedman, *Capitalism and Freedom* (Chicago: University of Chicago Press, 1962).

41. Friedrich A. Hayek, "Why I Am Not a Conservative," in *The Essence of Hayek*, ed. Chiaki Nishiyana and Kurt R. Leube (Stanford, Calif.: Hoover Institution Press, 1992 [1960]), 281–98.

42. Economic liberals also remained vocal opponents of Keynesian economics and presented some of the earliest critiques of fiscal policy. For a compendium of these critiques, see Friedrich A. Hayek, *Contra Keynes and Cambridge: Essays, Correspondences*, ed. Bruce Caldwell (Chicago: University of Chicago Press, 1995).

43. What they really support is the right to quit, which is not problematic. See Hayek, *Constitution of Liberty*, 269, and Lionel Robbins, "Aspects of Postwar Economic Policy," in *Explorations in Economic Liberalism: The Wincott Lectures*, ed. Geoffrey E. Wood (New York: St. Martin's, 1996), 72.

44. Shenfield, *What Right to Strike?*, 13.

45. Hayek, *Constitution of Liberty*, 269.

46. Simons, "Some Reflections on Syndicalism," 152–53.

47. W. H. Hutt, *The Theory of Collective Bargaining, 1930–1980* (San Francisco: Cato Institute, 1980), 116.

48. Friedrich A. Hayek, *Law, Legislation, and Liberty, Volume 1: Rules and Order* (Chicago: University of Chicago Press, 1973), 35–54. Hayek refers to this misplaced faith in social planning as "rational constructivism." See *Fatal Conceit*, 69–70.

49. Arthur Okun, *Equality and Efficiency: The Big Tradeoff* (Washington, D.C.: Brookings, 1975), 10.

50. Kornhauser, Dubin, and Ross, eds., *Industrial Conflict*, 8, 10.

51. Philip Taft and Philip Ross, "American Labor Violence: Its Causes, Character, and Outcomes," in *Violence in America*, ed. Hugh Graham and Ted Gurr (New York: Bantam, 1969), 385–86.

52. David Hume, *A Treatise of Human Nature* (London: Oxford University Press, 1973 [1739]), 526; emphasis in original. On Hayek's debt to Hume, see Friedrich A. Hayek, "The Legal and Political Philosophy of David Hume (1711–1776)," in a collection of Hayek's essays, *The Trend of Economic Thinking: Essays on Political Economists and Economic History*, ed. W. W. Bartley III and Stephen Kresge (London: Routledge, 1991), 101–18.

53. Hayek, *Fatal Conceit*, 114–17.

54. Hayek, *Constitution of Liberty*, 13.

55. Ibid., 207–14.

56. Ibid., 134.

57. "Because striking has been accepted as a legitimate weapon for unions, it has come to be believed that they must be allowed to do whatever is necessary to make a strike successful" (Hayek, *Constitution of Liberty*, 274).

58. Quoted by Hayek, *Fatal Conceit*, 34.

59. Hayek, *Constitution of Liberty*, 140. "Several" refers to full possession of one's property, as well as the liberty to sell one's property.

60. Michael J. Sandel, *Democracy's Discontent: America in Search of a Public Philosophy* (Cambridge: Harvard University Press, 1996), 168–200.

61. Hayek, *Constitution of Liberty*, 137.

62. Robert J. Steinfeld, *The Invention of Free labor: The Employment Relation in English and American Law and Culture, 1350–1870* (Chapel Hill: University of North Carolina Press, 1991), 5.

63. Eric Foner, *A Short History of Reconstruction, 1863–1877* (New York: Harper and Row, 1990), 46–47.

64. *Ritchie v. People* (Illinois, 1888); *Lochner v. New York* 198 U.S. 45 (1905); *Wabash R.R. v. Young* (Indiana, 1904); *Adair v. United States* 208 U.S. 161(1908); *Coppage v. Kansas* 236 U.S. 1 (1915).

65. David Hume, "Of the Original Contract," in *David Hume's Political Essays*, ed. Charles W. Hendel (New York: Liberal Arts Press, 1953), 56–57.

66. *Truax v. Corrigan* 257 U.S. 312 (1921).

67. On the resurgence in right-based liberalism, see Mary Ann Glendon, *Rights Talk: The Impoverishment of Political Discourse* (New York: Free Press, 1991), 1–17.

68. On the international human rights movement, see Maurice Cranston, *What Are Human Rights?* (London: Brodley Head, 1973); James W. Nickel, *Making Sense of Human Rights: Philosophical Reflections on the International Declaration of Human Rights* (Berkeley: University of California Press, 1987).

69. Quoted by Cranston, *What Are Human Rights?*, 13.

70. Hume, *Treatise of Human Nature*, 484–98.

71. H.L.A. Hart, "Are There Any Natural Rights?" in *Theories of Rights*, ed. Jeremy Waldron (Oxford: Oxford University Press, 1984 [1955]); John Rawls, *A Theory of Justice* (Cambridge: Harvard University Press, 1971); Ronald Dworkin, *Taking Rights Seriously* (Cambridge: Harvard University Press, 1977). See also S. I. Benn and R. S. Peters, *The Principles of Political Thought* (New York: Free Press, 1959), 101–20; and Cranston, *What Are Human Rights?*. Although I appreciate the significant differences among these theorists, this section focuses on their shared interest in rights.

72. Hart, "Are There Any Natural Rights?" 79.

73. Dworkin, *Taking Rights Seriously*, xi. Compare this to the following quotation from Rawls: "Each person possesses an inviolability founded on justice that even the welfare of society as a whole cannot override. For this reason justice denies that the loss of freedom for some is made right by a greater good shared by others. . . . The rights secured by justice are not subject to political bargaining or to the calculus of social interests." Rawls, *A Theory of Justice*, 3–4.

74. Cranston, *What Are Human Rights?*, 19.

75. Hart, "Are There Any Natural Rights?" 77.

76. Dworkin, *Taking Rights Seriously*, xii.

77. John Dewey, *Liberalism and Social Action* (New York: Putnam, 1980 [1935]), 33–34.

78. Dworkin, *Taking Rights Seriously*, 273–74.

79. Cranston argues that economic rights are subordinate to civil and political rights, that the rights enumerated in the International Covenant of Civil and Political Rights have priority over those enumerated in the International Covenant of Economic, Social and Cultural Rights. The distinction between civil rights and economic rights is somewhat arbitrary, however, since the right to property and the freedom from slavery are affirmed by the International Covenant of Civil and Political Rights. Moreover, why consider the right to one's livelihood as less important than the right to one's opinions? See *What Are Human Rights?*, 34–42.

80. Dworkin, *Taking Rights Seriously*, 91.

81. Hart, "Are There Any Natural Rights?" 83.

82. Benn and Peters, *Principles of Political Thought*, 101.

83. Rawls, *A Theory of Justice*, 3.

84. Glendon, *Rights Talk*, 115.

85. Michael J. Sandel, *Liberalism and the Limits of Justice* (Cambridge: Cambridge University Press, 1982), 179.

86. Although affirmative action policies establish a sort of group right, their purpose is to remove the barriers to equal opportunity that individuals face. Affirmative action policies nonetheless remain controversial within modern American liberal discourse because they extend a group right.

87. Karen Orren, *Belated Feudalism: Labor, the Law, and Liberal Development in the United States* (Cambridge: Cambridge University Press, 1991).

88. Charles E. Lindblom made this point regarding the large private corporation in *Politics and Markets: The World's Political-Economic Systems* (New York: Basic Books: 1977), 356. Lindblom's first book makes a similar point concerning labor

unions and liberal capitalism. See *Unions and Capitalism* (New Haven: Yale University Press, 1949).

10. "Something of slavery still remains"

1. T. H. Marshall and Tom Bottomore, *Citizenship and Social Class* (London: Pluto Press, 1991 [1950]), 18.

2. H.L.A. Hart, "Are There Natural Rights?" in *Theories of Rights,* ed. Jeremy Waldrom (New York: Oxford, 1984), 83; emphasis in original.

3. Marshall and Bottomore, *Citizenship and Social Class,* 24.

4. Mary Ann Glendon, *Rights Talk: The Impoverishment of Political Discourse* (New York: Free Press, 1991), chap. 5; Michael Sandel, *Liberalism and the Limits of Justice* (Cambridge: Cambridge University Press, 1982), 178–83.

5. Marshall and Bottomore, *Citizenship and Social Class,* 12.

6. Marshall and Bottomore, *Citizenship and Social Class,* 26.

7. Judith Shklar, *American Citizenship: The Quest for Inclusion* (Cambridge: Harvard University Press, 1991), 64.

8. Shklar, *American Citizenship,* 100–101.

9. Marshall and Bottomore, *Citizenship and Social Class,* 40–46, 26.

10. Marshall and Bottomore, *Citizenship and Social Class,* 24.

11. On the rational actor model and nonvoting, see Anthony Downs, *An Economic Theory of Democracy* (New York: Harper and Row, 1957), chap. 14. See also William H. Riker and Peter Ordeshook, "A Theory of the Calculus of Voting," *American Political Science Review* 62 (1968): 25–42.

12. See, for example, Robert B. Westbrook, *John Dewey and American Democracy* (Ithaca: Cornell University Press, 1991), chap. 6. This conception of public education for citizenship has its origins in the Jacksonian era.

13. Hence, a main argument against school vouchers is that they weaken the common school.

14. Michael J. Sandel, *Democracy's Discontent: America in Search of a Public Philosophy* (Cambridge: Harvard University Press, 1996), 6–7.

15. Glendon, *Rights Talk,* 171; Lawrence Mead, *Beyond Entitlement: The Social Obligations of Citizenship* (New York: Free Press, 1986).

16. Robert Weibe, *Self Rule: A Cultural History of American Democracy* (Chicago: University of Chicago Press, 1995), also emphasizes this theme.

17. James Gray Pope, "Labor and the Constitution: From Abolition to Deindustrialization," *Texas Law Review* 65, no. 6 (May 1987): 1071–1136; Sidney Fine, "Frank Murphy, the Thornhill Decision, and Picketing as Free Speech," in *The Labor History Reader,* ed. Daniel J. Loeb (Urbana: University of Illinois Press, 1985 [1965]), 361–82; Sheldon Leader, *Freedom of Association: A Study in Labor Law and Political Theory* (New Haven: Yale University Press, 1992), 180–210.

18. 336 U.S. 251 (1949); see also *United States v. Kozminski* 487 U.S. 931 (1988), in which the court ruled that psychological coercion of underpaid, mentally retarded workers did not constitute involuntary servitude.

19. *United States v. United Mine Workers of America* 330 U.S. 307 (1947).

20. James Gray Pope, "The Thirteenth Amendment versus the Commerce Clause: Labor and the Shaping of American Constitutional Law, 1921–1957," *Columbia Law Review* 102, no. 1 (January 2002): 15–38.

21. Sumner Slichter, *The Challenge of Industrial Relations: Trade Unions, Management, and the Public Interest* (Ithaca: Cornell University Press, 1947), 158–59.

22. Arthur Kornhauser, Robert Dubin, and Arthur M. Ross, eds., *Industrial Conflict* (New York: McGraw-Hill, 1954), 8.

23. United States Bureau of Labor Statistics, *Current Wages and Working Conditions* 34, no. 2 (1982): 17. USBLS publishes this data monthly.

24. Philip Taft and Philip Ross, "American Labor Violence: Its Causes, Character, and Outcome," in *Violence in America: Historical and Comparative Perspectives*, ed. Hugh Davis Graham and Ted Robert Gurr (New York: Bantam, 1969), 282.

25. Taft and Ross, "American Labor Violence," 382.

26. Taft and Ross, "American Labor Violence," 380.

27. 316 U.S. 489, 496 (1960).

28. See, for example, Ruth Bandzak, "The Strike as Management Strategy," *Journal of Economic Issues* 26, no. 2 (June 1992): 645–59.

29. Walter Korpi and Michael Shalev, "Strikes, Industrial Relations, and Class Conflict in Western Nations," *British Journal of Sociology* 30 (1979): 164–97.

30. On the role of the presidency in reshaping authority relations, see Stephen Skowronek, *The Politics Presidents Make: Leadership from John Adams to George Bush* (Cambridge: Harvard University Press, 1993), esp. 17–32.

31. Quoted by Westbrook, *John Dewey and American Democracy*, 49.

32. W. Edwards Deming, *Out of the Crisis* (Cambridge: Massachusetts Institute of Technology, 1984). "With the storehouse of skills and knowledge contained in its millions of unemployed, and with the even more appalling underuse, misuse, and abuse of skills and knowledge in the army of employed people in all ranks in all industries, the United States may be today the most underdeveloped nation in the world" (6).

33. Leon H. Keyserling, "The Wagner Act: Its Origin and Current Significance," *George Washington Law Review* 29 (1960): 221.

34. Nick Salvatore, *Eugene Debs, Citizen and Socialist* (Urbana: University of Illinois, 1982), 223–24.

35. Rogers Smith, *Civic Ideals: Conflicting Visions of Citizenship in U.S. History* (New Haven: Yale University Press, 1997).

36. Robert Wiebe, *Self-Rule: A Cultural History of American Democracy* (Chicago: University of Chicago Press), 39; emphasis added.

37. Salvatore, *Eugene Debs*, 129. For further discussion of Debs, the cult of masculinity in nineteenth-century working-class culture, and the social construction of gender, see Paul Michel Taillon, " 'What We Want Is Good, Sober Men': Masculinity, Respectability, and Temperance in the Railroad Brotherhoods, c. 1870–1910," *Journal of Social History* 36, 2 (winter 2002): 319–38.

38. Salvatore, *Eugene Debs*, 137.

39. Eric Foner, *Politics and Ideology in the Age of the Civil War* (New York: Oxford University Press, 1980), 74.

40. David Montgomery, *Citizen Worker: The Experience of Workers in the United States with Democracy and the Free Market during the Nineteenth Century* (Cambridge: Cambridge University Press, 1993), 56.

41. Bruce Laurie, *Working People of Philadelphia, 1800–1850* (Philadelphia: Temple University Press, 1980), 65.

42. Herbert Hill, *Black Labor and the American Legal System: Race, Work, and the Law* (Madison: University of Wisconsin Press, 1985), 15.

43. Gwendolyn Mink, *Old Labor and New Immigrants in American Political Development: Union, Party, and State, 1875–1920* (Ithaca: Cornell University Press, 1986), 82–83.

44. Mink, *Old Labor and New Immigrants,* 107.

45. Salvatore, *Eugene Debs,* 104.

46. Mink, *Old Labor and New Immigrants* 71.

47. Hill, *Black Labor and the American Legal System.*

48. Ronald Takaki, *A Different Mirror: A History of Multicultural America* (Boston: Little, Brown, 1993), 149.

49. Stephen W. Norwood, *Strikebreaking and Intimidation: Mercenaries and Masculinity in Twentieth-Century America* (Chapel Hill: University of North Carolina Press, 2002), 78.

50. Salvatore, *Eugene Debs,* 105–7; Mink, *Old Labor and New Immigrants,* 85, 95.

51. Cesar Chavez, address to the Commonwealth Club, November 4, 1984, San Francisco. Available at www.ufw.org/commonwealth.htm.

Index